Cognition through Color

Issues in the Biology of Language and Cognition
John C. Marshall, editor

What the Hands Reveal about the Brain
Howard Poizner, Edward S. Klima, and Ursula Bellugi, 1987

Disorders of Syntactic Comprehension
David N. Caplan and Nancy Hildebrandt, 1987

Missing the Meaning? A Cognitive Neuropsychological Study of the Processing of Words by an Aphasic Patient
David Howard and Sue Franklin, 1988

The Psychobiology of Down Syndrome
edited by Lynn Nadel, 1988

From Reading to Neurons
edited by Albert M. Galaburda, 1989

Visual Agnosia: Disorders of Object Recognition and What They Tell Us about Normal Vision
Martha J. Farah, 1990

Theoretical Perspectives on Language Deficits
Yosef Grodzinsky, 1990

Modular Deficits in Alzheimer-Type Dementia
Myrna F. Schwartz, 1990

Laura: A Case for the Modularity of Language
Jeni Yamada, 1990

Cognition through Color
Jules Davidoff, 1991

Cognition through Color

Jules Davidoff

A Bradford Book
The MIT Press
Cambridge, Massachusetts
London, England

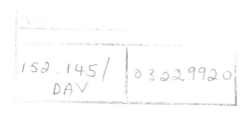
This book was set in Palatino by DEKR Corporation, Woburn, Massachusetts and printed and bound in the United States of America.

Library of Congress Cataloging-in-Publication Data

Davidoff, Jules B.
    Cognition through color / Jules Davidoff.
        p.   cm. — (Issues in the biology of language and cognition)
    "A Bradford book."
    Includes bibliographical references and index.
    ISBN 0-262-04115-4
    1. Visual perception.   2. Color vision.   3. Cognition.
    4. Cognitive disorders.   I. Title.   II. Series.
    [DNLM: 1. Cognition.   2. Color Perception.   3. Color Vision
Defects.   WW 150 D249c]
    QP441.D38   1991
    152. 14'5—dc20
    DNLM/DLC
    for Library of Congress   90-13643
                                                              CIP

I know how to react if you tell me that you have seen a white or a pink elephant.
Umberto Eco

Contents

Foreword by John C. Marshall   ix

Preface   xiii

Chapter 1
Introduction   1
1.1 An Object Lesson   1
1.2 Representations   5
1.3 The Organization of Chapters   6

Chapter 2
The Neurophysiology of Modularity   11
2.1 Parallel Pathways   11
2.2 Color Blindsight   25
2.3 Arguments against Modularity   26
2.4 Conclusions   28

Chapter 3
The Neuropsychology of the Color Module   31
3.1 Achromatopsia   31
3.2 Dissociated Input Modules   39

Chapter 4
Modularity Studied by Equiluminance   41
4.1 Introduction   41
4.2 Color Blind Modules   42
4.3 Summary Comment   49

Chapter 5
The Temporary Representation: Modular Approaches   51
5.1 The Pictorial Register   51
5.2 Feature Integration   52
5.3 Domain Models   60
5.4 Summary   67

Chapter 6
Boundaries and Surfaces   69
6.1 The Temporary Representation: Modular and Nonmodular Accounts Compared   69
6.2 The Colors of Surfaces   75
6.3 Apperceptive Visual Disorders: Modular and Nonmodular Accounts Compared   81
6.4 Summary and Progression to Object Recognition   83

Chapter 7
Object Knowledge   87
7.1 In Normals   87
7.2 After Brain Damage   92
7.3 A Model for the Division of Object Knowledge   96
7.4 Relationships to Other Models   99

Chapter 8
Colors without Objects   103
8.1 Functional Modularity   103
8.2 Associations with Color   111

Chapter 9
The Colors of Objects   121
9.1 The Role of Color in Object Recognition   121
9.2 The Role of Object Knowledge in the Perception of Color   124
9.3 The Recognition and Retrieval of Object Color   128

Chapter 10
Objects and Their Names   139
10.1 The Role of Object Knowledge   139
10.2 Object Knowledge and the Retrieval of Object Names in Aphasia   142
10.3 Conclusions   146

Chapter 11
Color Naming   147
11.1 In Normals   147
11.2 Disorders of Color Naming   156
11.3 Color Naming and Word Naming: Interference   163

Chapter 12
Overview   169

References   173
Index   211

Foreword
Long Live VIBGYOR!
John C. Marshall

Our lives are informed by color at all levels, from the most utilitarian (stop at the red light) to the most metaphorical (a colorful personality). Yet we have little difficulty in imagining (or seeing) a world without color—at night, all cats are gray, and many of us prefer black-and-white photography to garish technicolor. Nonetheless, the ubiquitous presence of (daytime) color experience, and our varied ways of talking about it, carve out a domain of scientific inquiry that is (paradoxically) both highly constrained and coextensive with human cognition.

Little wonder, then, that the study of normal color cognition should, for many centuries, have exercised the minds of physicists, physiologists, psychologists, and linguists (to say nothing of artists, interior decorators, and those nameless creatures who nowadays add artificial coloring to our apple pies). The prismic observation of Isaac Newton (1704) that a beam of white light can be separated into a spectral band of colors is easy enough to replicate; but the poet who fondly imagines drinking *white* wine by the banks of the *blue* Danube is indulging in poetic license. As indeed was Newton himself when he "saw" "only seven separate homogeneal colors" (Boring, 1942) dispersed on the screen by his prism. The percept VIBGYOR (violet, indigo, blue, green, yellow, orange, and red) may have owed as much to linguistics as it did to visual sensation (Berlin and Kay, 1969). As an exercise in understanding the relationship between biology and culture, the investigation of color has proved remarkably successful.

The basic mechanisms of color vision should be universal across all (normal) members of the human species, although subject to limited parametric variation consequent upon "environmental adaptation to ultraviolet components in sunlight and/or dietary habit" (Bornstein, 1973). On the other hand, languages have such varied color-naming systems that it was (once) possible to believe that "words for basic colors are not translatable across languages, and that each language expresses color perception in arbitrary color words" (Ratliff, 1976). Yet one (of many) exciting conclusions from recent study is that "the linguistics of color terms *corroborate* the neurophysiological basis of the opponent color theory; they do not conflict with it" (Von Wattenwyl and Zollinger, 1979). Even for those whose primary interest is *not* in color cognition, the topic may well provide a salutary example of an unbroken explanatory chain from the retina (Dowling, 1987) to language as a mirror of the mind (Chomsky, 1966).

That chain can, however, be broken by brain damage, thereby causing (relatively selective) deficits that range all the way from disorder of color discrimination to disorder of color naming and memory. As in all other domains of human neuropsychology, the fractionation of color cognition by discrete cerebral injury has provided important constraints on the theory of normal functioning (Shallice, 1988).

Central achromatopsia, with well-preserved acuity, was first observed by Robert Boyle (1688) and has subsequently continued to provide crucial evidence for the modular structure of early processing mechanisms (Mollon, Newcombe, Polden, and Ratcliff, 1980; Heywood, Wilson, and Cowey, 1987). At "higher" levels of processing, we seem to need a large range of distinctions between and within such taxonomic categories as color agnosia (Kinsbourne and Warrington, 1964), color anomia (Oxbury, Oxbury, and Humphrey, 1969), and color amnesia (Varney, 1982). There is a bewildering variety of color-tasks that patients without primary loss of color discrimination can and cannot perform (Lewandowsky, 1908; Meadows, 1974; Beauvois and Saillant, 1985). "Knowledge" of colors is distinct from perception thereof. The patient who no longer knows that grass is (typically or paradigmatically) green is not suffering from a perceptual disorder; and likewise the patient who can accurately sort tokens of varied hues into conventionally acceptable categories, but calls the green ones red.

Jules Davidoff's *Cognition through Color* covers (in brief outline at least) most of the spectrum of scientific knowledge of color, from the cones and ganglion cells of the retina to the child's acquisition of color vocabulary. And at most points along the way, a serious integration of studies of normal and impaired color perception is attempted. To achieve this breadth of coverage *and* include full details of everything that is currently known about color would, of course, require a hundred-volume encyclopedia (and even more authors than volumes).

The structure of Davidoff's (one-volume) book is accordingly of some consequence. What he has written is actually an essay concerning the neuropsychology of object recognition. At first blush, this might appear to extend the scope of the monograph to a ridiculously broad extent: color cognition *and* object recognition! The careful reader will, however, soon see that the object of the exercise is to restrict the core of the monograph to a domain that is both manageable and theoretically motivated. The organization of the brain appears to be such that initial input stages are characterized by separate channels or streams for such "stimulus" properties as shape, size, orientation, motion, depth, color. . . . But the organism as a whole will usually have little interest in these properties per se. What the "ego" wants to know is what is out there (and where out there is it, and what is it doing). It is this information that allows the subject to plan and execute an appropriate response to the environment. And it is in this sense that Davidoff's monograph is concerned with the role that color plays in object recognition. The shape of the text concerns not color but rather the colors of *things*: how they are seen, represented in memory, talked about (and otherwise responded to).

It is thus my conviction, then, that the new theory of color cognition in Davidoff's book cuts nature at the joints. I accordingly expect that this monograph will play an important role in stimulating and steering further advances in the cognitive neuropsychology of color.

References

Beauvois, M.-F., and Saillant, B. (1985). Optic aphasia for colours and colour agnosia: A distinction between visual and visuo-verbal impairments in the processing of colours. *Cognitive Neuropsychology* 2: 1–48.

Berlin, B., and Kay, P. (1969). *Basic Color Terms: Their Universality and Evolution.* Berkeley: University of California Press.

Boring, E. G. (1942). *Sensation and Perception in the History of Experimental Psychology.* New York: Appleton-Century.

Bornstein, M. H. (1973). Color vision and color naming: A psychophysiological hypothesis of cultural difference. *Psychological Bulletin* 80: 257–285.

Boyle, R. (1688). *Uncommon Observations about Vitiated Sight.* London: Taylor.

Chomsky, N. (1966). *Cartesian Linguistics.* New York: Harper and Row.

Dowling, J. E. (1987). *The Retina: An approachable part of the brain.* Cambridge, Mass.: Belknap Press.

Heywood, C. A., Wilson, B., and Cowey, A. (1987). A case study of cortical colour "blindness" with relatively intact achromatic discrimination. *Journal of Neurology, Neurosurgery, and Psychiatry* 50: 22–29.

Kinsbourne, M., and Warrington, E. K. (1964). Observations on colour agnosia. *Journal of Neurology, Neurosurgery, and Psychiatry* 27: 296–299.

Lewandowsky, M. (1908). Ueber abspalting des farbensinnes. *Monatsschrift für Psychiatrie und Neurologie* 23: 488–510.

Meadows, J. C. (1974). Disturbed perception of colours associated with localized cerebral lesions. *Brain* 97: 615–632.

Mollon, J. D., Newcombe, F., Polden, P. G., and Ratcliff, G. (1980). On the presence of three cone mechanisms in a case of total achromatopsia. In G. Verriest, ed., *Colour Vision Deficiencies*, Vol. 5. Bristol: Hilger.

Newton, I. (1704). *Opticks.* London: Smith.

Oxbury, J. M., Oxbury, S. M., and Humphrey, N. K. (1969). Varieties of color anomia. *Brain* 92: 847–860.

Ratliff, F. (1976). On the psychophysiological bases of universal color terms. *Proceedings of the American Philosophical Society* 120: 311–330.

Shallice, T. (1988). *From Neuropsychology to Mental Structure*. Cambridge: Cambridge University Press.

Varney, N. R. (1982). Color associations and "color amnesia" in aphasia. *Journal of Neurology, Neurosurgery, and Psychiatry* 45: 248–252.

Von Waltenwyl, A., and Zollinger, H. (1979). Color-term salience and neurophysiology of color vision. *American Anthropologist* 81: 279–288.

Preface

The starting point of *Cognition through Color* was a patient who was referred to me when I was working in the MRC Neuropsychology Unit at the University of Oxford. One of the patient's problems was an inability to name colors. More than that, despite normal color vision, his memory for colors and the colors of objects was "split off" from all other aspects of his memory. The patient's memory for shapes of objects was excellent, but he could not recognize their colors. Color would thus appear to qualify as one of the basic building blocks—input modules—from which perception is constructed and our memories organized. A research program was subsequently initiated, the consequence of which is *Cognition through Color*.

Modular input is compatible with some approaches to the study of perception but not to other philosophical and experimental accounts. To the latter, a color cannot exist without being the color of something. My own work with normal individuals also raised doubts concerning modularity. While there indeed appeared to be several tasks in which, perhaps counterintuitively, color played little role; for object-naming tasks, color was beneficial. Thus it became clear that in order to understand how color is remembered, we must know how objects are identified. The book, therefore, develops a model in which the understanding of objects is linked to the knowledge concerning their color.

Cognition through Color is, like most academic texts, mainly a summary of other people's research effort. Wherever possible, ignorance and sloth permitting, I have tried to give credit to the originators of ideas or lines of research. To those whose ideas have been omitted or misrepresented I apologize. There is also thanks to be expressed for help given. The excellent recent texts that have become available were particularly useful in getting color into a more general perspective of object recognition. Without them, the inaccuracies would assuredly have been greater. There are individuals whom I would like to thank by name. They read parts, sometimes only a few pages, and by so doing made significant improvements to them. I am, therefore, extremely grateful to Chris Barry, Patrick Cavanagh, Ilham Dilman, Jon Driver, Julie Evans, Charlie Heywood, Kathy Mullen, Keith Ruddock, Rodger Weddell, and Sean Wilkie. There are some individuals whom I cannot thank by name, as they were the anonymous reviewers of earlier drafts for MIT Press. To those people I owe a great debt. Gratitude must also be extended to the conscientious attention to the draft manuscript given by the series editor, John Marshall. It was through his good efforts that I was able to spend a few months at the Université de Montreal, and it was there that the first few stabs were made at the keyboard. To Roch Lecours and all others there who provided such excellent facilities, I would like also to express my gratitude. For some obscure reason, the emblem of their lab is a pink elephant.

Chapter 1
Introduction

1.1 An Object Lesson

When phrenologists (bump readers) had their heyday in the nine-teenth century, their diagram of faculties included a bump for color, situated just above the eyebrow. Today, the notion of a color center has returned, but its locus is considerably different. The site of the color center or color module, to give the contemporary terminology, is at or near the visual cortex. The phrenologists' argument was based on spurious correlations; the modern modular approach to the organization of the visual cortex (Zeki, 1978; Cowey, 1985) is considerably more sophisticated. However, the essence is the same. All modular descriptions hold that there are brain areas solely dedicated to partic-ular aspects of perception; these modules include not only color but also those for the analysis of motion, stereopsis, and shape. The critical word is *solely*. In a modular system, these brain areas are computa-tionally autonomous. They are, as Fodor (1983) describes them, infor-mationally encapsulated. Indeed, part of the credit—if credit is the right word—for the widespread acceptance of modular input systems within neurophysiology must be given to Fodor's philosophical ac-count. As part, albeit not the most significant, of his influential thesis ("Modularity of Mind"), he allows *input* modules a substantial place. Fodor writes (p. 132): "Generally speaking, the more peripheral a mechanism is in the process of analysis . . . the better candidate for modularity it is likely to be. . . . There is recent, striking evidence owing to Treisman and her colleagues that the detection of such stimulus "features" as shape and color is typically parallel, preatten-tive, and *prior* to the identification of the object in which the features, as it were inhere. . . . There is analogous evidence for the modularity of (other) detectors. . . ." It is such claims with respect to color that are considered and rejected in the first chapters of this book. Other (noninput) versions of modularity are not rejected. Indeed, in subse-quent chapters a proposal of functional modularity will emerge that has relevance to a psychological understanding of object knowledge and its mental representation.

Input modules have their historical roots in the philosophical tradition of Locke, which breaks down objects into separate sensations of shape, motion, color, and the like. The neurophysiological instantiation of that tradition requires evidence for a separate pathway from which those sensations might arise. Its genesis has been detected in the writing of Newton (Hilbert, 1987). Newton wrote, ". . . so colours in the object are nothing but their dispositions to propagate this or that motion into the sensorium, and in the sensorium they are sensations of those motions under the forms of colours." However, the status of Newton's version of color perception is unclear with respect to modularity. More than generalized brain activity is required for a system to be described as modular. Before arriving at even a simple modular input account, brain activity needs to be organized by, for example, Mueller's (or perhaps more properly Elliot's see Mollon, 1987) principle of the specific energies of nerves. Only by such means could one imagine a processing system solely dedicated to color. Or, at least, one could try to imagine it. The difficulty would come in imagining a color that had no extent (spatial constraint). Thus, inherent in the straightforward modular account of color perception is the problem of how color is integrated with other stimulus aspects. As John Stuart Mill put it (Westphal, 1987, p. 109), "whatever hidden links we might detect in the chain of causation terminating in the colour, the last link would still be a law of colour, not a law of motion nor of any other phenomenon whatsoever." The problem of how modules might be integrated is addressed in the opening chapters of this book.

The philosophical tradition that holds objects rather than sensations to be basic for perception (Strawson, 1979) provides a potential solution to the problem of integrating modular inputs. Historically, one can see Goethe's refusal to divide color into parts as being in that tradition. Goethe (see Ribe, 1985) said upon conducting the Newtonian experiment of projecting light through a prism: "How astonished I was that . . . no trace of coloring was to be seen on the light grey sky outside. It did not require much deliberation for me to realize that a boundary is necessary to produce colors, and I immediately said aloud to myself as if by instinct that the Newtonian theory was false." Goethe took as his primary percept (*Urphaenomen*) the color of a surface rather than Newton's spectral colors. A surface is not possible without a boundary; hence, Goethe believed that color is an edge phenomenon. In the spirit of Goethe, Westphal (1987) talks not of color but of "being coloured" as a property of colored things. The proposal that color was a property of surfaces was greeted with ridicule by color theorists working in the Newtonian tradition. On reviewing Goethe's work, Young (1814) denigrated it as follows (Ribe, 1985): "Our attention has been less directed to this work of Mr. von Goethe, by the hopes of acquiring from it anything like information, than by a curiosity to contemplate a striking example of the perversion of the human faculties." Goethe's observations are not so easily dismissed; they are intrinsic to theories of color perception concerned with color contrast (Hering, 1964; Land, 1977). However, to be fair to Newton, it is worth recording (Mollon, 1988) that color-contrast phenomena were documented prior to Goethe's outburst. Goethe was aware of these reports; thus, his observations did not have quite the originality he claimed for them.

There must be considerable sympathy for the philosophical position that has a "commonsense" preference for a world of objects rather than giving primacy to isolated input modules (Kelley, 1986). We are not aware of color, depth, and motion but of their combination in objects; thus, attempts to analyze perceived objects into discrete features by distinct independent modules can be regarded as artificial. However, textbooks on the psychology of color perception provide examples of supposedly pure color percepts (Beck, 1972). For example, a red light viewed through a small aperture fills the aperture with a so-called film color that appears to be at an indeterminate distance from the observer. The film percept is in contrast to most of our day-to-day percepts, where it is completely clear that the color is at the surface of an object. There are exceptions—the sky, for example—but these are few. Although the same name (red, green, and the like) can be applied to both film and surface colors, the two percepts are different. Film colors are luminous (i.e., they glow) or are transparent; surface colors are, almost always, nonluminous and opaque. When intensity is increased, a film color becomes luminous, never shiny, as does a surface. Katz (1935) says that spectral (film) colors are always seen in a vertical plane to the observer and often at an indeterminate distance; surface colors are seen at any orientation but at a particular place. The colors of objects are surface colors, but the background, according to Rubin (1921), has a film appearance; the film color is the "smooth or space-filling quale" of Hering (quoted in Katz, 1935).

We argue that neither film nor surface color is *pure* color. Following many others (see Kelley, 1986) we maintain that there can be no sensation of red, only the perception of a *red object*; even film color has a location in the visual field and is, in principle, no different from other examples of color. Kelley's argument can be extended to colored surfaces that are transparent or glow with color. These sensations are also not of pure color. Whether a surface is seen as glowing (luminous) or nonluminous depends on the relative amounts of light transmitted from it and surrounding surfaces. Thus, Mach reported the following important observation in the nineteenth century. He bent a rectangular piece of white card along the midline and placed it upright on the table in front of him with the open ends nearer to his eye. After he had looked at the vertex for a little while, an alternative three-dimensional interpretation appeared. The edges that were, in fact, nearer appeared farther away. (The demonstration works best if one eye is closed so that stereoscopic depth cues are not present.) Mach then introduced a beam of light from one side. He found that the brightness of the two visible surfaces changed when the three-dimensional interpretation changed. Normally, the visual system compensates to some extent for shadowing, so that differently illuminated surfaces of the same reflectance are not seen as different brightnesses. But when we have the incorrect three-dimensional interpretation, the slant of the surfaces relative to the light source is wrong. The unshadowed side is seen as reflecting more light than the shadowed side and also as being in shadow; this can occur only if it is "psychologically" a light source and, therefore, it appears to glow (see Hochberg, 1978 for other similar observations).

Transparency, like luminosity, in a surface color also depends on the amount of light reflected from a wide field and not just from a local area (see Metelli, 1974 for a historical review of research into the necessary conditions for the perception of transparency). There are circumstances in which materials that let light through will be seen as opaque and others in which opaque materials will be seen as transparent. It has been shown that transparency requires that the "transparent" object and the object "seen" through it are perceived as independent objects. Thus, percepts of luminosity or transparency are not to be taken as evidence of a "pure" color percept. They are not devoid of content derived from other modules and are always part of an object.

When Wittgenstein (1978) asked, "Why cannot grey be luminous?" and "Why can there be transparent green but not transparent white?", he was not concerned with the difference between film and surface colors but with the logic of language. Nevertheless, Wittgenstein's problem with imagining a transparent white is resolved according to Westphal (1987, but see Gilbert, 1987) by limiting white to the color of a surface. White is the color name that is given to a surface with the appropriate reflectance distribution. White is the color seen when a surface reflects all wavelengths equally. It is, therefore, not possible to cast a white shadow. We do not, as Wittgenstein says, talk of a "whitish cast on things" as we do a "reddish cast." Therefore, lights ought to be called bright rather than white, though we often blur the distinction. A broad-band spectrum film color is normally called white, but it ought to be modified by the adjective "glowing"; the same applies to white highlights. Water, being transparent, is never called white. When, in California, they talk of white water, they mean the surf. However, if Wittgenstein's question is expressed as "why is white limited to the lightest color of a surface?", one has to resort to the reply "that is how it is." There is no similar ratio of reflectances for a surface of an object with respect to the surrounding surfaces that is seen any other way.

The present work is not preoccupied with these different appearances of colors. Rather, consideration is given to whether color forms an independent input to the construction of mental representations. It is more productive to consider the representation as a boundaried surface and, therefore, color as surface detail contained by boundaries, or so it will be argued. In any case, the point of forming these representations is to act upon them. Action often requires recognition of that constructed representation. The relationship between the temporary representation (boundaried surface) and the objects stored in permanent memory will be considered at length. In particular, questions will be asked concerning the storage of colors connected to objects.

1.2 Representations

For some theorists, perception is "direct" and does not need representations (Gibson, 1959; 1979). The visual input is taken to be rich, to be capable of much division, and to contain all the information required for perception. Direct perception is opposed by representationalists, who, apart from recent connectionist theorists, are in the mainstream of current cognitive science. Gibsonian theorists differ from representationalists on at least three grounds, but two of these are not critical. The possibility of error in perception can be explained with or without recourse to representations. Another noncritical distinction between the views held by proponents of direct perception and representationalism concerns consciousness. Representationalists often consider that consciousness is constructed from stored knowledge by the act of paying attention. In general, direct perception theorists do not talk of the conscious percept; but when they do, it is not as a result of conceptual mediation. Kelley (1986) talks of attention as "a ladder that can be thrown away."

The critical distinction between direct perception and representationalism concerns conceptual mediation. Malcolm (1963) warns of the infinite regress he believes to be inevitable when cognition is mediated by a decision process that is representational. One mediated concept will have to hide another to decide on the output of the first and so on ad infinitum. Therefore, Kelley (1986) wishes to argue that no "epistemological glue" is required to perceive objects. He argues thus (p. 178): "To undertake such a project (the construction of abstract representations) merely for the sake of explaining perceptual judgements would be to let a very small tail wag an enormous dog." Direct perception removes Malcolm's problem of the infinite regress but only at the cost of ignoring decisions based on memory. It is by no means clear that the extraction of invariances, however subtle, could allow all identity judgments to be made between percepts (Fodor and Pylyshyn, 1981). For that, a representation or its connectionist alter ego (Rumelhart and McClelland, 1986) is required. Categorization of the input by abstract mediating constructs is central to representational approaches in contemporary psychology (Fodor and Pylyshyn); it is what really distinguishes representationalists from the believers in direct perception. Jackendoff (1988), for example, claims that people have things to talk about only by virtue of having them mentally represented. What is not represented is simply not available and cannot be referred to. However, representations need not be conceptual for us to have things to label; they are conceptual only if we apply the same label to a class of things. If object recognition requires categorization of a potentially infinite number of stimuli, then naming an object requires an abstract mediating representation.

1.3 The Organization of Chapters

Some aspects of the study of color vision are not included in the following chapters. The omitted areas concern the measurement of color and its genetic basis; other sources deal with these matters (Pokorny and Smith 1986; Wyszecki, 1986; Foster, 1990). This volume is concerned with color as it relates to a philosophical position known as modularity. The widespread acceptance of modularity in current models of cognition is largely due to the susceptibility of cognitive science to a reductionist argument. Cognitive science has the need to verify hypotheses, which requires well-defined variables. Modules provide, by a division of large processes into several smaller units, manageable analyses that are also flexible enough to allow modification by experience (Barlow, 1986). Fodor's (1983) input modules have had several agents to perform their work; they have been presented as acting through channels (Broadbent, 1958), features (Treisman and Gelade, 1980), and domains (Cavanagh, 1987). The definition of input modules and the consequent estimation of their number are critical issues; these are discussed in chapters 2 to 5. In Fodor's analysis, an input module must have its own rules for information extraction. A color module therefore has to be independent of other modules. The evidence for an input module devoted to color are considered with respect to the underlying neurophysiology (chapter 2), the effects of damage to the human brain (chapter 3), and in normal perception (chapter 4).

Comprehensive accounts of modularity have been given in neuro-physiology by Zeki (1978) and by Livingstone and Hubel (1987a). Concentrating on what Livingstone and Hubel call the color "stream," chapter 2 considers the neurophysiological evidence for input modularity. The criticisms (DeYoe and Van Essen, 1988) of the claim by Livingstone and Hubel that there is a pure color stream, that is, one that carries information only about color, are assessed. Those readers not concerned with the detail of neurophysiology may wish to read only the concluding sections, which demonstrate that the criticisms are largely justified. Neurophysiological explanations are particularly weak in their account of module integration. So too are modular accounts based on attention (Treisman, 1986), which are considered in chapter 5. The neuropsychological evidence for modularity is stronger; it concentrates on reports of individuals who have lost modules of perception (Warrington, 1985). Achromatopsia—loss of all color vision after cortical lesions—provides the best available evidence for a color module. However, even that evidence is not found to be perfectly secure after reassessment.

The view that boundaried surfaces and their corresponding object representations are primary to perception is developed in chapters 6 and 7. Special consideration is given to theories of object recognition that distinguish between object boundaries and object surfaces. The distinction between object boundaries and their surfaces might appear reminiscent of the historical division between primary and secondary properties. Locke called those properties that were essential to the object *primary*, whereas those that were produced by our sensory apparatus he called *secondary*; this distinction is somewhat confusing. When considering information received, color is equally primary (Reid, 1813/1970). Recent advances in neurophysiology certainly make it difficult to argue that the perception of shape is any less constructed than is color. Wavelength differences do not directly produce color differences, but neither do brightness differences give the total explanation of shape perception (Gilchrist, 1979). The distinction between shape boundaries and their surfaces is much clearer. Color is primarily a surface property—Thus, when we speak of seeing an elephant, we refer to both its boundary and surface qualities. However, color need not be a criterion for elephantness; elephants can be green, white, or pink, but they remain elephants (Eco, 1988). Even a simple line drawing with its surface left uncolored is interpreted as an elephant.

Chapter 7 proposes a model in which both immediate and mediated percepts have a place. The model benefits from observations made in neuropsychology, but its eventual development relies on ideas developed in many disciplines. It takes from direct perception the notion of an external object represented unmediated at a pictorial register and from the representationalist the notion of a mediating category. Information is extracted from the temporary representation held at the pictorial register to be matched against that held in permanent storage. At this point it becomes possible to consider pure (modular) color. The chromatically derived surface information can be categorized at what is called the *internal color space*; its role for color is conceptually similar to that carried out elsewhere in the model for object recognition. The establishment of abstract categories (red, blue, and the like) from surface information allows color to be stored independently from shape. The internal color space and the meanings of colors are considered in chapter 8; color as concerned with objects is discussed in chapter 9. In chapter 7 the model considers the "entry" level representation that provides the critical initial categorization of objects (e.g., chair, face). A further distinction is made between representations for appearance and other sensory properties ("hasa") and functional ("isa") object properties. The model proposes that stored knowledge of color is part of the hasa representations. Only the entry level representations, or isa knowledge, are needed for certain tasks; it will be shown, for example, that color contributes little to recognition or to judgments of function. Object color is, therefore, stored independently of object shape. If the communicating links between the separate storage systems are lost, then the color associated with the object will be irretrievable. Thus, a role for object color separate from object shape can be derived from both normal and brain-damaged populations. Chapter 9 also discusses how stored knowledge might interact with the directly perceived "boundaried surfaces" at the pictorial register. Stored knowledge can be activated both with and without the presence of an object. Whether exactly the same neural pathways are involved in the two cases will be discussed.

Chapter 10 is concerned with naming objects. Visually presented objects are given names primarily as a result of activation of the entry level description. Intervening between the entry level representation and name output are the stores of knowledge introduced in chapter 7. It will be argued that the hasa rather than isa store of knowledge gives more assistance in the production of an object's name. Therefore, being a hasa object property, color is a likely candidate for name output facilitation. Color thus has an interesting property: it serves as a marker for the flow of information from visual input to name output. The use of color as a marker of function somewhat parallels the use of tracing agents (see chapter 2) by the neurophysiologists to isolate visual pathways.

Chapter 11 deals with color names and considers several issues. One of these is the universality of the internal color space compared with the variety of color names in the world's languages. The discussion leads to a further consideration of how stored knowledge, this time of color names, might affect the perception of information held at the pictorial register. Another issue considered is the remarkable difficulty that children have in the acquisition of color names. An explanation is offered for the difficulty that incorporates the different procedures used for object and (modular) color categorization.

Chapter 2
The Neurophysiology of Modularity

2.1 Parallel Pathways

2.1.1 Introduction
Twenty years ago there was talk of two visual systems (Schneider, 1969). To the well-established primary retinogeniculate-striate system was added a parallel, secondary pathway. These pathways were said to distinguish *where* from *what* information. The major (what) pathway (see figure 2.1) proceeds from the retina to a relay station in the

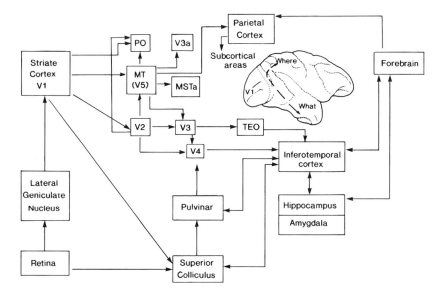

Figure 2.1
The major cortical areas concerned with vision and the major connections between them. The what and where streams ending at the temporal and parietal cortices are inset upon a monkey brain. The Livingstone and Hubel streams are within Schneider's what pathway.

midbrain known as the lateral geniculate nucleus. It then travels directly to the visual reception areas—situated at the back of the brain—in the striate cortex of the occipital lobe before turning in an anterior direction. The reception area (striate cortex) corresponds to area 17 of Brodmann and is known to contain a single representation or "map" of visual space. Unfortunately, a different label applies to area 17 in electrophysiology; there it is called V1. The visual areas anterior to the striate cortex are sometimes referred to as prestriate cortex and correspond to areas 18 and 19 of Brodmann. These areas contain multiple maps of the visual world. Figure 2.2 shows the position, in the monkey brain, of some of the visual areas to be considered; figures 3.1a and 3.1b, to some extent, do the same for the human brain.

Schneider's second visual pathway also reaches the cortex via the midbrain but by a different route. It travels from the retina via the superior colliculus and pulvinar (see figure 2.1)—vestiges of our amphibian evolution—to many areas of the cortex, including those that may be responsible for turning the gaze toward an object (Andersen, 1988), but does not go to area 17. The existence of a second visual system is consistent with an initially surprising set of findings on what has become known as *blindsight*. Patients with totally destroyed parts of the striate cortex respond, without conscious awareness, to the presence of a stimulus in their blind visual field (Weiskrantz, 1986).

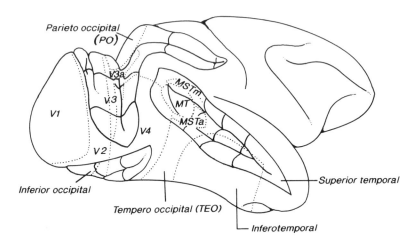

Figure 2.2
Diagram of the right hemisphere of a rhesus monkey showing the positions of various visual areas (adapted from Cowey, 1985). Parts of the cortex have been opened to give some indication of their depth.

These fascinating experiments are examined more fully toward the end of this chapter.

Parallel routes abound in the visual system. It is now known that there is extensive parallel processing at the retina and that this functional segregation of information is maintained at the lateral geniculate nucleus. The parallel pathways become even more numerous at the cortex. There are now thought to be around twenty-four areas of the monkey cortex (DeYoe and Van Essen, 1988) that show relative specialization for vision. The prestriate visual areas have connections to each other—certainly more than are shown in figure 2.1—that allow both parallel and serial processing. There is even a well-founded new division between where and what information (see figure 2.1) *within* Schneider's what pathway (Mishkin, Ungerleider, and Macko, 1983). The where and what pathways shown in figure 2.1 reflect current terminology rather than that of Schneider (1969).

The case made from neurophysiology for perceptual input modules in the main retino-geniculate-striate cortex-prestriate cortex pathway (Zeki, 1974, 1978; Cowey, 1985; Livingstone and Hubel, 1987a) is not new. The argument for "streams" of visual information has been traced back by Zeki (1989) at least to Poppelreuter (1923). The argument considers parallel processing for form, motion, stereopsis, and color, but here the concentration is on the role of color. The main stations in the processing chain from retina to cortex will be considered in sequence, and the types of cells present and their function will be described. The essence of the neurophysiological approach is that differences in behavior can be correlated to differences in anatomy and physiology; it is unashamedly reductionist.

The search for the neurophysiological substrate for color (Livingstone and Hubel, 1987a) has a different aim from the earlier work of Hubel and Wiesel (1965). The earlier work was concerned with the discovery of cells that perform multiple functions. In 1965 Hubel and Wiesel saw the visual system as hierarchical; this fitted nicely with then current theories of pattern recognition such as the Pandemonium model of Selfridge (1959). The farther from initial sensory reception, both in the Pandemonium model and physiology, the more complex the function that each level or neuron has to perform (Barlow, Narasimhar, and Rosenfeld, 1972). The logical consequence of the hierarchical approach would be to find neurons at the end of the processing chain that respond to objects (the so-called grandmother cells). There is convincing evidence that such neurons or groups of neurons exist in the temporal lobes (Gross, Desimone, Albright, and Schwartz, 1985; Baylis, Rolls, and Leonard, 1985). Livingstone and Hubel (1987a) now think that these neurons receive input from, and are part of, neuro-physiologically defined modules or streams.

2.1.2 Retina

According to Walls (1956), it was Palmer in 1777 who first deduced the way the retina must function in order to process color. In a line of reasoning often ascribed to Young (1802), Palmer argued that it was most unlikely that there is, at every spot on the retina, a separate receptor for each discriminable hue. If that were the case, it would be necessary to have minute receptors and to make continuous eye movements of quite a large extent in order to verify the presence of any color. It would be much better to have only a few different light-sensitive receptors and, by a comparison of their respective outputs, to recreate the color of the stimulus. Best of all would be to have the minimum number of different types of retinal receptors to generate all the colors that can be seen. What Palmer did not realize (Mollon, 1987) was that the receptors were stimulated by a continuously variable source of information (frequency of electromagnetic radiation); Elliot (1780) deduced that. Young's insight was to put the ideas together.

The minimum number of light sources necessary to produce all colors, as Newton discovered, is three, and this is precisely the number of different pigment types in the retinal receptors (cones) responsible for color vision. There are three types of cones, and these are maximally responsive to short (S), middle (M), or long (L) wavelengths. They are commonly referred to as blue, green, and red cones, but one must not be misled into thinking that the individual output of these cones would produce the sensations of blue, green, and red. Green (M) and red (L) cones predominate at the center (fovea) of the retina. Along with rod receptors, which are responsible for night vision, these three receptors are responsible for all our vision.

Palmer's argument could equally have been applied to shape. It would not be practical to have, at each retinal location, a separate receptor dedicated to each discriminable orientation. But if the cones are also to transmit shape information, a modular visual system has to find a way of keeping the two sorts of information separate. The first intimation from neurophysiology that information is channeled in some systematic spatial fashion came from investigations of the ganglion cells of the retina that receive input from the cones (Barlow, 1953). Each ganglion cell, like other visually responsive cells, has what is termed a *receptive field* on the retina that corresponds to the area of the visual field that activates the cell. Kuffler (1953) found that the receptive fields of ganglion cells are not uniformally responsive to light. Some ganglion cells have an on center (i.e., stimulation of the center raises the output from the cell above its resting level); the others have an off center, (i.e., similar stimulation reduces the cell's output below that of the resting level). These centers are surrounded by an annulus (ring) of the opposite polarity. The function of the on/off center-surround system is to detect increments and decrements in brightness and thus to detect contrast. Using pharmacological substances with the remarkable properties of affecting only on or off firing (Slaughter and Miller, 1983) it has been found that the on/off pathways are kept separate—thus giving more parallel pathways—by some inhibition system until the information reaches area 17 (V1) of the visual cortex (see figures 2.1 and 2.2).

Cells at the retinal ganglion level show a range of preferences for spatial and temporal frequencies. Some cells respond best to low spatial and high temporal frequency, others to high spatial and low temporal frequencies. Two types of ganglion cells are of particular interest in the primate. They have high or low contrast sensitivity, different sensitivities to colored stimuli (Kaplan and Shapley, 1986), and project to different layers of the lateral geniculate nucleus (Schiller and Colby, 1983; Perry, Oehler, and Cowey, 1984) and possibly to the pulvinar (Felsten, Benevento, and Burman, 1983).

2.1.3 Lateral Geniculate Nucleus
It has been known for centuries that the lateral geniculate nucleus of the main retino-cortical visual pathway is divided into two anatomically distinct sections. However, only recent research has shown the importance of this division in the development of pathways responsible for "discrete" perceptual functions. In primates, the parvocellular (four dorsal) and magnocellular (two ventral) layers receive input from two different types of retinal ganglion cells maintaining the on/off center distinction by layers. Livingstone and Hubel (1984; 1987a) have documented their own and others' research showing differences in the functions of these two divisions of the lateral geniculate nucleus. They propose four main differences (color, contrast sensitivity, spatial resolution, and temporal resolution) between the magnocellular and parvocellular layers (see table 2.1).

With respect to color, it was found that the most common type of color-sensitive cell is type 1 with receptive fields that are color-opponent center-surround (see figure 2.3). These account for about 80 percent of the neurons analyzed in the parvocellular layers and have not been found in the magnocellular layers. Their small on or off centers receive input from one cone type and are surrounded by an antagonistic (i.e., wavelength-opponent) annulus of a different spec-

Table 2.1
Parvocellular and magnocellular differences

	Parvocellular	Magnocellular
Color	Yes (color opponent)	No (broad band)
Contrast sensitivity	Lower: threshold > 10 percent	Higher: threshold < 2 percent
Spatial resolution	Higher	Lower
Temporal resolution	Slow (sustained responses, low conduction velocity)	Fast (transient responses, high conduction velocity)

Source: Taken from Livingstone and Hubel, 1987a, table 1.

tral sensitivity. Type 1 cells are mostly red (L) versus green (M) (56 percent), or blue (S) versus green (M) + red (L) (i.e., blue versus yellow (18 percent)), with 3 to 4 percent each of green (M) versus blue (S) + red (L), and red (L) versus blue (S) + green (M). Type 2 cells are color-opponent center-only cells (see figure 2.3), which make up roughly another 10 percent of the parvocellular layer neurons. Like type 1 cells, they have not been observed in the magnocellular layers. They have no field surround, but are fed by two completely antagonistic sets of cones, either red (L) versus green (M) or blue (S) versus yellow (M + L).

The neuronal organization with respect to color has thus undergone a dramatic change at the lateral geniculate nucleus; it no longer behaves as the trichromatic system (Young-Helmholtz) of the retina but as a Hering opponent process (Hurvich, 1981; Derrington, Krauskopf, and Lennie, 1984). Hering noted that the afterimages of colors were paired. Continued exposure to yellow (blue) made a white surface appear blue (yellow), and exposure to red (green) made the white look green (red). Hering therefore argued for opponent processes in color perception.

All parvocellular cells are capable of signaling luminance information, but there are some that apparently have only that function. Broad-band cells, called type 3 (see figure 2.3), make up the remaining 10 percent of the cells in the parvocellular layers. These are center-surround cells that show no opponent wavelength effects. In particular, spectral sensitivities are identical for center and surround. Adapting these cells to a particular color has revealed that they receive input from more than one cone type, perhaps most frequently from red and green (De Monasterio and Gouras, 1975) and possibly from all three (Wiesel and Hubel, 1966).

Receptive fields of magnocellular neurons are of the broad-band type, so individual magnocellular neurons cannot play a part in determining color differences within their receptive fields. However, the spectral tunings of the cells differ so much that they could have some role in color vision for a larger stimulus. A characteristic of magnocellular neurons, according to Livingstone and Hubel (1987a), is that they show color selectivity for their receptive field-surround, which is indicative of a red cone input. These cells are tonically (i.e., for long durations) suppressed by diffuse red light but not by diffuse white light.

The magnocellular and parvocellular layers differ according to their sensitivity to luminance contrast; magnocellular neurons are ten times more sensitive (Livingstone and Hubel, 1987a). Parvocellular neurons do not respond well to borders with less than 10 percent contrast, unlike magnocellular neurons, which respond well to low contrast and are unresponsive to high contrast. The two layers also differ in their spatial resolution. Magnocellular neurons have receptive field sizes two to three times larger than parvocellular neurons. Finally, they differ according to their temporal properties. The magnocellular layers contain a type of neuron, originally termed type 4, that is not found in parvocellular layers. These neurons are different from broad-

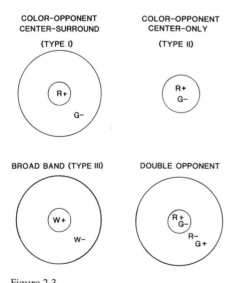

Figure 2.3
Types of cells in the primate visual system that have radially symmetrical receptive fields. The double-opponent cells are the outstanding characteristic of the blobs in V1 (taken from Livingstone and Hubel, 1984).

band cells in that the center and surround produce responses with different time courses. Responses from the center are very quick and, depending on the cell, may be to onset or offset of stimulation. Decay times are very brief. They can follow higher frequency stimulation and respond to rates of flicker higher than the parvocellular, which are more sluggish. Parvocellular cells have a sustained output, which suggests that they are insensitive to temporally varying input. Magnocellular neurons tend to have their spontaneous and evoked discharges grouped in bursts at 25 to 35 per second with discharge rates within bursts reaching levels of about 200 per second. The bursts tend to be synchronized, so that the unresolved background activity, like the cells, when converted to sound energy produces a buzz; this type of firing pattern does not occur in the parvocellular layers.

2.1.4 Area 17

2.1.4.1 Layer 4   Area 17, like all sensory cortex, is divided into six layers (see figure 2.4). The main projections from the lateral geniculate nucleus arrive at a section of layer 4 called 4C. Projections from the magnocellular layers of the lateral geniculate nucleus arrive at area 17

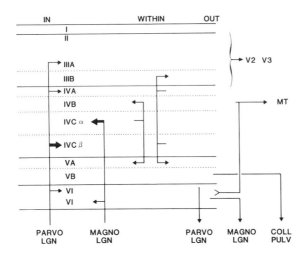

Figure 2.4
Diagram of the striate cortex (V1) in the monkey showing in and out pathways. The two major inputs from the parvocellular (parvo) and magnocellular (magno) layers of the lateral geniculate nucleus (LGN) are shown by heavy arrows. There are connections between layers of V1 and, most importantly, segregated outputs to other visual areas including back to the LGN (not marked in 2.1) and to the superior colliculus (COLL) and pulvinar (PULV). Diagram adapted from Cowey (1985).

in layer 4Cα. The neuronal projections from layer 4Cα are predominantly to layer 4B. The main projection from the parvocellular layers of the lateral geniculate nucleus arrives at area 17 in a physiologically distinct section of layer 4C called 4Cβ and at layer 4A. The defining characteristics of magnocellular cells in the lateral geniculate nucleus are carried forward to layers 4Cα and 4B, though there are some differences (Malpeli, Schiller, and Colby, 1981). The most important, as discovered by Hubel and Wiesel (1965), is that the receptive fields of layer 4B neurons are of remarkably different shapes from those of the lateral geniculate nucleus. At layer 4B—and subsequently also found to be the case at layer 4Cα—the so-called simple cells have receptive fields responsive to a bar or an edge of a particular orientation. Hubel and Wiesel found that there are other cells that respond to the same orientation over a larger area of the retina. They called these complex cells. Neurons that respond to more specific bar lengths were originally called hypercomplex but are now referred to as *endstopped;* roughly a third are of this type.

Layer 4Cβ contains cells indistinguishable from the parvocellular geniculate cells; they are unoriented in the Hubel and Wiesel (1965) sense and are either broad band or color-opponent center-surround. In one typical microelectrode penetration from which recordings were taken from 124 cells, Livingstone and Hubel (1984) found that 46 were broad band, and 78 were color-opponent center-surround.

Hubel and Wiesel (1965) made the important observation that neurons in the striate cortex are anatomically organized according to the visual characteristics to which they best respond. For example, penetrations with their microelectrodes perpendicular to the surface of area 17 provided evidence for columns of cells with a systematic organization. These columns of cells are driven by one eye and are known as *ocular dominance columns.* Cells of a similar orientation were found to be close to each other in the columns. Thus, the neurophysiological foundations of a modular structure for orientation and stereopsis is well established by area 17. However, it was not clear where color fitted into the modular picture emerging in visual physiology; that was to change in the 1980s. Livingstone and Hubel (1987a) proposed that it is one module in a neurophysiologically determined set of modules. These modules or streams are dedicated to color, form, and motion/stereopsis (see table 2.2).

2.1.4.2 Blobs   It is possible to tell if neurons are involved in the transmission of visual information by staining the cells for the presence of an enzyme that results from neuronal activity. Using this technique, Wong-Riley reported in 1978 that visual input seemed to be having

Table 2.2
Information in the Livingstone and Hubel streams

	Streams		
Property	Form (parvocellular-4Cβ-interblobs-pale stripes)	Color (blobs-thin stripes-V4)	Motion/stereopsis (magnocellular-4Cα-4B-thick stripes-MT)
Color	No[a]	Yes	No
Contrast	Low	High	High
Spatial resolution	High	Low	Low
Orientation sensitivity	Yes	No	Yes
Movement sensitivity	Yes	No	Yes
Directionality	No	No	Yes
Stereopsis	Disputed	No	Yes

Source: Adapted from Livingstone and Hubel, 1987a, table 2.
a. Depends on definition of a color-coded cell. See section 2.3.

some decided effect in other parts of area 17 besides in layer 4. Horton and Hubel (1981) followed up the observation and confirmed that there was a pattern of regularly repeating structures in area 17, with the most conspicuous staining for a particular enzyme (cytochrome oxidase) in layers 2 and 3 (see figure 2.4). Hubel and Livingstone (1987) called them *blobs* from their appearance in tangential section. They have been found in all primates studied but not in any nonprimates. Blobs extend throughout the full thickness of layers 2 and 3 in area 17 and may be seen more faintly in layers 4B, 5, and 6, where they lie exactly underneath the overlying upper-layer blobs. Staining reveals that there are no blobs in layers 4A and 4C.

Livingstone and Hubel (1984) found that the outstanding feature of the blobs was the abundance of double-opponent cells. These cells, originally described by Daw (1968) in the goldfish retina, were absent in the lateral geniculate nucleus and in layer 4Cβ of the striate cortex, although the latter is disputed by Michael (1988). According to Livingstone and Hubel, primate double-opponent cells are organized (see figure 2.3) like those found in the goldfish (but see Martin, 1988). In double-opponent cells, both center and surround of the receptive field show color opponency. The center resembles the receptive field of a color-opponent center-only (type 2) cell. For example, a cell may have a field center R+G− and surround R−G+, where R and G refer to (L) and (M) cones (see section 2.1.3). Such a cell tends to respond poorly or not at all to "white" light spots of any size or shape or to diffuse light of any spectral composition. Double-opponent cells were the most common class of blob cells. There was a preponderance of R+G− cells over all other types, with B−Y+ cells being rare. Livingstone and Hubel also found what they called 3/4 double-opponent cells, which resemble double-opponent cells except for an absence or weakness of one of the two surround systems. Although not rare, they were less common than proper double-opponent cells.

The blobs apparently lack color-opponent center-surround cells, which were the most common type found in the lateral geniculate nucleus. There were also relatively few (13 percent) center-only color-opponent cells. Next only to the double-opponent cells, broad-band cells were the most important class. The broad-band cells had relatively strong surround antagonism. On-center cells outnumbered off-center cells by more than two to one. Most of these cells gave vigorous responses at all wavelengths from 440 nanometers to 680 nanometers; thus, they probably receive input from all three cone types. Hubel and Livingstone (1987) have speculated that any individual blob contains only one of these cell types.

The anatomical connections between the lateral geniculate nucleus and the blobs are uncertain. A projection from layer 4Cβ to the blobs seems unlikely because of the profound differences between the color-opponent center-surround cells of layer 4Cβ and the double-opponent cells in the blobs. Hubel and Livingstone (1987) maintain that it is extremely difficult to conceive of a way in which a double-opponent cell could be generated from any straightforward combination of color-opponent center-surround cells, because the surrounds would have the wrong polarity. So, at the moment, any connection between layer 4Cβ and the blobs is based solely on anatomical proximity. The blobs may also receive input directly from the lateral geniculate nucleus.

Blob cells give vigorous responses to stationary round spots placed in their receptive fields. A particularly striking aspect of the blob cells is their lack of orientation specificity. Cells close to the blobs are orientation specific. On approaching a blob with their microelectrodes, Livingstone and Hubel (1984) found that cells showed a sudden decline in orientation selectivity. Within the blob itself, there was a complete absence of cells with orientation selectivity thus producing the same effect as if the electrode had entered the lateral geniculate nucleus or layer 4Cβ of area 17. A lack of orientation selectivity in the blob cells could be due to their receiving input from neurons with center-surround receptive fields like those of layer 4Cβ or the lateral geniculate nucleus, but the connections are not proven. Hubel and Livingstone (1987) argue that it cannot be due to the blob cells' pooling the inputs of the neighboring orientation-specific cells and consequently responding to line segments in all orientations.

2.1.4.3 Interblobs   Livingstone and Hubel (1987a) found that a blob is made up of a core of unoriented cells 100–150 nanometers in width surrounded by a shell of poorly oriented cells. Away from this shell, in what they call the *interblob* region (i.e., surrounding and between the blobs), are cells that show an orientation specificity even greater than the cells of layer 4Cα. Cells outside the blobs in layers 2 and 3 are mostly complex (see section 2.1.4.1), but some are simple. They have relatively small receptive fields and are precisely tuned for orientation but are not obviously selective to direction of motion or wavelength. Only a quarter are endstopped. Some nonblob cells respond poorly or not at all to "white" light but vigorously to "colored" light regardless of the stimulus intensities. These orientation color-coded cells (including cells responding best to dark bars) make up 17 percent of the nonblob population receiving input from 6 to 8 degrees from the fovea; at 0 to 2 degrees, there is a higher proportion (38 percent). Interblob neurons have smaller field centers than the blobs. The interblob cells receive projections from layer 4Cβ, but their properties are clearly different.

2.1.4.4 Summary   The most striking feature of area 17 (see Cowey, 1985) is the segregation (see figure 2.4) of its output to the different visually sensitive areas. It also feeds back information to the lateral geniculate nucleus. Modularity would clearly require such an organization. The beginnings of three streams of organized neuronal activity can be detected in area 17. The blobs are part of a system separate from that of the orientation tuned cells in layer 4B, but running parallel with it. Livingstone and Hubel (1987a) propose that the blobs are concerned with color vision. The interblob neurons would appear to have properties different from both the blob stream and the one arising from the magnocellular layer of the lateral geniculate nucleus. These differences are extended in area 18, which receives projections from area 17 (see figure 2.1).

2.1.5 Area 18

2.1.5.1 Organization of V2   In the monkey, area 18 contains the visually responsive prestriate regions known as V2, V3, V3A, and V4 (see figures 2.1 and 2.2). In humans there is as yet only circumstantial evidence for a separate V2 area (Cowey, 1979). V2 receives a topographically organized input from area 17 (V1). Staining with cytochrome oxidase reveals alternating dark and light stripes about 1 mm wide running perpendicular to the area 17/18 border (Tootell et al., 1983). The dark stripes are of two sorts (thick and thin), which are much harder to tell apart in the macaque than in the squirrel monkey. Livingstone and Hubel suspected that the blobs in area 17 projected to the stripes in area 18. A direct way of showing the neuronal connections is to inject into the cell body a substance (label) that can be carried to a synapse that it cannot cross. Post mortem preparations can then reveal the labeled neural pathway. With this method it has been shown that the blobs connect to the thin stripes of area 18.

2.1.5.2 Thin Stripes   Cells in the thin stripes, like cells in the blobs of area 17 to which they are connected, are not orientation specific, and many of them are color coded. Thin-stripe neurons of area 18 show less specialization with respect to spatial localization, although the optimum stimulus size to make the neuron respond is the same as in area 17. The cells in the thin stripes were, like those of area 17, mostly double-opponent. Hubel and Livingstone (1987) concluded that over half of the unoriented cells in area 18 were similar in every way to the blob cells of area 17. However, they regarded their subgrouping of colour responsive cells for area 18 as uncertain because they did not carry out the time-consuming chromatic adaptation or other procedures (Derrington et al., 1984) necessary to distinguish red/green from yellow/blue neurons.

The interactions between center and surround of thin-stripe neurons were found to be complex with respect to colour. The response to a red spot and a green annulus was not necessarily stronger than the response to a red spot alone. Indeed, it was sometimes weaker. There were also color-opponent cells (see figure 2.3), comprising 10 percent of the thin-stripe neurons, with very odd properties. For example, neurons were found that were red on/green off in one eye and the reverse in the other. These cells would, with both the animal's eyes open, respond only to out-of-focus colored objects and not to large colored objects at all distances. There were also "complex" unoriented cells that responded to the optimum spot size (1/4–1/2 degrees) up to 4 degrees from the center of the receptive field. Twelve percent of the cells were unoriented, in sharp contrast to cells found in other stripes, where they were orientation tuned and responded poorly, if at all, to stationary stimuli.

2.1.5.3 Pale Stripes   The pale stripes of area 18 receive their input from the interblob regions of area 17 and exhibit similar properties. However, in area 18, a higher proportion of cells are endstopped, that is, they respond to short but not to long lines or edges. The pale stripes also contain many complex orientation-specific cells.

2.1.5.4 Thick Stripes   Livingstone and Hubel (1987b) originally had some difficulty tracing the pathway from the thick stripes back to area 17. Large injections of label (see section 2.1.5.1) into area 17 do not spread uniformly to area 18; little goes to the thick stripes. They appear to be connected to layer 4B of area 17 but also probably receive input from elsewhere—for example, the pulvinar (see figure 2.1). It appears that the thick stripes respond only to moving stimuli. They contain neurons tuned for binocular disparity, but they have rather less directional specificity than those at layer 4B. The thick stripes also have orientation-specific neurons of the complex type.

2.1.6 Beyond V2
The three streams of information proceed out of area V2 in an anterior direction within area 18 and beyond. However, all their connections to the multiplicity of visual areas in the cortex are not yet known. Thin stripes certainly project to the area V4 (see figure 2.1) that Zeki (1980, 1983) discovered has interesting properties with respect to color. V4 cells can be suppressed by a stimulus as much as 30 degrees outside their receptive fields. Such stimuli are "silent," that is, they have no effect unless the cell's receptive field is stimulated. The suppression is wavelength dependent. V4 cells also have the property of color constancy (see section 6.2.2.); they respond to a particular color independent of the wavelength of incident light. V4 neurons are not the only cells that have been accredited with color constancy, but their large receptive field sizes make them more suitable than other candidates, for example, the retinal cells (Poppel, 1986) or the double-opponent cells of area 17 (Hubel and Livingstone, 1987). Studies with brain-damaged humans have given conflicting results with respect to a retinal or cortical site for color constancy (Poppel, 1986; Land et al., 1983).

    Pale stripes may also project to V4 and to the little-investigated area V3 (see figures 2.1 and 2.2). Thick stripes show connections with the superior temporal sulcus in the macaque, an area that is also known as MT or V5 in the Old World monkey. MT also has connections with layer 4B of area 17 (see figure 2.1) and contains cells with a similar directional selectivity; it might even be considered as part of a movement pathway separate from the where and what pathways.

2.1.7 Résumé

According to Hubel and Livingstone (see table 2.2), the retinocortical pathway splits as follows: a pathway or stream (blobs-thin stripes-V4) concerned with color, another (parvocellular-4Cβ-interblobs-pale stripes) concerned with high-resolution form perception, and another (magnocellular-4Cα-4B-thick stripes-MT) concerned with movement and stereopsis.

2.2 Color Blindsight

The particular claim for the color stream has gained further support from studies of human brain damage. The complete removal of the color module is considered in the following chapter. Other, more limited, support concerns the blindsight phenomenon mentioned earlier (see section 2.1.1). Blindsight studies reveal that stimuli are "detected" and that orientation is "discriminated" (Poppel, Held, and Frost, 1973; Weiskrantz, 1986), even if area 17 is destroyed and the patient is not conscious of seeing any stimulus. Inverted commas are placed around detected and discriminated because one would normally use these words only if the observer was aware of the stimulus. Even ignoring the question of the extent of conscious activation (Marcel, 1983; De Haan, Young, and Newcombe, 1987; Marshall and Halligan, 1988), these are important findings. Blindsight implies that the pathways (see figure 2.1) from subcortical areas to area 18 and other parts of the prestriate cortex are capable of carrying considerable amounts of information. Recent studies suggest that the information carried may include color.

Bender and Krieger (1951) were perhaps the first to report that wavelength discrimination was possible in the blind fields of patients with lesions to the geniculate-striate cortex pathway. Subsequent studies (Perenin, Ruel, and Hecaen, 1980; Barbur, Ruddock, and Waterfield, 1980; Weiskrantz, 1987) reported differently; the residual vision of blindsight patients appeared to show the spectral characteristics of rod rather than cone vision (Barbur, Ruddock, and Waterfield). Recently, the preservation of at least rudimentary color vision was again claimed for blindsight (Blythe, Kennard, and Ruddock, 1987; Stoerig, 1987). Stoerig even presented clear evidence of red/green discrimination in the absence of an implicit brightness discrimination. However, the dissociation between color and brightness was probably an artefict of using large stimuli. Cells at the lateral geniculate nucleus respond better to changes in the appropriate wavelength than to changes in luminance if they have more than their receptive field center stimulated (Wiesel and Hubel, 1966; DeValois et al., 1977). So the evidence for color blindsight needs to be treated with a little caution until it is reliably distinguished from achromatic blindsight.

It is by no means certain which residual pathway would permit color blindsight. The problem to be resolved concerns the route from the retina to the prestriate cortex after loss of area 17. Intact retinal ganglion cells would still allow processing of chromatic information. Indeed, it is known that these cells survive after removal of the striate cortex of monkeys (Cowey, Stoerig, and Perry, 1989). However, the route cannot use the midbrain (collicular) pathway that allows achromatic blindsight because this is not color coded (Wolin, Massopust, and Meder, 1966; Perry, Oehler, and Cowey, 1984). If there is residual processing, it must occur in the retinothalamic pathway, but it is not yet clear how. Some little-used pathways must be involved. It was shown previously (see section 2.1.3) that the main pathway for color information begins at the retina (Kaplan and Shapley, 1986) and can be argued to remain separate in the geniculo-striate pathway to V4; this will be unavailable. Color-specific ganglion cells also project to the parvocellular layers of the lateral geniculate nucleus (Perry, Oehler, and Cowey) and possibly to the lateral pulvinar nucleus, where a small proportion of color-opponent cells have been found (Felsten, Benevento, and Burman, 1983). Thus, from the monkey research, it would have to be the pulvinar extrastriate pathway (not marked precisely in figure 2.1) or perhaps the sparse but direct projection (not marked in figure 2.1) from the lateral geniculate nucleus to area 18 (Yukie and Iwai, 1981) that is responsible for color blindsight.

2.3 Arguments against Modularity

The clarity of Hubel and Livingstone's presentation has not prevented some substantial criticism of their model by others carrying out neurophysiological research into the visual pathways. The claims made for strict modularity (streams) are central to the dispute. De Yoe and Van Essen (1988) claim that there is no area that has cells that are selective for only one of the defining features of the Hubel and Livingstone scheme. Doubts about the specificity of the color stream have been expressed for all its stages from area 17 onward. First, the blobs, even if primarily concerned with color, contain cells similar to those in layer 4Cα that are not color coded. Second, the role of the double-opponent cells, which are found only in the blobs, is not clear. There is no straightforward cross-species connection between blobs and color vision. It is true that macaques, which behaviorally have better color vision than squirrel monkeys, also have more blobs, but blobs and thin stripes are prominent in bushbabies and owl monkeys (Tootell, Hamilton, and Silverman, 1985), which have poor color vision. DeYoe and Van Essen (1988) therefore insist that the color "stream must serve other functions besides hue discrimination." A third doubt concerns the supposedly specifically color-coded region, V4.

V4 is part of the main color pathway from area 18 to the temporal lobe but not with the same opponent-process organization as seen earlier in the pathway (Desimone et al., 1985). However, V4 cannot be regarded as a color center. Zeki originally reported that V4 cells were exclusively and highly selective for wavelength, but later studies (Kruger and Gouras, 1980; Schein, Marrocco, and DeMonasterio, 1982) denied the claim that it is more selective for color than are other areas. Despite having a peak response to one wavelength, most V4 cells give some response to all. Across cells, the average response to the least favored color was 20 percent of the best; "white" light elicited 60 percent of the best response. Thus, V4 cells do not respond only to narrow ranges of the spectrum even if they show spectral selectivity. Furthermore, small lesions in V4 had little effect on hue-discrimination thresholds (Dean, 1979). Larger lesions produced impairments for pattern, orientation, and hue discrimination but not for brightness discrimination (Heywood and Cowey, 1987). Only one study (Wild et al., 1985) of the monkey V4 area found pattern and hue discrimination to be normal while color constancy was impaired, but histology was not available. Moreover, in that study it was not clear whether the tasks were matched for difficulty, and conclusions were based on only two animals.

V4 is concerned with more than color. There are more unoriented cells in V4 than in V1 or V2, but there are still many cells that are orientation tuned. In fact, these cells show as full a range of spatial frequency tuning, though more to low frequencies, as cells in the striate cortex. V4 also contains cells with reasonably large receptive fields that operate like simple or complex cells, being sensitive to the width and length of the bar within them. It would therefore appear that V4 must form part of an object-recognition system that extends from the striate cortex into the temporal lobe. Cells that have a dual function for color and edge detection would be ideal for color constancy and would have consequent benefits for breaking camouflage.

Some sort of color coding has been found in all three streams. Concern has also been expressed about the specificity of function given by Hubel and Livingstone for the two other streams (Schiller, Logothetis, and Charles, 1990; Mollon, 1990). Indeed, the streams cannot be so completely separate as shown in table 2.2. For example, velocity cues can benefit other visually based functions besides motion detection per se. Motion cues are certainly helpful in object recognition, so there must be links between MT and V4 (DeYoe and Van Essen, 1988) for the two to become combined. It is clear that these prestriate visual areas beyond V2 are concerned with many diverse aspects of the stimulus. MT is certainly involved with texture and figure-ground resolution as well as binocular disparity (Livingstone and Hubel, 1987a). Therefore, a network of differentiated neurons does not necessarily have to operate in modular streams.

2.4 Conclusions

Disagreements with the Hubel and Livingstone position may be a matter of different definitions of color coding for a cell. DeYoe and Van Essen (1985), for example, give the number of neurons that are color coded to be 86 percent in the thin stripes and 64 percent in the pale stripes. However, they use a different procedure from Hubel and Livingstone's for assessing whether cells are color coded. Hubel and Livingstone look for cone input antagonism in the cell's receptive field, whereas DeYoe and Van Essen assess the cell's response to bars of different colors. Hubel and Livingstone, quite reasonably, argue that only cells that give opposite responses to different wavelengths and respond weakly if at all to white light should properly be called color-coded cells. They do not dispute that there are other cells that respond to chromatic input. Indeed, they agree that about half of the complex cells in the interblob regions (layers 2 and 3) of area 17 in the macaque respond to chromatic borders irrespective of their luminances (Gouras and Kruger, 1979; Thorell, DeValois, and Albrecht, 1984). However, for these cells, no information about polarity or color of contrast is present. These cells project to the pale stripes in area V2, so it might be expected that half the cells in the pale stripes would be responsive to chromatic borders at all luminance contrasts. Hubel and Livingstone argue that the color contrast is being used to detect an edge, not to detect the colors themselves. Nevertheless, the distinction between the color and other streams appears to be somewhat more blurred than popular accounts (Livingstone, 1988) lead one to expect.

One might have predicted that even if the color module was not defined at the retina, it would become more so as the distance from the retina increased. This does not appear to be the case. There is better evidence for a color module in area 17 than there is at the prestriate cortex. However, the responses of cells in the striate and prestriate cortex are clearly not equipotential with respect to stimulus attributes of color, form, and motion. Cells in V2 and V4, for example, have more color coding than in other visually responsive areas such as V3. One might, therefore, wish to ignore the limited extent to which the streams are not informationally encapsulated (Fodor, 1983; see section 1.2), but to do so would remove the force of the argument.

On a more global level than the Livingstone and Hubel proposal, different neurophysiological substrates for the whereness and whatness of objects (see figure 2.1) seem more certain (Mishkin, Ungerleider, and Macko, 1983; Newcombe and Russell, 1969; Levine, Warach, and Farah, 1985). In primates, where and what functions have been associated with anatomically distinct areas, namely, the parietal and temporal cortex, respectively. Removal of parietal cortex tissue in monkeys did not prevent them from knowing what an object was but did prevent them from using spatial information (Pohl, 1973). Conversely, removal of temporal cortex affects object identification (Gross et al., 1985). These results suggest that one could recognize an object but not know where it is; that seems unlikely. An isolated color stream would be equally difficult to imagine. However, the modularity argument would certainly be reinforced if cortical insult in humans resulted in the discrete loss of a module. Such a loss has been reported for color vision and is considered some of the best evidence for modularity. It is dealt with at greater length in the next chapter.

Chapter 3
The Neuropsychology of the Color Module

3.1 Achromatopsia

3.1.1 Introduction
The proposal for modular input requires that brain damage could completely remove color vision and leave all other visual functions intact. Clinical evidence is available to support that conclusion. Both partial and total loss of color vision have been reported, but it is only complete loss of color vision that is of critical interest and will be referred to here as *achromatopsia*. Less than total loss, whether congenital or acquired, will be termed *dyschromatopsia*. In other accounts, perhaps because of the rarity of the pure form, the term achromatopsia is sometimes used for all conditions resulting in a loss of some color vision.

Acquired cortical achromatopsia was not observed until comparatively recently. Its late arrival into the medical literature must be deemed somewhat surprising, because achromatopsia can be inherited and was recorded in the seventeenth century (Porkorny, Smith, and Verriest, 1979; Mollon et al., 1980). A brief account of inherited achromatopsia is given first, followed by a longer discussion of the acquired version.

3.1.2 Inherited Achromatopsia (Monochromatic Vision)
Mammals more primitive than the higher primates have a two-cone (dichromat) color system, which allows a comparison between a cone with a peak absorbance at 430 nanometers (S cone) and another with a peak between 510 nanometers and 570 nanometers. The longer-wavelength channel is morphologically and neurophysiologically distinct (Mariani, 1984). Higher primates divide the second peak into two, with cones showing maximum sensitivity at 530 nanometers (M) and 560 nanometers (L). S cones are slow in action, fewer in number, and predominantly used for color vision. Spatial discrimination, flicker, and the other functions required for object detection arise from

the output of other cones. Impairments to the action of the cones will produce deficits of color vision. Inherited achromatopsia and dyschromatopsia arise from such deficits of a genetic origin. It is now known why red/green confusion is the most common type of genetically caused dyschromatopsia. Recent research into the inheritance of color vision (Nathans, Thomas, and Hogness, 1986; Nathans, Piantanida, Eddy, Shows, and Hogness, 1986) has shown that genes for the M and L cones are in the same region on an X chromosome and are chemically very much more similar than the gene controlling the short-wave pigment. Therefore, Mollon (1986) argues that there is much more chance of a genetic disturbance causing red/green color blindness.

The incidence of congenital achromatopsia is 0.003 percent (Pokorny, Smith, and Verriest, 1979) and can occur in male or female children without there being any necessity for other cases in the family. In a high proportion of cases there is a history of consanguinity. In congenital achromatopsia the rod system is generally assumed to be intact, but the cones are missing. However, the picture is somewhat confused with respect to a complete absence of cones. There are types of congenital "achromatopsia" (Birch et al., 1979) where the patient is, in fact, a dichromat.

The absence of cones causes differences besides that of color appearance in the vision of achromats. Achromats do not observe the change in the brightness of objects at twilight (Purkinje shift) as vision shifts from cone to rod vision. Also, as cones dark-adapt at a different rate from the rods, normal color sighted individuals show a duplex function for dark adaptation (Bartley, 1951); achromats do not. In general, there is a drop in acuity because of the lost cone contribution except for the few cases of so-called cone or atypical monochromats (Pokorny, Smith, and Verriest 1979). With respect to their color vision, congenital dyschromatopsic conditions can be distinguished from the similar conditions of acquired origin by their more regular confusion of opponent colors. Acquired conditions do not always have the pronounced confusion between red/green as in the congenital case.

3.1.3 Acquired Achromatopsia
Acquired achromatopsia of a central origin was first reported in the nineteenth century. The first well-described case was that of Samelsohn in 1881, though Zihl and Von Cramon (1986) also note a less well documented case due to Treitel (1879) and two other cases reported in the same year (Steffan, 1881; Von Seggern, 1881). An early case, presented by Verrey in 1888 (Damasio and Damasio, 1986), is most interesting. Verrey's patient had a lesion of the infracalcarine region

involving the lingual gyrus and underlying white matter (see figure 3.1b) that resulted—as it did for Samelsohn's patient—in achromatopsia confined to one visual field. There was little damage to area 17, so visual reception was generally good. The lesion was relatively shallow, so there was very little disturbance of other cortical sites and hence no other cognitive impairments. The patient was therefore able to be his own control and compare his normal color vision with his achromatopsia. Many similar reports of achromatopsia confined to a hemifield were presented in the German neurological literature around the turn of the century (see Zihl and Von Cramon, 1986); the first such case in English was perhaps that reported by Abney (1913).

The first reports of a full-field acquired achromatopsia were due to Von Seggern and Steffan, both in 1881; the first in English was by Mackay and Dunlop (1899). However, many such cases (see list in Zihl and Von Cramon, 1986) might be better described as dyschromatopsic; the patients reported surfaces as "washed-out" or "colors by twilight" rather than as shades of gray. Irrespective of any consideration of whether color vision was totally lost, it is a remarkable fact that these early reports were not part of received opinion in the medical establishment until comparatively recently. Neither Holmes (1918) nor Teuber, Battersby, and Bender (1960) observed any cases of achromatopsia in their large-scale studies of missile wounds to the brain and therefore denied its existence.

There are several good reasons for their unwillingness to admit the possibility of acquired achromatopsia. First, the area that Verrey indicated was outside the visual reception area and did not appear to be a likely candidate for producing achromatopsia. Second, at that time neurophysiologists required regions of the cortex to be visually distinct or have different cell types if they were to subserve different functions. Third, because the lesion necessary to cause achromatopsia is deep within the brain, and a missile wound causing such damage would very likely cause death, they never saw such cases. Fourth, there are a vast number of medical conditions that, by injuring the retina or the optic nerve, can preferentially impair color vision (see Mullen and Plant, 1986). Achromatopsia of a cortical origin would have to be distinguished from these. To take the achromatopsia seriously, one would also have to show that brain damage had not caused some general loss of visual functions. Fifth, Teuber argued that color vision was particularly vulnerable to general cortical damage. Although this argument does admit a difference between color and other sensory functions, it is only a matter of degree, not of kind. Despite these good reasons it is, as Damasio and Damasio (1986) report, "surprising that Holmes dismissed, on the sole basis of his negative ex-

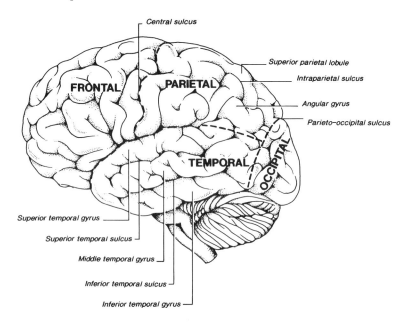

Figure 3.1a
Lateral surface of the left hemisphere of a human brain.

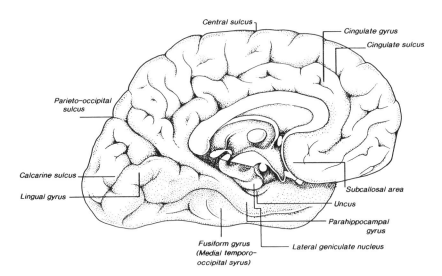

Figure 3.1b
Medial view of an isolated left hemisphere with brain stem removed to show the medial surface of the temporal lobe.

perience, the powerful and unequivocal findings of four investigators published in leading scientific periodicals of the epoch. It is even more surprising that it took five decades for Holmes' opinion to be reversed."

In more recent times, reports of cases where patients claim that "everything appears in various shades of grey" (Pallis, 1955; Critchley, 1965; Meadows, 1974) did not fall on such deaf ears. By that time, a modular approach to cortical function was more acceptable. Meadows, in what is still the largest survey in English, compared fourteen cases of achromatopsia (some dyschromatopsic) with the intention of finding the anatomical locus and concomitant symptoms that they all shared. His survey found that all patients had visual field defects—though Zihl and Von Cramon give two exceptions (Steffan, 1881; Young, Fishman, and Chen, 1980)—especially for the left upper quadrant, usually with some loss of acuity. Prosopagnosia (disorder of face recognition) and topographical disorientation were very common accompanying symptoms. From the survey, Meadows concluded that the critical lesion to produce achromatopsia affects the anterior inferior part of the occipital lobe (see figure 3.1a).

A most informative description of the anatomy and associated symptoms for acquired achromatopsia comes from two cases reported by Damasio et al. (1980). Case 1 of Damasio et al. is particularly interesting because in this hemiachromatopsic patient all other sensory functions appeared intact except for a left upper quadrantal scotoma. Depth perception in the colorless field was normal, and acuity was 20/20. Visual evoked potentials to black-and-white patterns did not differ from those to colored patterns in the left visual field. However, in the right visual field there was a clear difference. Color naming and matching were normal in the intact field, and the patient reported no loss of color imagery. None of the disorders that could potentially accompany a posterior right hemisphere lesion, such as visual disorientation, topographic disorientation, left-sided neglect and dressing apraxia, was present. Visual short-term memory was normal, as was judgment of orientation and unfamiliar face recognition. The patient was able to read letters and words, identify small objects such as paper clips or buttons, whether moving or stationary, in either hemifield. Apparently, it was a pure case of acquired achromatopsia. Heywood, Wilson, and Cowey (1987) do add the one caveat that they would have liked to see, as in their own study, evidence of normal ability to make discriminations among grays.

The anatomical damage in case 1 of Damasio et al. (1980) appeared restricted to area 18 and adjacent areas 19 and 37. In all likelihood, the lingual and fusiform (medial tempero-occipital) gyri were compromised, but the calcarine region (see figure 3.1b), which sits at the higher level, was spared as was the white matter containing the optic radiations traveling to the lips of the calcarine sulcus. The damage was consonant with the visual field loss, which revealed only a left upper quadrantanopia that was possibly related to the small amount of damage either to the inferior lip of the calcarine cortex or to part of the inferior contingent of the optic radiation.

The second case of Damasio et al. (1980) had bilateral lesions. There was visual field loss in both upper quadrants, but more on the right. Acuity was normal. The evoked potentials for color were similar to those for achromatic patterns. As predicted from the study of Jeffreys (1971), visual evoked potentials to color were not differentiated in upper and lower visual fields. Jeffreys found, in normals, that only the upper fields distinguished between black-and-white and color. It would have been even more interesting if the left and right visual fields had been compared in a similar fashion for case 1. Besides prosopagnosia, the patient had no associated intellectual deficits, such as aphasia or alexia. There was a reported loss of voluntary color imagery, but the patient nevertheless claimed to dream in color.

Figure 3.2 shows the lesions that produced full-field achromatopsia in case 2. Damage had occurred to the ventromedial sector of the posterior region of the hemispheres. The lesion destroyed white matter of the posterior and inferior temporal lobes, undercutting areas 21,

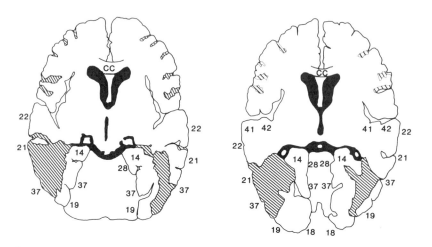

Figure 3.2
Diagrams of two sections from a CT scan performed on case 2 of Damasio et al. (1980). The hatched areas show the lesioned areas that produced the full-field achromatopsia. (Adapted from Damasio et al., 1980.)

36, 37, and possibly 19; on the right it also involved the cortex of area 36. In summary, the lesion appeared to undercut or involve the lingual and fusiform gyri; areas 17 and 18 were held to be intact. The lesion did not affect the callosal pathways. Posterior lesions of the type producing achromatopsia would only have to be slightly larger in order to produce cortical blindness or some disorder of form perception, so these cases are rare. The lesions have to be small enough not to involve the optic radiations or the calcarine regions. It appears that there is a ring of maximal coding of color located in a generous ring of visual association area encompassing the lingual and fusiform gyri as well as some of the cortex of the inferior and lateral surfaces of the occipital lobe. Recent investigations (Lueck et al., 1989) using blood flow labeled with a radioactive tracer support the localization given by Verrey (1888) and Damasio et al. (1980). The Lueck et al. methodology compared brain activity for colored to equally bright achromatic surfaces. Subtracting the brain activity for the grays from the colored stimuli revealed no differences for striate cortex (V1, V2) activity but showed pronounced differences in the region of the fusiform and lingual gyri.

In achromatopsia, one finds not a total loss of knowledge concerning color but rather a simple loss of color vision arising from a locus appropriately close to the visual reception areas. The loss is presumed to be for color alone and hence, most importantly for the modular input argument, it follows that the brain area concerned is a color "center." The argument is not so secure. The cases of achromatopsia provide only certain support that the damaged area does not contain a well-organized topographic map for colors. Although it is important that cortically acquired achromatopsia arises for a visual field quadrant, a half-field, or a full field but never as a spatially irregular loss, that is not sufficient to show the existence of a color center. Rather, it would be necessary to show, as Damasio et al. (1980) may have done, that all other sensory functions were intact.

Meadows (1974) and Damasio et al. (1980) believe that achromatopsia reveals a color center that they take to be a homologue of the visual area V4 known from monkey research (Zeki, 1980) to be of special importance for color vision. However, the counterpart of color loss in humans does not have the same cortical site as in monkeys. V4 is predominantly on the lateral surface of the hemisphere, whereas the critical damage in humans is ventromedial and points to area 37 rather than area 18. In fact, none of their cases of achromatopsia provide any support for or against the view that there is a human equivalent of V4 as proposed by Zeki (1980). Zeki's conclusions (see section 2.1.5) would require (Heywood, Wilson, and Cowey, 1987) loss of the human

V4 area to bring about, not achromatopsia, but impaired color constancy with preserved wavelength discrimination. Such a case in which hue discrimination has been claimed to be normal was reported recently in a cortically colorblind patient (Sacks et al., 1988).

3.1.4 Achromatopsia and the Right Hemisphere

It has been speculated, with some cause, that achromatopsia might arise from a unilateral right hemisphere lesion. First, it can be seen from Meadows's (1974) study that it is a left rather than a right upper quadrantanopia that appears to be critical. It could therefore be argued that the left hemisphere lesions are not involved in any critical sense with color perception. That argument is found to be false from the scan data illustrated in figure 3.2 taken from Damasio et al. (1980); essentially symmetrical lesions are required to produce bilateral achromatopsia. Second, the association of color vision loss with prosopagnosia—twelve out fourteen in Meadows's sample (1974)—might lead one to conclude that achromatopsia could arise from a unilateral right hemisphere lesion. Of course, the strength of the argument depends on the assumption that prosopagnosia also arises from a unilateral right hemisphere lesion. Damasio, Damasio, and Van Hoesen (1982) strongly deny that unilateral right hemisphere lesions can cause prosopagnosia. They argue that the only cases verified by histology have bilateral lesions. Recent cases (Landis et al., 1986; De Renzi, 1986) provide stronger support for the production of prosopagnosia by unilateral right hemisphere lesions, but there is still no more than a correlational link to achromatopsia. The association to prosopagnosia could mean nothing more than that the two areas subserving these function are close together. In fact, the argument by association is just as easy to maintain for the correlation of achromatopsia with topographical disorientation. An equal number (twelve out of fourteen) of Meadows's sample suffered from topographical disorientation, which nowadays (DeRenzi, 1982), though not in the past, is associated with unilateral right hemisphere lesions. The cortical distance involved between the lesion for achromatopsia and the parietal lesion for topographical disorientation makes a causal connection unlikely. Nevertheless, the correlation is much the same. The conclusion must be that complete loss of color vision cannot arise from a unilateral lesion. It is rather the case that both hemispheres independently process chromatic information; therefore, like simple disorders of shape processing (Charnallet, Carbonnel, and Pellat, 1986), achromatopsia can be present in only one hemifield.

A right hemisphere dominance, rather than total specialization, for color discrimination has been proposed by DeRenzi and Spinnler

(1967). It has been consistently found in large-scale studies of brain damage that dyschromatopsia is more likely to arise from right than left hemisphere lesions (DeRenzi and Spinnler, 1967; Scotti and Spinnler, 1970; Capitani, Scotti, and Spinnler, 1978). Data from normals have confirmed the preferential involvement of the right hemisphere. Rapid presentations of colored stimuli to a normal hemifield produce both latency (Pennal, 1977) and accuracy advantages (Davidoff, 1976) for the right hemisphere. However, neither population produces results that are completely compelling in showing that the right hemisphere advantage is for color discrimination per se.

The poor performance of patients in complex color-sorting tasks could well be due to the difficulties in matching that result from a visual field loss and spatial disturbance (Zihl et al., 1988). Right hemisphere damage could also reduce the efficiency with which all visual stimuli are processed. It has been found that even after controlling lesion size, right hemisphere damage slows responses to a light flash more than left hemisphere damage (Benson and Barton, 1970). The right hemisphere could, therefore, be a more efficient processor of all visual information. Discrimination could also be superior for the right hemisphere in normals because stimuli appear to last longer in the left visual field (Kappauf and Yeatman, 1970) and therefore look brighter (Dallenbach, 1923; Davidoff, 1975). Latency and accuracy advantages for color discrimination in the right hemisphere are, therefore, open to interpretation.

3.2 Dissociated Input Modules

Acquired achromatopsia provides some of the best evidence for input modularity in the visual system. A series of patients with occipital lobe lesions collected by Warrington (1985) showed the modularity most clearly. Every possible double dissociation between color discrimination, shape discrimination, visual acuity, and visual location estimation was reported. Although it is more common in cases of severe brain damage to lose the ability to recognize both colors and form, Warrington's cases are by no means the only reports of dissociation. Lissauer (1890; Shallice and Jackson, 1988) in his classic paper on disorders of object recognition noted that his patient had normal color vision. In another similar case where color vision was intact, objects were considered to be identical if they had the same color (Marin, Glenn, and Rafal, 1983). Most remarkable of all, patients have been reported who can discriminate color considerably better than lightness (Rovamo, Hyvarinen, and Hari, 1982; Milner and Heywood, 1989). A comparison can be made between these last two studies and inferotemporal lesions on monkeys, which cause great difficulty in learning color discrimination (Wilson et al., 1972; Dean, 1979; Heywood, Shields, and Cowey, 1988) but not a gray discrimination (Heywood et al., 1988). All these findings argue strongly for an independent input module devoted to color. Further support for modularity comes from the selective loss of other streams. While being extremely rare, selective loss can occur for both motion (Zihl, von Cramon, and Mai, 1983) and stereopsis (Riddoch, 1917). Loss of stereopsis is correlated with lesions in the occipital-parietal (where system) rather than occipito-temporal (what system) lesions (Rizzo and Damasio, 1985). The locus of damage in these patients therefore points to the involvement of streams receiving magnocellular input and hence (see table 1) not the involvement of color.

The argument that double dissociation implies modular function is a popular one in neuropsychology. Shallice (1988a) has cogently argued that the reasoning is based more on parsimony than logical necessity. It is logically possible for damage to nonmodular systems also to produce double dissociations and thus to appear to be modular. However, the argument becomes involved when the dissociation is profound. The weakness of the double-dissociation argument with respect to the evidence for achromatopsia is not so much the lack of logical necessity as concern that the dissociations are complete. In fact, the dissociations between color, form, and motion shown in neuropsychology are sharp but seldom, perhaps never, absolute. The case of Zihl et al. (1983), for example, was able to detect some movement, and achromatopsic patients usually have some acuity or object recognition impairment. There are exceptions (Damasio et al., 1980) one is prepared to accept but not so much because of the rigorous clinical testing but because it *is* possible to imagine the visual world that some clean dissociations would produce. Cortical damage could, say, disturb a chemical pathway—much as in inherited achromatopsia—leaving an otherwise normal but colorblind world. The reverse dissociation of perfect color vision with *no* form perception is less easy to understand. Indeed, what would perception in such cases be like? Presumably, it would be a perfectly discriminable color that would have no boundaries and would fill the visual space as film color (see section 1.1); there are no such reports.

Chapter 4
Modularity Studied by Equiluminance

Modularity within the visual system is shown most clearly in the important distinction between the where and the what systems. It would appear (see chapter 2) that where information is associated with the magnocellular pathway, which is not color coded. Thus, chromatic information should not be necessary to direct attention to a particular location. Within the what system, there are three streams of information that have been shown from neurophysiology (chapter 2) to be at least moderately encapsulated. Livingstone and Hubel (1987a) hoped to bolster their claim for these modular streams by demonstrating a corresponding effect in perception. However, what should constitute the basic modules for perception is no clearer than it is in neurophysiology. We do not see colors (but see section 1.1) as some philosophers (Price, 1933) might suggest. Of necessity, it is an object located at a particular distance, perhaps traveling at a particular speed, that is seen to be green, red, or whatever color. To determine whether the perceived color is independent of other aspects of the percept it is necessary to carry out experiments in which stimulus parameters are systematically covaried.

If color is functionally independent of shape, motion, and stereoscopic information, then the colored percept will be stable across their variation. However, any independence that may be established is achieved only with reference to the context of unexamined modules. To be certain that color is functionally modular, its independence from every other module and combination of modules would be required. The establishment of a module is, in effect, an attempt to prove the null hypothesis. Nevertheless, Livingstone and Hubel (1987a) believe that perceptual evidence for a color module warrants consideration. Their basic belief is that three of the main contenders for the status of modules, namely, shape, motion, and stereopsis, contain no color information. They are, therefore, "color blind." The following sections, in dialectical form, present the evidence for and against the proposal of Livingstone and Hubel. The independence of color from other modules is often verified by use of stimuli that are equiluminant (or, more commonly, isoluminant for most of us who have no objection to the use of words combining Greek and Latin roots). Equiluminant stimuli are those in which the luminance levels of all colors are equated. Livingstone and Hubel (1987a) have examined the effect of removing luminance information on shape, motion, and depth perception. So much work has been carried out with equiluminant stimuli that this chapter is devoted to the subject. However, the arguments concerning modular streams are essentially the same as those in the following two chapters, which also concern integration.

4.2 Color Blind Modules

4.2.1 Shape Perception Is Color Blind
Given the properties of the form stream, Livingstone (1988) argues that stimuli defined entirely by color should never produce clear perception of form. In fact, it is well known that sharp equiluminant colored borders look less distinct than sharp luminance-defined borders (Lehmann, 1904; Koffka and Harrower, 1931), but Livingstone and Hubel (1987a) wish to claim more than that. They would argue that boundaries formed by equiluminant colors are possible only to the extent that the parvo-interblob (form) stream can detect color contrast. It is only in those limited circumstances that interblob neurons are capable of forming a border.

According to Livingstone and Hubel, the properties of the form stream (see table 2.2) explain many aspects of shape perception. They explain, for example, the effects produced by fixation and by stabilizing retinal images. Equiluminant stimuli fade with fixation because the low spatial frequencies are adapted. However, voluntary fixation does not remove the rapid tremor of the eye. This is sufficient to prevent the high-acuity form stream from adapting; thus, luminance-modulated stimuli do not fade. All stimuli fade with completely stabilized retinal images, since these procedures counter the rapid tremor of the eye. Completely stabilized images can, however, be made to reappear with slow, but not fast, movements of the object (Krauskopf, 1957). The ineffectiveness of the high-frequency vibrations in restoring the image would be consistent with an adapted magnocellular system. The parvocellular system with its slow temporal properties (see table

2.1) is not adapted; hence, object perception is reinstated when it is moved slowly.

Color and size interact in the perception of colored forms to produce a phenomenon known as *assimilation* or the *Von Bezold spreading effect*. When a colored background is interlaced with a pattern of a different color, there is, with the appropriate stimulus parameters, a blending of colors. The effects of assimilation are critically dependent on the size of the elements of the display. In the Livingstone and Hubel model, assimilation may be explained from the different spatial properties of the form (parvo-interblob) and color (blob) pathways (see table 2.2). Extrapolating from their work with single cells, Livingstone and Hubel argue that the field centers of color-coded blob cells are at least twice as large as the interblob system, so "bleeding" occurs when a fine pattern can be resolved by the form system but not by the color system. Thus, because of its better spatial resolution, the form stream can resolve outlines in some displays, but because it is color blind cannot hold the precise position of the colors within them.

The color blindness of the form system, according to Livingstone (1988), has been used implicitly by artists to link color with shape. For example, in the pointillist paintings of Seurat, the small dots of color have different effects depending on the distance of the viewer. At some distance, even the high-resolution form stream will not be able to stop the colors from merging. At closer distances, the color will bleed out of the object boundaries. The same effects can be seen in mosaics and on color television monitors. Another technique, well known to watercolor artists, can be seen to have its origin in the low-contrast resolution of the form pathway. There is no need for artists to be precise about the color/form boundaries when using pale watercolors. The pale colors themselves are too low in contrast to produce boundaries using the interblob neurons, so the strong achromatic object boundaries can appear to hold colors that, in fact, are substantially out of register with them.

Livingstone and Hubel (1987a) make the further claim that visual form illusions disappear at equiluminance. They replicated earlier findings (Lehmann, 1904) showing that visual illusions (e.g., Munsterberg, Poggendorf, and Zollner illusions) in which angles are distorted (see Robinson, 1972) break down at equiluminance. Their reasoning is somewhat supported by the dependence of these illusions on achromatic rather than color contrast (Benussi, 1902; Oyama, 1962) and the poor vernier acuity with equiluminous stimuli (Morgan and Aiba, 1985; Troscianko, 1987). Interblob neurons should show only the contrast sensitivity of the parvocellular pathway; therefore, these illusions break down for nonequiluminant figures at appropriately (see table 2.1) low contrasts (below 10 percent). A similar explanation is offered for the breakdown of other illusions dependent on boundary contrast. Mach bands (illusory lines of brightness at boundaries of contrasting luminance) are held to be impossible to generate with equiluminant stimuli (Pease, 1978), as are Hermann grids (the illusory change in brightness at line intersections).

4.2.2 Shape Perception Is Not Color Blind
There appears to be a simple disagreement about the perception of shapes and lines at equiluminance. Gregory (1977) calls equiluminant borders jazzy but is unwilling to say that they disappear; the perception of global form symmetry is also claimed to be intact (Troscianko, 1987). Furthermore, Ware and Cowan (1987) say that Mach bands *are* seen at equiluminance, Farell and Krauskopf (1989) that vernier acuity *is not* worse at equiluminance, and Mullen (1985) that equiluminant chromatic gratings *can* be seen with reasonably distinct borders over a wide range of spatial frequencies.

Gregory insisted that the only equiluminant stimuli for which form perception was difficult were those where boundary lines were not continuous. Low-resolution stimuli were difficult to see as shapes only when it was unclear which line formed part of which object. Only stimuli requiring high-resolution shape discriminations were impaired at equiluminance (Troscianko and Harris, 1988). It is therefore argued (Troscianko, 1987) that the indistinct boundaries for equiluminant stimuli reflect nothing more than the poor spatial resolution obtainable with chromatic stimuli.

There is considerable evidence that chromatic stimuli provide poor spatial resolution (Hilz and Cavonius, 1970; Granger and Heurtly, 1973; Mullen, 1985). The spatial resolution determined with chromatic differences was only half that obtained with luminance contrast (Hilz and Cavonius, 1970). Subsequent research (DeValois and Switkes, 1983; Kelly, 1983; Mullen, 1985; Livingstone and Hubel, 1987a) confirmed these findings. The comparatively poor acuity for colored stimuli can also be shown by measuring spectral sensitivity against a white background (Stiles and Crawford, 1933)—a procedure that, for certain stimulus parameters, activates only the color-opponent process (Mollon, 1982).

It is worth noting that the poor spatial resolution of the chromatic pathway must make one circumspect about recommendations (McLean, 1965; Matthews, 1987) to use color as a means of resolving stimuli presented on television monitors. There is an advantage for color contrast over luminance contrast only at low spatial frequencies (Mullen, 1985). It is most likely that the claimed benefit (Neri, Luria, and Kobus, 1986; Santucci, Menu, and Valot, 1982) is due to uncontrolled brightness differences between the color phosphors or advantages in segmenting the display (see chapter 6). The only possible use of added color for resolving stimuli would be under circumstances where the contrast was so low that luminance mechanisms were inoperative (Guth and Eastman, 1970; Bruce and Foster, 1982).

The dispute over the Livingstone and Hubel (1987a) claim that shape is color blind reduces to whether the perception of shape disappears at equiluminance or whether it only reduces in accord with the spatial resolution possible for chromatically modulated stimuli. Livingstone and Hubel maintain that their argument depends on both a proper definition of color coding (see section 2.3) and strict control of the display to ensure its equiluminance. They argue that differences in the distribution of each cone type (Marc and Sperling, 1977) mean that the red/green balance needed for equiluminance differs with retinal eccentricity. However, other workers (Stabell and Stabell, 1981) report little variation for the M and L cones with eccentricity. Livingstone and Hubel further argue that stimuli balanced for equiluminance at one spatial frequency will not be balanced at others. So, in most large displays, there are likely to be residual luminance differences responsible for the enhanced acuity and form perception. But not all studies that produce results of the shape is not color blind variety use large stimuli.

4.2.3 Motion Perception Is Color Blind
Livingstone and Hubel (1987a) claim that the perception of flicker and motion is derived from the color blind motion stream. They base their claim on both established and new psychophysical findings. It has been found that the effect of temporal oscillation on luminance-modulated light sources is different from those that are chromatically modulated. Luminance-modulated sources must be oscillated faster to remove flicker (Ives, 1923), and illusory brightness changes produced by flicker are independent of wavelength (Walters and Harwerth, 1978). Therefore, color may not be concerned with the sensation of flicker (Kelly and Van Norren, 1977). The same is claimed for motion perception. Livingstone and Hubel found, for equiluminant stimuli, that apparent motion disappeared at a different oscillation rate than flicker. They claim that the perception of motion, like flicker, is solely determined by the achromatic, magnocellular system but reliant on different properties of it (Campbell and Maffei, 1981). For example, at very low luminance contrasts, very little, if any, movement is seen in slowly moving stimuli. In the Livingstone and Hubel model, equiluminant stimuli will not activate the magnocellularly dri-

ven motion stream. Therefore, equiluminant stimuli ought to carry no information on either real or apparent motion (Ramachandran and Gregory, 1978; Moreland, 1980). Indeed, when luminance differences are removed, the abrupt transition from organized directional to random movement can be very striking.

The illusory effects of movement provide further evidence for the independence of the color and motion pathways. Livingstone and Hubel (1987a) produced a colored version of the Mackay illusion (1957) that observers fixated while the luminance difference between the colors was changed. In the original illusion, staring for some time at a high-resolution (narrow-stripe) achromatic display produced an impression of orthogonal streaming lines as an aftereffect. In Livingstone and Hubel's colored version, when the equiluminance point was reached, the streaming effect was seen but without the observer's looking away! Livingstone and Hubel interpret their observation as showing the dependence of the Mackay effect on luminance contrast. Further indication that the strength of motion aftereffects depends only on the luminance parameters of the stimulus comes from Troscianko and Fahle (1988).

4.2.4 Motion Perception Is Not Color Blind

There are two main arguments against the motion is color blind proposal. The first (Troscianko and Harris, 1988) is that based on "positional uncertainty." It derives from a model of Ingling and Martinez (1983) in which the red/green opponent cells carry both luminance and chromatic information with different powers for spatial resolution. The reduction in perceived motion for equiluminant stimuli is believed to be due to their boundaries' being indistinct. Thus, there is no difficulty in seeing the sudden introduction of a new stimulus in an equiluminant display; it is hard to detect only when it moves (Troscianko, 1987). Troscianko and Harris (1988) have shown that *luminance*-modulated gratings can mimic the loss, at equiluminance, of both global and local motion if "positional uncertainty" is added to the displays. Positional uncertainty is achieved by the addition of a random jitter to the moving elements of the display. Troscianko and Harris (1988) therefore consider the effects of equiluminance on motion to arise from the poor spatial resolution of color-sensitive neurons. However, it is not clear why it should. Contrast sensitivity for moving gratings is best, not worst, at the low spatial frequencies at which the color-sensitive neurons excel. The positional uncertainty hypothesis has equal difficulty explaining why global motion and other long-distance effects of motion (Breitmeyer and Valberg, 1979) also weaken or disappear at equiluminance (Ramachandran and Gregory, 1978). One possibility is that positional uncertainty causes the loss of boundary information in the display. Ramachandran (1987) argues that a border locking system (Gregory, 1977) is required for color to be linked to the moving form. If that goes with the removal of achromatic differences, there could be a global disturbance of movement.

The second main argument against the motion is color blind proposal essentially affirms that motion really is color coded despite its apparent disappearance at equiluminance. For example, the loss of apparent movement at equiluminance observed by Ramachandran and Gregory (1978) is considered artifactual (Cavanagh, Boeglin, and Favreau, 1985) because a blank interval is used between the frames of the display. The effect of the blank intervals is to weaken the effect of apparent movement from an already weak source. Cavanagh (1987) maintains that color-modulated stimuli carry motion information, but the threshold for the detection of motion is higher than for luminance modulation. Cavanagh, Tyler, and Favreau (1984) asked their observers to adjust the speeds of gratings, modulated either by luminance or wavelength, so that they appeared equal. The chromatically modulated gratings appeared to move more slowly, but it was only at very low speeds that they appeared not to move.

Chromatic information has been shown to affect motion in other experimental procedures. Cavanagh, McLeod, and Anstis (1987), for example, asked whether a luminance-modulated grating drifting in the direction opposite of a chromatically modulated grating would remove its motion. They found that it did and therefore argued that the isolated color stream must be carrying motion information. A similar experiment (Cavanagh and Anstis, 1988) showed that red/ green opponent cells contribute to motion at low spatial frequencies. Added weight to the rejection of the motion is color blind proposal is given by studies making use of the blue cones, which may have no input to the shape and motion streams (Eisner and McLeod, 1980). For the green/purple stimuli that differentially stimulate these cones, there is less possibility that, at most temporal and spatial frequencies, information is also being carried by the luminance "pathway." Furthermore, there are positive studies that show, in contrast to the negative motion is color blind results already discussed, that motion aftereffects *can* be obtained with equiluminant stimuli (Cavanagh and Favreau, 1985; Derrington and Badcock, 1985; Mullen and Baker, 1985). In summary, there is now good evidence that the isolated color stream carries motion information for both real and apparent motion. Gorea and Papathomas (1989) even claim that there are circumstances where apparent motion induced by chromatic differences alone can be *stronger* than that produced from luminance cues.

4.2.5 Depth Perception Is Color Blind

Depth perception can be achieved by both monocular and binocular (stereopsis) cues. Livingstone and Hubel (1987a) derive the monocular cues from the form module and the binocular cues from the stereopsis module. In their model, neither is color coded. The claim, therefore, is that monocular depth cues of perspective, overlap and the like (Livingstone and Hubel, 1987a), and stereopsis (Lu and Fender, 1972; Gregory, 1977; Livingstone and Hubel, 1987a) disappear at equiluminance. The proposal that all our depth perception is color blind (Livingstone, 1988) gains support from the disappearance at equiluminance of other depth effects that are known to depend on luminance. For example, the illusory elliptical movement produced by a swinging pendulum (Pulfrich effect) disappears, and binocular rivalry is much reduced.

4.2.6 Depth Perception Is Not Color Blind

Some of the demonstrations in Livingstone (1988) concern illusory size distortions, which Gregory (1970) has suggested are due to explicit or implicit depth cues. Presumably, it is these cues that are lost at equiluminance. However, the depth-cues explanation of the illusions has been contested (Hotopf, 1966; Blakemore, Carpenter, and Georgeson, 1970). If the illusions are really due to mutual inhibition between display elements (Blakemore, Carpenter, and Georgeson), then the loss of depth information at equiluminance could be due to the positional uncertainty associated with color-modulated stimuli. In that case, the illusions would be weaker but would not completely disappear. Gregory (1977) certainly denies their disappearance.

It is unclear whether or not large figural stimuli are seen stereoscopically at equiluminance (Comerford, 1974; Gregory, 1977; De Weert and Sadza, 1983). Livingstone and Hubel argue that with smaller figures it is possible, though with considerable subject variability, to show that stereopsis always reduces at some ratio of red/green brightness. Nevertheless, the impression of depth does not completely go away (DeWeert and Sadza). Furthermore, it appears possible to obtain, albeit weak, stereopsis under blue illumination (Grinberg and Williams, 1985). On the assumption that the S cones input only to the color stream, this should not happen.

4.3 Summary Comment

The independence of color from other streams of information has been examined by the technique of equiluminance. Some element of color coding has been found present in all streams and, therefore, a color module is denied. However, if the stimuli used were not properly equiluminant, there is a possible "let out" for the color module. It could then be argued that effects apparently due to chromatic differences were caused by residual luminance differences. Bradley, Switkes, and DeValois (1988) discuss these potential artifacts. Size and chromatic aberration are the main problems. Size is a problem because stimuli set to be equiluminant at one spatial frequency will not be equiluminant at others. Chromatic aberration is a problem because the optics of the eye produces differential blur and magnification according to wavelength. Bradley et al. (1988) conclude that it may not be possible to totally balance chromatic stimuli for luminance or to prevent the luminance "stream" from being differentially affected by different (albeit equiluminant) wavelengths. If it is impossible to completely remove luminance differences, the modular approach does not have to worry about reports of limited shape and motion perception found with equiluminant stimuli. Opinions differ, but the evidence (see especially Gorea and Papathomas, 1989) is that the effects are not so limited. It must be concluded that the modular input approach derived from neurophysiology—which is itself contested—has not been strengthened by studies using equiluminant stimuli.

In essence, the Livingstone and Hubel proposal is that perception mirrors the properties of cells in their form, color, and motion streams; this extrapolation from single-cell data to psychophysics should be approached with caution. The perception of shape is not the property of single cells, especially those in area 17 and 18 with restricted field sizes. For none of the streams does our perception conclusively parallel their version of the action of single neurons. Indeed, in turning to perception for support of their modular input streams, Livingstone and Hubel skate around the important issue of module integration. The problem is well illustrated by a supporter of the modular approach (Savoy, 1987). He writes: "Let me emphasize that the collection of subsystems chosen . . . may mask rather deep problems. A given neuron showing preference for some orientation will likely show some specificity for direction of movement and ocularity and be dependent upon the magnitude of the luminance contrast. How is it possible to think about an orientation system (to which this neuron supposedly belongs) without simultaneously considering other systems?" How then are the supposed streams of information (color, shape, and motion) integrated in normal perception? As the Gestalt psychologists stressed, perception is organized for object recognition. Advocates of the modular approach will, therefore, have to explain how that integration into objects takes place. One proposal has concerned attentional processes. From that proposal, discussed in the next chapter, will develop an alternative modular approach based on boundary-forming "domains."

Chapter 5
The Temporary Representation:
Modular Approaches

5.1 The Pictorial Register

The retina receives patterns of light energy that change both spatially and temporally. An essential function of the temporary representations created from these luminance and chromatic differences is to mark objects simultaneously present and thereby to allow otherwise identical objects in different places to be distinguished. The representations are held in a buffer that has been given various names. As a generic for all the alternatives, the term *pictorial register* will be used. The pictorial register incorporates, or results from, a more direct sensory store called *iconic* memory (Sperling, 1960; Neisser, 1967). Iconic storage is said to have different properties (Phillips, 1974) from a more durable short-term visual buffer that is here called the pictorial register. However, the distinctions have been disputed (Coltheart, 1983; Haber, 1983). The pictorial register also operates as the short-term visual memory store known as the *visuo-spatial scratch pad* (Baddeley and Hitch, 1984). Maintenance of information in the pictorial register involves the visual memory maps found in the frontal lobes (Goldman-Rakic, 1987); these are part of a neural network connected to the where and what systems of the posterior cortex. A different register deals with auditory material (Brooks, 1968; Logie, 1986).

Formation of the temporary representation in the pictorial register is rapid but nevertheless can be disrupted (masked) by a subsequent stimulus. No part of a picture, not even luminance differences, can be perceived if it is immediately followed by a bright mask. Luminance, but not shape, differences are seen if the picture is followed after a slightly longer delay by a patterned mask (Turvey, 1973). A patterned mask at 100 ms can even remove the illusory appearance of geometric patterns (Reynolds, 1978). However, at some time interval around 100 milliseconds it is generally too late to prevent the formation of temporary representations by any type of mask.

As its name implies, the contents of the register are pictorial. Posner and Keele (1967) talk of a visual code, which can survive for up to 25 seconds (Kroll et al., 1970). The visual code has interesting properties. Subjects are particularly quick to assess that two simultaneous or successive stimuli are identical (Bertelson, 1961; Jordan and Rabbitt, 1977; Kroll and Ramskov, 1984). Nonidentical shapes that differ only by orientation are also easy to match (Kelter et al., 1984), but less facilitation occurs compared with an identical repetition (Bartram, 1973). Thus, the pictorial register is the site at which unmediated visual information is represented. It is also capable of some interactions with stored knowledge (see chapter 7), but for the present, only the un- mediated nature of the pictorial register will be considered. The central issue of this and the following chapter is whether the contents of the pictorial register (temporary representations) are formed from isolated input modules. Arguments that it is so derived come from both neu- ropsychology and the study of attentional processes in normal vision.

5.2 Feature Integration

5.2.1 Disorders of Module Integration
There are a vast number of medical conditions that can produce dis- turbances in the integration of form and color. They give support to the Livingstone and Hubel (1987a) model for independent streams of information. The disturbances range from the pink elephants of chronic alcohol toxicity to the auras associated with temporal lobe epilepsy. However, the most striking examples come from the break- down of normal perception after occipital lobe damage in which color and form are no longer in register. Critchley (1965) reports patients who see every object as red or yellow and, more interestingly, those for whom the color spreads out over the object boundaries. Skin, for example, can take on the colors of clothes. In Critchley's words, "they see colours much as we smell an odour. . . . (It) enfolds and intrudes upon them without occupying any specific form or extension in a more definable way." Von Senden (reported in Critchley, 1965) described the visual appearance of the world for such patients as swimming in colors. There have been other similar reports. A spreading over bound- aries, more marked for red than for other colors, was described by Hendricks, Holliday, and Ruddock (1981). The patient reported by Gelb (1921; Katz, 1935) talked of having to reach *into* the color in order to touch the surface of an object. Colors were so dissociated from the surfaces of objects that the patient never used the words "black" and

"white," which normally refer to surfaces, but talked instead of "bright" and "dark" (see section 1.1).

During the recovery of vision after brain damage, it is recorded that features of objects return one at a time. Riddoch (1917) described the sequence of return as beginning with the sensation of light and motion, followed by form perception and, finally, color vision. Poetzl (1928), in describing a similar sequence, reported that red was the first color to return and blue the last. These early case histories strongly imply modular function. A recent investigation of the recovery of cortical blindness (Merrill and Kewman, 1986) does likewise. It stresses the difficulty patients have in getting both object color and object shape correct at the same time—as if it is the "glue" that has been lost.

The neuropsychological evidence once more gives support for input modules. However, the clinical reports could be interpreted differently. It could be that the patients' difficulty lies in an inability to form a coherent object boundary rather than in the nonintegration of input modules. A similar debate has taken place in the literature concerning normal vision. Normal performance can also be interpreted in both modular and nonmodular theoretical frameworks. Modular accounts are given in this chapter, and the nonmodular is reserved for the next.

5.2.2 Pop-out

The modular account of visual processing (Treisman, 1986; Broadbent, 1958) proposes that different sensory dimensions such as color, orientation, size, and direction of movement are coded separately in specialized temporary representations that map positions in the visual field. In Treisman's model (see figure 5.1), maps are formed for each of the pathways. For color there are many maps (see figure 5.1). Activity within a module is monitored without conscious attention by mechanisms that Neisser (1967) called preattentive. Thus, if there is only one item active in the red map, it can be detected by activity per se without requiring any discrimination among stimulus values. Phenomenologically, the unique color appears to stand out from the rest of the achromatic display or from other chromatic maps; it is said to "pop out." For Treisman, pop-out is the most important defining characteristic of a feature. Operationally, its definition is the independence of search time from the number of items in the display. Therefore, the time taken to search for a red object among green objects is not substantially affected by the range or number of other shapes present (Green and Anderson, 1956; Noble and Sanders, 1980; Treisman and Gelade, 1980). Pop-out is not present if search time increases with number of items in the display.

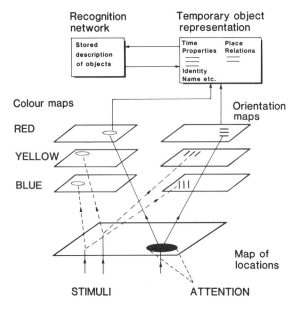

Figure 5.1
A model for the integration of stimulus features (adapted from Treisman, 1988). An attentional spotlight is shown upon the master map (map of locations) at which the features in that location are integrated from the individual maps. A temporary representation (object file) is formed as a result of the integration.

Features pop out in other modules besides color; for example, a single vertical line pops out from horizontal lines. Furthermore, it is possible under certain conditions, to search for several different feature targets simultaneously (Quinlan and Humphreys, 1987; Treisman, 1988). The important restrictions concern the similarity of distractor (nontarget) items to the target. Thus, pop-out can be found even if the targets are features from different dimensions. Quinlan and Humphreys found that there was a small increase in search time for three modules (dimensions) compared with the one-module condition because each module needs to be checked to see which contains the target. However, the time taken to spot the target did not increase with the number of distractor items in the feature map.

5.2.3 The Attentional Spotlight
A visual system that is functionally modular at its early stages will require a "glue" to bind together features such as red and circle (Treisman and Gelade, 1980). Integration is linked (see Treisman, 1986, 1988 for reviews) to mechanisms of attention. It is determined by spatial

location and not by the temporal synchronicity of color and shape information (Keele et al., 1988). Treisman (1988) proposes that there is a master map (see figure 5.1) that gives the location of all feature boundaries. An attentional spotlight trained on a particular location in the master map allows integration of information from that position in all the feature maps. Only at the place where the attentional spotlight falls is information in the feature maps made available to control responses *and* to consciousness. Thus, a single feature target can be identified without first being accurately localized, but to identify a target defined by a combination (conjunction) of features, knowledge of location is also required. When targets are defined by a conjunction of features, attention has to be allocated to each object in turn, and the targets should not pop out. The time to find a target should increase linearly with the number of items in the display. For example, a search for a red item among green items takes place in parallel but not a search for a red circle among red and green shapes (Treisman and Gelade, 1980). Resources are stretched when it is necessary to combine information from more than one map, and under pressure, incorrect combinations ("illusory conjunctions") of color and shape can sometimes arise (Treisman and Schmidt, 1982). In the preceding example, a red circle might occasionally be seen as a green circle if there are other green shapes in the display. It has been shown, contrary to Treisman and Schmidt (1982), that illusory conjunctions occur only from nearby objects (Snyder, 1972; Prinzmetal, Presti, and Posner, 1986).

The metaphor of attention operating in the beam of a spotlight comes from Posner (1980). There have been several interesting demonstrations (Eriksen and Eriksen, 1974; Posner, Snyder, and Davidson, 1980; Eriksen and Yeh, 1985) of its usefulness. Information close to a target requires very limited processing resources. At distances greater than 1 degree from a target, such "automatic" processing diminishes (Kahneman and Chajczyk, 1983) until at more than 4 degrees it disappears (Kahneman, Treisman, and Burkell, 1983). The diameter of the spotlight is, therefore, usually quite small. However, estimates for the diameter of the spotlight vary (Keele et al., 1988) perhaps because the control mechanisms—probably thalamic (Crick, 1984)—are able to direct attention to different sizes of visual field. According to task demands, the spotlight can be focused strongly over a narrow area or weakly over a larger one; consequently, the attentional spotlight might be better described as a "zoom lens" (Eriksen and Murphy, 1987).

Helmholtz argued (James, 1890) that when fixation is tightly controlled, attention cannot be divided between locations. Posner's account of the attentional spotlight is similar and has confirmed some interesting predictions. He showed that prior knowledge of where a target would appear (warning cue) made it easier to join together information from the different feature maps on the master map of locations (Posner, 1980; Posner et al., 1980). Posner's model is supported by electroencephalographic evidence (Previc and Harter, 1982) showing that evoked potentials for color at an expected locus differ from those at other loci. The limitations to the usefulness of warning cues are also compatible with Treisman's model. For a target defined by conjunctions of features, subjects benefited from cues indicating its position (Posner and Snyder, 1975); for targets in only one feature map, the validity of the warning cue was largely irrelevant (Prinzmetal, Presti, and Posner 1986), but see Briand and Klein (1987).

Posner sees the attentional spotlight as a mechanism by which information in the where system can be integrated with the what system. Damage to the parietal lobe (where system) reduces the effectiveness of the spotlight (Posner et al., 1984). The neurophysiological substrate for the what system of the attentional spotlight is being discovered. For example, neurons exist in V4 (Spitzer, Desimone, and Moran, 1988) and the inferotemporal cortex (Fuster, 1988) that have the property of responding differentially when attention to color is required. These cells do not respond to the same extent when the stimulus is simply placed, without attentional task demands, within the cell's receptive field. Fuster locates these attentional-sensitive cells in the lower bank of the superior temporal sulcus (see figures 2.2 and 3.1a). Furthermore, microelectrode implantations in the inferotemporal regions of the macaque monkey have shown that the appropriate neurons exist to represent a whole visual scene (Gross et al., 1985) and that the locus of attention can be varied to small or large areas within it.

There is a modular basis to the models of attention proposed by Posner and Treisman. Color is one of the modules. It is a stimulus feature that directs the attentional spotlight to a location where stimuli require further specification (Williams, 1966). It is, perhaps, one of the preattentive mechanisms (Neisser, 1967), which Posner (1980) calls exogenous. Moving, flashing, and perhaps colored stimuli in the periphery of vision automatically shift attention to that location so that voluntary controlled (endogenous) attention can operate.

5.2.4 Prior Entry: A Modular Alternative to the Spotlight
The spotlight account of attention gives particular emphasis to stimulus location. Tsal (1983) has even proposed that spatial location is different in kind from other physical properties of a display. However, the priority of location information over other features may not be

mandatory. As Broadbent and Broadbent (1986) point out, a more general notion of "prior entry" (Titchener, 1908) has had a long history in experimental psychology and deserves consideration for explaining feature integration. The prior entry view of attention simply proposes that preference is given to any aspect of the stimulus processed first. Prior entry is now sometimes considered as part of the problem in determining the width of the "attentional gate" (Reeves and Sperling, 1986), that is, how much information can be dealt with at any one time. Thus, data explained by means of the attentional spotlight may also be interpreted in terms of the temporal order of processing (Gathercole and Broadbent, 1987).

The prior entry account considers that attentional resources are allocated according to task demands. Location is considered special only in so far as it is very often a critical aspect of objects in the visual world. Subjects, unless instructed otherwise, would give it attentional priority over, say, color. Muller and Findlay (1987) reported that attentional mechanisms are, in that way, flexible and respond best to whatever attribute is available first. If color is given priority, then it will be processed first, and likewise for location.

Information processing by order of priority should mean that preference is given to those features that are available earlier. Availability may be determined by neurophysiological as well as psychological constraints. The superior ability of observers to segment the left visual field by color (Harms and Bundesen, 1983) could be explained by the faster rate for processing visuo-spatial information in the right hemisphere (Davidoff, 1982). One might also expect that the slower color stream (see table 2.2) would have a somewhat limited priority over the faster shape stream. However, in general, task demands will determine the order of feature processing. If an observer is asked about the color of an object, the object (shape) gets priority; if the observer is asked about the object in a particular color, the color gets priority.

A prior entry account will also predict illusory conjunctions (McLean, Broadbent, and Broadbent, 1982; Gathercole and Broadbent, 1984; Broadbent and Broadbent, 1986). Furthermore, it makes definite predictions about the time course of these intrusions. Broadbent and Broadbent (1986) argue that illusory conjunctions are formed with objectively subsequent features only when the target feature is encoded less rapidly than the other task-salient features. They should all occur (see Sternberg and Knoll, 1973; Reeves and Sperling, 1986) from objectively later items than the target. Since color is generally slower to code than shape, the intrusion errors for "what color was the three?" will be from earlier items than those for the question "what digit was red?" However, in their early experiments McLean, Broadbent, and Broadbent (1982) found that location cues were producing intrusion errors of a type that could not be explained by prior entry; the intrusion errors were as likely to be from earlier items than later ones. A later study (Broadbent and Broadbent, 1986) showed that the symmetrical pattern of intrusion errors was, itself, an artifact of the slower encoding for color. A different pattern of intrusion errors is associated with a category search ("what color was the digit?"). In category search, the delay before "gating of attention" is lengthened, and prior entry becomes unimportant.

5.2.5 Is Integration Based on Features?
There is a class of aftereffect that considers the adaptation to combinations of modules. These aftereffects are called *contingent* and, on first analysis, provide evidence that complex shapes can be built up from combinations of features from various dimensions. Research into contingent aftereffects began with McCollough (1965); she discovered an aftereffect dependent on the combined "modules" of color and form. McCollough found that the continued alternation of red vertical gratings with green horizontal gratings induced red in a horizontal achromatic grating and green in a vertical one. The use of two orientations is not mandatory, but its use clearly removes any concern that the McCollough effect is a simple afterimage color. There have been a considerable number of variations using many modules besides color and orientation (see Treisman, 1986). These include those of color contingent on movement (Hepler, 1968) and movement contingent on color (Favreau, Emerson, and Corballis, 1972; Mayhew and Antis, 1972). According to Treisman, the Mayhew and Anstis study shows best the action of the dimension of color. Subjects were adapted to a red clockwise-moving disk alternating with yellow counterclockwise. When tested with a stationary disk, the subject saw counterclockwise motion if it were red and clockwise if it were yellow. But, when tested with yellow and green stationary disks, the subject saw a counterclockwise motion with the yellow disk. Subjects appeared to be responding to relative values within the color module.

On the Treisman and Gelade (1980) model, color, orientation, and motion are represented on different feature maps. Therefore, focused attention should be necessary for their conjunction, yet Houck and Hoffman (1986) found that neither attentional monitoring tasks (peripheral or central) nor number of items in the display affected the production of the McCollough effect. To accommodate these results, Treisman (1988) suggests that the McCollough effect results from a processing stage prior to the formation of feature maps. She suggests area 17 as a possible anatomical site, since some cells there are, in a sense (see chapter 2), coded on several features. However, the Mc-Collough and related effects can last for several hours, even days or weeks (Stromeyer and Mansfield, 1970; Riggs, White, and Eimas, 1974; Jones and Holding, 1975), suggesting a rather more central locus. There is also conflicting evidence with respect to anatomical site from the effects of color contrast (see chapter 6) and other induced colors on the production of McCollough effect (Murch and Hirsch, 1972; Thompson and Latchford, 1986; Webster, Day, and Willenberg, 1988).

More basic objections to the feature-integration theory are that location acts like a feature in a conjunction task (Arguin and Cavanagh, 1988) and that many targets defined by feature conjunctions can be searched for in parallel, especially if there are only a small number of items in the display (Pashler, 1987). Pop-out can occur for targets defined by conjunctions of color with motion (Nakayama and Silverman, 1986; Treisman, 1988), disparity with many other dimensions including color, spatial frequency with both direction of contrast and color (Nakayama and Silverman, 1986), form with motion (McLeod, Driver, and Crisp, 1988) and stimuli whose elements form "good" (Koffka, 1935) figures (Humphreys, Quinlan, and Riddoch, 1989). There is even a report that searches for triple conjunctions (color, size, and form) can be performed more quickly than double conjunctions (Wolfe, Cave, and Franzel (1989). Pop-out has, therefore, been shown for targets that have multiple features in common with the distractors. If pop-out really is the defining characteristic of features, then features are not input modules.

Feature-integration theory could explain pop-out based on feature conjunction if the targets were restricted spatially (Treisman, 1982). However, that is not always the case. Treisman is able to accommodate pop-out for feature conjunctions only by somehow allocating pop-out to a plane at which attention can be directed. The plane could be the master map of locations, but as Treisman (1988) points out, her theory would require modification for that to be so. Treisman's solution to the problem is to suggest that locations on the master map are capable of being selectively activated or inhibited from the links to particular feature maps. Whereas focused attention to a cued location seems to be limited to one region (Posner, Snyder, and Davidson, 1980), it is proposed that selective inhibition need not be restricted in the same way. So, inhibition of the unwanted features in the master map could produce the effect of a segmented field. Treisman thus uses inhibition to create a plane that could be called "distractor free." Feature inhibition can thus be used (Treisman, 1988) to explain figure-ground segmentation. The figural aspect of a display can be intermingled with the background and still stand out. Where targets are from the same master map as distractors there cannot be inhibition; therefore, they will never pop out.

Treisman's theory of feature integration is salvaged (Treisman, 1988) by paying greater account to the effect of similarity between target and distractor items. Attentional load is determined by the number of separate representations—Treisman calls these object files—constructed at the pictorial register. The ease of dividing attention between two different features depends on whether they are seen as features of the same or different objects (Treisman, Kahneman, and Burkell, 1983). Treisman (1988) points out that it is the features, not the objects, that change places in illusory conjunctions. When colors migrate in illusory conjunctions, they do so between objects and not between the object and its background. Treisman is now forced to talk not of feature integration but of a distinction between the medium (shape-defining properties) as opposed to the message (values on a dimension). She says, "Discontinuities of luminance and colour can either directly form the boundaries of objects, or they can define the local elements of a texture medium in which a second class of properties defines the boundaries of objects." A distinction is being made here between shapes (boundaries) and surfaces. Treisman now wonders whether attention is needed only to prevent illusory conjunctions *within* a medium and not between the properties of the medium and the message it carries. Thus, colors might be exchanged between objects but not between the object and the background. Treisman deduces—preempting work to be discussed in later chapters—that color will not be essential for the differentiation of one shape from another.

The demonstration that values of a dimension (e.g., red) can pop out when another feature (e.g., luminance) defines the shape of the red object (Cavanagh, Arguin, and Treisman, 1989) presents a challenge to feature-integration theory. The problem has been dealt with by giving different properties to the shape-defining features than to the features within them. These shape-defining features are called *domains* in other modular theories of integration.

5.3 Domain Models

5.3.1 Domains
The information at the pictorial register is derived from spatial and temporal variations in chromatic or luminance input. Marr (1982) realized that constructing a mental representation of the objects that produced these variations was a formidable problem. He adopted a

modular account for its solution. His modules were based on the neurophysiological streams. There have been several similar accounts. In Cavanagh's (1987) model, there are functional modules called domains that have two important defining characteristics. First, each domain is capable of producing shape boundaries from the relevant stimulus attribute. These boundaries could then independently contribute to perceptual phenomena such as apparent motion (Cavanagh, Arguin, and von Grunau, 1989). Second, the same features or coding primitives are the building blocks of the attributes of every domain. The domains correspond only approximately to the Livingstone and Hubel streams. Figure 5.2 shows that in the domain model luminance information contributes to the luminance, motion, stereopsis, and texture domains. Color information contributes to the color, motion, and stereopsis domains. There are five domains for the production of shape (see figure 5.2). Boundaries may be harder to form in some domains. The color domain, as we saw in chapter 4, is particularly controversial with respect to its ability to produce shape. However, given the conclusions reached in that chapter, the color domain ought to produce (see Savoy, 1987) weak McCollough effects from equiluminant stimuli rather than none, as has been reported (Stromeyer and Dawson, 1978).

An interesting experiment (Carney, Shadlen, and Switkes, 1987) illustrates that color contributes to more than one domain. Carney,

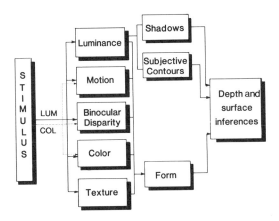

Figure 5.2
A domain model for the processing of form. Luminance (LUM) information contributes to all domains capable of providing form. Color (COL) contributes only to color, stereopsis (binocular disparity), and motion domains. All domains are fed by stimulus attributes that carry the coding primitives of size and orientation. (Adapted from Cavanagh, 1987.)

Shadlen, and Switkes presented differently colored bars to the two eyes in a situation that would make it difficult for them to fuse into an integrated percept. They found that binocular rivalry for the two color/orientation combinations occurred simultaneously with their combination for motion. It is, therefore, possible to use color information to define motion, whereas the same information does not contribute to stereopsis. Similar conclusions come from some observations on brain-damaged patients. These observations indicate that some domains may have their chromatic input preserved, whereas it is lost in others. They are, in a way, similar to blindsight (see chapter 2), as these effects have been demonstrated in patients with deficits in their color vision (Ruddock and Waterfield, 1978; Mollon et al., 1980). Ruddock and Waterfield found that a "red-blind" patient was able to use the red color of which he was unaware to form a stereoscopic image. Furthermore, the patient was able to use the red input to promote binocular rivalry between the two eyes. Mollon et al. showed that a cortically color blind patient could use color to enhance a movement aftereffect. Most interestingly, this patient could read the numbers of the Ishihara color vision test at 2 meters, though he failed completely at normal reading distance. At the greater distance the numbers could be read using the high-resolution parvocellular-interblob pathway. The color information could be used to form a boundary even if the color itself was undetected. The patient of Mollon et al. is important for the further reason that color vision was proven to be intact at the retina.

Gregory (1977) argues, from the results of studies with equiluminant stimuli (see chapter 4), that boundary contours are primarily produced by the luminance domain, though they are also strongly achieved through motion (Ramachandran and Anstis, 1986). Certainly, it is the luminance contrast rather than the color contrast of a target which mostly determines its detection in visual search (Barbur and Forsyth, 1990). The special role of the luminance domain is also seen in the analysis of shadows. Cavanagh (1987) has shown that shadows, which contribute to object recognition (see figure 5.3), are not color coded. A shadow is properly interpreted only if the shadow region is darker that the nonshadow region (Cavanagh and Leclerc, 1989). Most importantly, making the shadows unnatural colors (see also section 9.1.1) did not interfere with object recognition as long as the correct brightness difference was maintained. Cavanagh and Leclerc (1989) further showed that the interpretation of shadows was not modified by the breaking of natural constraints such as those of possible disparity. The brightness constraint was the important factor and it "appears to be verified particularly at the edge of shadow regions." However, it is

Figure 5.3
A demonstration that shadows are important in reconstructing depth and surface information. The versions of the face (a) and letter (c) with high contrast are easily seen. In (b) and (d) the boundaries are formed by texture differences, and the depth is hard to see. (Taken from Cavanagh, 1987.)

possible to argue (see Cavanagh, 1989) that there is nothing special, apart from its superior resolution (see section 4.2.2), about boundaries formed from the luminance domain. Indeed, the problem of confusable shadow areas might, in nature, favor boundaries formed from texture or color because they are not contaminated by unwanted shadow regions. Only in the line drawings favored in many experimental procedures will luminance boundaries come into their own.

5.3.2 The Color Domain

Electrophysiological evidence supports the specific distinction between achromatic and chromatic edge boundaries. Tansley, Robertson, and Maughan (1983) showed that evoked potentials to a border marked by a luminance and color contrast have two components, whereas those to a border marked only by color contrast have one. Thus, if color information can separately produce shape boundaries, it should be easy to allocate attention to colored items in a display (Von Wright, 1970). In fact, it can be so easy that care must be taken to avoid unwanted segmentation from the use of irrelevant colors

(Eriksen, 1952; Smith and Thomas, 1964; Wright and Fox, 1970; Christ, 1975; Poulton and Edwards, 1977; Foster and Bruce, 1982). Conversely, color can be extremely useful if you need to break up a coherent display (Wickens and Andre, 1990).

Overlapping areas that contain the same colors are particularly difficult to keep separate (Julesz, 1965; Beck, 1982; Callaghan, Lasaga, and Garner, 1986). Color is, therefore, ideal for denoting areas of a display in which identical items should be seen as connected. For example, it has been found excellent for defining the track of a particular aircraft (Poulton and Edwards, 1977), showing the number of aircraft at a particular altitude (Wedell and Alden, 1973), and, by coloring it pink on nineteenth-century maps, showing the world status of the British Empire from a single glance. Color can even help pick out noncolored items. Harms and Bundesen (1983) asked their subjects to respond to a target letter in a known location. Noise (nontarget) letters were presented on either side of the target. The target was easier to detect if one of the flanking noise letters was a different color to the target and easier still if both were.

The time to perform a task when there are two colors present need not be longer than when there is only one (Willows and McKinnon, 1973; Carter, 1982). Nevertheless, the segmentation of a display by color is generally affected by the number of colors it contains. The Treisman model would predict some difficulty in sorting out the different features from the color maps to the extent that spectrally similar colors simultaneously activate more than one map. However, the increase in latency depends on more than the number of colors in the display. It is also affected by the spatial arrangement of the colors; a "good" layout facilitates segmentation. The time to segment the display is equal to the number of perceived units in the display. For "good" figures, Bundesen and Pedersen (1983) found that the time to segment a display was equal to the number of colors. Each color was said to be a Gestalt. For more random displays, segmentation could still be performed by color, but there was more than one "unit" for any color. In general, Bundesen and Pedersen (1983) found that the latency to segment a display was proportional to:

$$n(c) + p(n(s) - n(c)),$$

where $n(c)$ was the number of colors, $n(s)$ the number of perceived units, and p a constant. Thus, there is a clear limitation on the use of color to segment the visual world that depends on the extent to which colors form shapes. If the same color is contained in different shapes, then segmentation by color will conflict with that determined by shape. In practice, it has been found that color stops being useful in segmenting a display when there are more than five colors present (Krebs and Wolf, 1979; Ware and Beaty, 1988).

In some circumstances, the color domain is of little importance for the formation of boundary contours (Ramachandran, 1987). Its use is most clearly seen (but note Cavanagh 1989; see section 5.3.2) in conditions where luminance boundaries are hard to form, as achieved deliberately in standard tests for color blindness. The Ishihara plates, for example, are constructed from small circles of different color saturation; only if a border can be formed by color alone can the numbers be seen. Boundaries formed in the color domain would be less sharp given the lower spatial resolution for color. Consequently, there are certain colors for which it is more difficult to maintain borders (Tansley and Boynton, 1978). The colored stimuli that produce the most difficulty are those that only activate the blue (S) cones (see section 4.2.4) and, therefore, contribute only to the color "stream." If a letter is printed in one of these colors with another such color as the background, it will be difficult to read (Mollon and Cavonius, 1986). Similarly, shapes are more likely to be perceived as crossing color boundaries for these color combinations (Stalmeier and DeWeert, 1988).

Highlighting target items in color has been recommended by Fisher and Tan (1989) for effective visual search. However, its use would appear to be limited to simple displays (see above) and occasions when the observer is aware that color segmentation is required (Philipsen, 1990). The limited importance of chromatic borders is also seen in the segmentation of shape by motion. Anstis (1989) has shown that segmentation by motion is determined by the boundary edge. Boundaries were hard to form from one of the secondary (e.g., color, texture) sources but easy with luminance-defined sources. The phenomenon of motion "capture" also illustrates the weakness of shape produced from chromatic boundaries. Moving stimuli can "capture" stimuli within their boundaries, thereby imparting illusory movement to stationary objects. One such illusion occurs when the moon appears to be "sailing" with the clouds when, in fact, it is the clouds alone that are moving. Colored borders do not appear to generate motion capture. Ramachandran (1987) found that an object was most easily captured if it were equiluminous to the background, presumably because its own borders were weak. However, chromatically defined borders can produce apparent motion (Green, 1986; Green and Odom, 1986; Cavanagh et al., 1989) and are useful in other circumstances (Gorea and Papathomas, 1989). A pattern whose movement is incoherent or ambiguous when seen in black and white produced an unambiguous percept of motion after the addition of color (Gorea and Papathomas,

1989). Thus, chromatic information acts as a valuable backup system for producing shape boundaries.

5.3.3 Coding Primitives

Each domain uses the same basic stimulus features (coding primitives) of the input (Barrow and Tenenbaum, 1978; Treisman and Souther, 1985). The most important primitives are those of size and orientation. The luminance domain can be shown to carry information concerning both these and perhaps also a curvature primitive (Dobbins, Zucker, and Cynader, 1987). Thus, achromatic stimuli produce aftereffects that can either be scaled by size (Pantle and Sekuler, 1968; Blakemore and Campbell, 1969; Blakemore and Sutton, 1969) or confined to particular orientations (Gilinsky, 1968; Blakemore and Nachmias, 1971; Campbell and Maffei, 1981). The same coding primitives operate in the color domain (DeValois, 1978; Favreau and Cavanagh, 1981; Javadnia and Ruddock, 1988), and the two domain-defined primitives are independent (Maudarbocus and Ruddock, 1973; Favreau and Cavanagh, 1981) or nearly so (Bradley et al., 1988). The independence can be illustrated by the studies using the tilt aftereffect (Gibson and Radner, 1937); although originally using luminance-defined bars, it also produces an aftereffect if defined by chromatic bars (Elsner, 1978). Flanagan et al. (1988) found that an equiluminant tilt aftereffect could be obtained at the same time as a similar effect defined by luminance. They adapted observers to 1 cycle/degree luminance gratings at 15 degrees clockwise from the vertical and alternated these with color-defined (red/green) gratings 15 degrees counterclockwise. When tested on a vertical grating, they found that the two aftereffects occurred simultaneously in opposite directions. It was subsequently shown that the color tilt aftereffect was present with the opponent color tuning (see section 4.2.4), which ought to use only the color "stream." Therefore, the orientation primitive in the color domain is independent of that in the luminance domain. It would be hard to accommodate such an effect into either the color "stream" or the parvo-interblob (form) "stream" of Livingstone and Hubel (1987a).

Cavanagh (1987, 1989) has demonstrated that the coding primitives are similar for all domains. The evidence comes from the production of visual illusions (see, for example, the above discussion of tilt aftereffect) and from the study of visual search. A defining characteristic of a coding primitive, like that of a feature (Treisman and Gelade, 1980), is that it can be processed simultaneously at all positions in the visual field. Therefore, whether a domain carries information concerning a coding primitive can be tested by varying the number of stimuli in a display. The unique level (e.g., the one large or vertical item) should pop out irrespective of the number of small or horizontal items in the display. Cavanagh, Arguin, and Treisman (1990) have recently shown that pop-out for size and orientation occurs with boundaries defined by luminance, color, texture, motion, and perhaps stereopsis.

5.4 Summary

We have seen that there are two basic problems for the modular explanation of the formation of representations at the pictorial register. First, there is the problem of definition of a module, whether it be a feature or domain. A color-input module is not sufficiently established from the fact that search for a color is achieved much more quickly than that for a colored form. A more precise operational definition is required but none, including pop-out, has been found satisfactory. Second, there is the problem of integrating the input modules. Treisman (1988) now allows that the important aspect of the output from feature maps is to somehow produce temporary representations (object files) that have boundaries. The production of boundaries could be achieved in parallel by several domains. However, the problem of integrating domains (see Todd, 1985) remains as problematic as that of integrating the information in the Livingstone and Hubel "streams." The modular proposal will require an executive process to decide which domain should be deployed for any particular input. With that requirement, there will be no escaping the infinite regress that Malcolm demanded we avoid (see section 1.2). Therefore, consideration will be given in the next chapter to procedures that allow the formation of temporary representations without recourse to input modules.

Chapter 6
Boundaries and Surfaces

6.1 The Temporary Representation: Modular and Nonmodular Accounts Compared

Neurons have different sensitivities to wavelength and to spatial and temporal aspects of the input; they are also spatially tagged with respect to the position of other neurons. In modular accounts, boundary formation at the pictorial register is determined within domains derived from these different sensitivities. A nonmodular procedure would achieve boundary formation by interactions within the total network of visually sensitive neurons. However, if only a small part of the network is activated, boundary formation may appear to be somewhat based on modular input given the differential sensitivities of the neurons.

Even parallel search, which is taken to be a powerful indicator of modular input, can be interpreted as the limiting case of boundary segmentation within a nonmodular network. Take, for example, searching for a single red item among green distractors, where phenomenologically the red color pops out. Here, the apparently modular search for color can be interpreted as a very easily achieved segmentation. More complicated search tasks require more complex segmentation. Targets defined as a conjunction of form and color will normally provide serial search, because segmentation must be by individual items of a display. Expressed more generally, ease of segmentation depends on the nature of the distractor items (Farmer and Taylor, 1980; Beck, 1982; Carter, 1982; Duncan, 1984; Duncan, 1989; Duncan and Humphreys, 1989; Zohary and Hochstein, 1989). Search difficulty increases with similarity between targets and distractors and also as distractors become more different from each other (Duncan and Humphreys, 1989). Therefore, segmentation is particularly easy for heterogeneous targets in a homogeneous background such as the single red target among green distractors. So, it can be concluded that popout of an item in a display is part of a more general segmentation process in which textured areas rather than items are the basic elements (Callaghan, 1990). Future research will clarify what is meant by similarity (Duncan and Humphreys, 1989) by an analysis of the processes producing segmentation.

"Computer vision" research has given both modular and nonmodular accounts of segmentation at the pictorial register. In one modular account (Marr, 1982), the representation is the end product of a multistage process in which information (tokens) at different places in the visual field is constructed into surfaces. These surfaces, produced from modular input, are held at what Marr called a two-and-a-half-dimensional sketch. The surfaces are then used to construct descriptions of shapes without any reference to object knowledge (see chapter 7). The first constructed description is viewer-centered. The final three-dimensional model or object-centered representation allows the surfaces of objects to be specified independently of the viewer's position. Thus, from such a description, it would be possible to tell if an object had been rotated, though one need not have any notion of what the object might be. Marr believed that the extraction of principal axes was critical for the construction of the object-centered view. His belief was based, in part, on clinical observations concerning object recognition (Warrington and Taylor, 1978).

The nonmodular account dispenses with the two-and-a-half-dimensional sketch. The shape of a surface cannot be accurately determined from the luminance gradients within the surface (Barrow and Tenenbaum, 1978; Todd and Mingolla, 1983); therefore, the boundary must be defined first. Grossberg and Mingolla (1985) proposed that the temporary representation of an object is formed by the cooperation of two systems, namely, boundary contours and feature contours. A plan of their proposal is shown in figure 6.1. However, omitted from figure 6.1 is the register—called by Grossberg a syncytium—at which the temporary representations are formed.

Grossberg and Mingolla (1985) argued that boundary contrasts formed in the analysis of the input are not by themselves visible. Visibility is achieved when, having segmented the visual input, the boundaries trigger an integration process that binds the features within a boundary. The boundary-contour system controls the emergence of a three-dimensional segmentation of a scene; it detects, sharpens, and completes boundaries. Within the boundary contour system there exist multiple spatial scales that activate corresponding scales in the feature-contour system concerned with surface detail. In other words, the completed boundaries organize surface detail (see also Bertulis and Glezer, 1984). The organized brightness and color differences arise within the feature-contour system at the boundary edges;

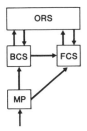

Figure 6.1
A macrocircuit for object recognition given in Grossberg (1987a). The boundary-contour system (BCS) organizes surface detail in the feature-contour system (FCS) at a temporary register (syncytium) not shown in the circuit. Preattentive segmentation within the BCS can directly activate the object-recognition system (ORS) to affect the final segmentation. Further interaction of the FCS with the ORS is then possible. The circuit shown is for monocular processed (MP) signals. Input from both eyes combine at a binocular syncytium.

they then generate a filling-in process. A separate boundary-contour and feature-contour system operates for each eye. The combined stereoscopic boundary information controls the organization of information in each monocular feature-contour system and its synthesis as a three-dimensional representation. The boundary-contour system and the feature-contour system obey different rules (Grossberg, 1987a,b). Boundaries are sensitive to orientation but not to direction of achromatic contrast; the featural filling-in is an outwardly directed, unoriented process sensitive to direction of contrast. Thus, the Grossberg and Mingolla model can explain an observation made by the Soviet physiologists Bertulis and Glezer (1984), who showed that a previously unnoticed difference in color between a spot and a background became apparent if different patterns were superimposed on the two areas. The new boundary contours differentiate between the contained surface colors without needing the further help of other discriminating procedures such as brightness enhancement.

Boundaries formed by color or brightness have different properties to those formed by other domains within the temporary representation. Whereas there are symmetrical interference effects on segmentation from boundaries formed from color and brightness (Callaghan, 1984), there are asymmetrical effects of color segmentation on boundaries formed by orientation (Callaghan, Lasaga, and Garner, 1986) or by item identity (Callaghan, 1989). It appears to be difficult to keep identical colors separate if they are contained within an adjacent boundary contour (see section 5.3.2).

The temporary representation that combines form and color in depth is placed by Grossberg (1987b) at V4 because that visual area contains cells highly sensitive to all these aspects (Desimone et al., 1985). Grossberg and Mingolla (1985) thus view the visual system as being designed to put the combined shape boundary and surface together at a very early stage. Grossberg (1987a) argues, in a fashion similar to Livingstone and Hubel (see sections 2.3 and 4.2), that an equiluminant stimulus provides some border information. However, in his model, the underlying neurophysiology is somewhat different. Grossberg and Mingolla link the boundary-contour system to the hypercolumns and the feature contours to the blobs. They argue that blobs are sensitive to all detail but not to orientation, whereas the hypercolumns are an early part of the boundary-contour system rather than just dealing with orientation. It is only the simple, not the complex, cells of the hypercolumns that are sensitive to direction of contrast (DeValois, Albrecht, and Thorell, 1982) and have double-opponent properties (Thorell, DeValois, and Albrecht, 1984). Grossberg (1987a) maintains that it is the simple cells that input to the blob neurons. Grossberg and Mingolla find support from their model from Von der Heydt, Peterhans, and Baumgartner (1984), who found cells sensitive to orientation that responded to magnitude of contrast. These area 18 cells were said to "extrapolate lines to connect parts of the stimulus which might belong to the same object." But, contrary to Grossberg's account, Peterhans and Von der Heydt (1989) are clear that at least some of their contour neurons are selective for the direction (polarity) of contrast. Peterhans and Von der Heydt also have difficulty finding a neural correlate for the supposed "short range competition" mechanism (Grossberg and Mingolla, 1985) underlying the removal of unwanted edges in the formation of the boundary. The Grossberg and Mingolla model requires more endstopped (hypercomplex) cells than have been found in V1 or V2.

Like Livingstone and Hubel (1987a), Grossberg (1987a,b) has used his model to explain a large number of visual illusions, including tissue contrast (Helmholtz, 1909/1962) and the suppression of colored flashes during binocular rivalry (Smith et al., 1982). He also provides an explanation for the McCollough effect (see section 5.2.4 and also Meyer and Dougherty, 1987) and illusory assimilation (see section 4.2.1). The McCollough effect is difficult to produce with equiluminant stimuli (see section 5.3.1), which suggests, according to Grossberg, that it requires information concerning both the boundary-contour and feature-contour systems. Illusory assimilation effects are also more convincingly explained by boundary- and feature-contour systems than with domains or modular input streams. Watanabe and Sato (1989) have shown that the color spreading can be attributed to the feature-contour system. Contrary to their model, Livingstone and Hubel (1987a) would need a blob system that deals with luminance information to explain all assimilation effects. Furthermore, it is not only the colors but also the brightnesses of stabilized retinal images that are unstable (Krauskopf, 1957; Yarbus, 1967). They both appear to flow across the edges that previously surrounded them until they are contained by the next boundary.

Grossberg claims the operation of the boundary-contour system to be generally "invisible" (i.e., unconscious). In the modular account, there are many preattentive pathways (dimensions). The two types of accounts have never been contrasted with respect to what might be unconsciously activated, but there are reports (see Dixon, 1981) that would make that investigation worth considering. A few studies have shown unconscious processing of color despite the evidence that subliminal perception is often unreliable and susceptible to response bias (Holender, 1986). In the course of a signal-detection study, Rollman and Nachmias (1972) presented their subjects with chromatic discs at low signal-to-noise levels. Each time subjects incorrectly reported "stimulus absent" they were asked to guess what color the disc would have been if it *had* been presented. Their guesses proved correct significantly more often than would have happened by chance. Furthermore, the results obtained with different color vision assessment procedures (Beauvois and Saillant, 1985) also suggest unconscious "awareness" of color. Beauvois and Saillant ascribe the discrepancies in the color vision assessment of their patient (RV) to the differential use of conscious or unconscious procedures. Abnormal color vision was shown if the test required "conscious" comparisons across the visual field—these involved comparisons of surfaces—but not when procedures used were tacit; these involved boundaries. So, modular and nonmodular accounts of the pictorial register might be usefully compared by using subliminally presented colored objects. Unconscious activation of boundary information might be more likely given the rapid time course of the luminance information, but it has never been specifically tested.

For Grossberg the unconscious activation of boundary information is seen in the production of illusory contours (Kanisza, 1979). Figure 6.2 shows that the boundary-contour system responds to orientation but is impervious to the direction of contrast. The edge at the bottom of the figure connects corners defined by white on the outside, but there is no difficulty forming vertical edges with the corners defined by black on the outside. Illusory contours, as Livingstone and Hubel (1987a) would predict (see chapters 2 and 4), are stronger when com-

Figure 6.2
Illusory contours are produced from corners of opposite polarity. The boundary-contour system is sensitive to orientation but indifferent to direction of contrast. (Taken from Grossberg, 1987a.)

bined with stereoposis or movement (Ramachandran and Cavanagh, 1985) and are not readily seen with equiluminant figures (Brigner and Gallagher, 1974; Frisby and Clatworthy, 1975; Brussell, Stober, and Bodinger, 1977; Gregory, 1977; Prazdny, 1985). However, equiluminant illusory contours have been reported (Ejima and Takahashi, 1988); they show the same saturation functions as for the production of a border between two equiluminant colors (Kaiser, Herzberg, and Boynton, 1971; Transley and Boynton, 1978) indicating involvement of the red/green opponent system but not the yellow/blue.

The production of illusory contours by chromatic contrast highlights the difficulty in distinguishing nonmodular from modular accounts from a consideration of boundary formation. Illusory, and for that matter, all other contours could be produced to the extent that a domain is capable of producing boundaries. Thus, both types of account stress the importance of boundary formation. The critical difference rests more on the separate status of the surface detail given by the nonmodular account. The perception of surface color will, therefore, be considered in more detail. The appearance of surface colors will be dependent, in a complex fashion, on the interaction of stimulus parameters but should show some resemblance to the properties of the blob neurons.

6.2 The Colors of Surfaces

6.2.1 Introduction

Several factors affect the color of a surface besides the spectral characteristics of incident illumination. The color of surfaces can be altered by interactions with other streams of sensory information (e.g., luminance, motion) present in the visual input, the colors of surrounding surfaces, and perhaps by our stored knowledge concerning object color. A discussion of the possible influence of memory on object color will be given in chapter 9; however, at this point, it is interesting to note that Helmholtz viewed identifying object colors as the main purpose of color constancy. He wrote (see Jameson and Hurvich, 1989) that by seeing the same objects under different illuminations "we learn to get a correct idea of object colours in spite of difference in illumination. We learn to judge how such an object would look in white light and since our interest lies entirely in the object colour, we become unconscious of the sensations on which the judgement rests." Therefore, we first consider color constancy and then briefly discuss the effects of lightness, motion, and depth information on perceived surface colors.

6.2.2 Color Constancy

Surfaces maintain approximately the same color appearance despite naturally occurring changes in the spectral composition of the illuminant. A red tomato, or any other shape for that matter, maintains much the same color appearance at various times of the day even though the proportion of short to long components in the illuminant varies. The extent to which color appearance is maintained despite these changes in illuminant is known as color constancy. There are two important and related questions that need to be answered with respect to this obviously adaptive capability. These questions concern the anatomical site of color constancy and the mechanisms by which it operates. The anatomical site of color constancy has been discussed previously (see section 2.1.5); it is unclear whether the locus is retinal or cortical. Psychophysical investigations into the mechanisms responsible for color constancy indicate that both sites are necessary but not equally important.

The retinal locus that has been traditionally proposed for color constancy is the cone receptors. Color constancy operates at these photoreceptors by Von Kries (1905) adaptation, which allows the output from the receptors to be weighted to take account of the illuminant. An increase in incident illumination from one part of the spectrum is compensated for by an equivalent reduction in sensitivity at the receptors. Von Kries adaptation is sufficient to explain color constancy, because spectral reflectance functions from surfaces under naturally occurring illuminations can be matched by the weighted output of three broad-band receptors (Maloney, 1986). The spectral sensitivities of the cone receptors are, of course, broad band and therefore satisfy that requirement. Further evidence for Von Kries adaptation is shown by the breakdown of color constancy if the illuminants are a small number of narrow-band primaries (McCann, McKee, and Taylor, 1976; Worthey, 1985).

It is not easy to prove that the receptors are the site of Von Kries adaptation. The computation of color constancy requires the spectral composition of the incident illumination to be known; this is normally obtained from comparisons of a surface with the distribution of light from surrounding surfaces. If the incident light is allowed to fall only on the surface under investigation, there will be no color constancy, so it is difficult to isolate the role of receptor adaptation from a secondary mechanism based on a comparison between surfaces. However, a clever technique introduced by Uchikawa, Uchikawa, and Boynton (1989) suggests that receptor adaptation by itself can provide at least partial constancy. These authors used separate light sources to illuminate the surface and to control the state of adaptation of the eye. Changing either of these alone showed a breakdown in color constancy, but changing them in synchrony made it return to a considerable extent.

Precise color constancy could be achieved only if the Von Kries adaptation for the three receptors could respond to the reflected light from many surfaces present in the scene (Hallett, Jepson, and Gershon, 1988). Thus, for cone adaptation to be the single site for color constancy, there would have to be some large-scale integration of information across space by eye movements. It could otherwise not be retinal, since neurons there do not have sufficiently large receptive fields. As eye movements are not essential for color constancy, a second anatomical site has been proposed. A second site is also required to explain the color constancy between objects presented to different eyes when they do not have the same chromatic adaptation (see Jameson and Hurvich, 1989). D'Zmura and Lennie (1986) propose that the second site is at opponent-process neurons, and, therefore, modulation of color appearance occurs probably at the lateral geniculate bodies. Hurvich (1981) suggests an adaptation level mechanism for which the equilibrium level also depends on the opponent-process systems, but could have its site at the double-opponent blob cells (see section 2.1.4). A different second subsidiary mechanism in the form of cortical neurons that separately compute luminance has been proposed by Dannemiller (1989a). The proposal has a similarity to the Land (1977) retinex theory (see section 6.2.5), for which a cortical site has also been proposed. Another likely cortical site is area V4 (see section 2.1.6). No locus that has been proposed for color constancy, not even V4 neurons (see section 2.1.5), acts as a color module.

6.2.3 Color Contrast

Effects of achromatic contrast are well known, even commonplace; it is the reason stars "come out" at night. Color appearance is also affected by nearby surfaces. The effect of color contrast is to alter color constancy in a systematic fashion. It works on opponent color principles—thus a red will induce a green in a nearby object; yellow will induce a blue. Both effects are reciprocal. The effects are stronger if one surface is surrounded by another, but Jameson and Hurvich (1955) have shown that color contrast occurs from distant as well as from nearby shapes. Color contrast has a long history (see section 1.1) and is important because substantial changes are produced in perceived color. For example, Chevreul, the chemist and director of dyes at the Gobelin tapestry factory in nineteenth-century Paris, was able to show doubting customers that an apparent green tinge to a black was due to color contrast and was not present unless a red was nearby.

The importance of boundaries in determining color contrast is shown by the phenomenon—known as long ago as the seventeenth century (Graham and Brown, 1965)—of colored shadows. Shadows of objects are colorless if illuminated by a single light source, but they may appear colored when illuminated by two light sources of different colors. A shadow will take on the opponent color of the surface that surrounds it. So, if an object is illuminated by "red" light and "white" light, a shadow that falls on a white surface will look green. The effect is very striking because the filling-in of color takes place not just at the boundary but over the whole shadow—at least up to 23 degrees (Walls, 1954), and probably more.

Boundaries are also involved in the explanation of an assimilation effect that incorporates color contrast. It is called, because of the induced illusory brightness, the spreading neon illusion (Van Tuijl, 1975). The blue diamond line pattern of Plate 1a is surrounded by, but separated from, a black crossed grating background. The blue spreads into the gap between the two parts of the pattern. When the blue and black are reversed, a contrast effect is observed: the gap becomes yellow. In Plate 1b, the blue does not induce yellow in the background because it is constrained by the boundary-contour signals in the black ground. The amount of "bleeding" depends on the contrast of the boundary contour (Van Tuijl and de Weert, 1979; Redies and Spillman, 1981), which fits the Grossberg and Mingolla model (see section 6.1). Another striking effect produced by segmenting the display by shape (boundaries) is demonstrated in the alteration of afterimage color found by staring at the whole versus a small section of Plate 2 (from Albers, 1971).

6.2.4 Boundary Size and Perceived Surface Color
For very small objects, color vision becomes dichromatic (produced by two cone types) and much like the rare color vision disorder trita-nopia. Small-field tritanopia, as it is called, is due to the relative sparsity of blue cones. Variation in cone distribution does *not* explain the more marked difference that size makes to perceived saturation. A stimulus increases in its perceived color purity (saturation) as the visual angle increases up to 20 degrees, but beyond this size, decreases in saturation. (Incidentally, this is a very important fact to bear in mind when choosing wall colors from small paint samples.) The feature-contour system (Grossberg, 1987a) is scaled for spatial frequencies, so neurophysiological mechanisms exist for these effects of size on color appearance. However, the locus for the interaction of size and color is not certain; the large field sizes involved could implicate V4.

6.2.5 Luminance and Perceived Surface Color

Some effects of luminance on color are, in a sense, trivial; they depend on the function of receptors in the retina. The cones and rods have different spectral sensitivities. At low levels of luminance—still sufficient to obtain achromatic vision from the rods—cones are not active, and so objects appear colorless. Therefore, at twilight, when there is a changeover from cone to rod vision, objects change color because of the different spectral sensitivity of the two systems.

The blobs (Livingstone and Hubel, 1987a) are fed by both the parvocellular and magnocellular pathways. If the blobs are providing the feature detail (Grossberg and Mingolla, 1985), one would expect interactions between perceived color and luminance. Indeed, it is well known that perceived color changes with intensity of illumination (the Bezold-Brucke effect). At low luminance levels, red and green hues predominate over yellow and blue. The reverse is true at high luminance. Increasing the intensity of colored lights causes colors with a wavelength greater than 505 nanometers to shift toward yellow; those with wavelengths shorter than 505 nanometers shift toward blue. There are three wavelengths for which there is no Bezold-Brucke effect. Interestingly these are the wavelengths judged to be the purest blue (470 nanometers), green (505 nanometers), and yellow (572 nanometers). Increases in intensity also produce changes in perceived saturation (Abney effect). Unsaturated blues and reds shift toward purple (Burns et al., 1984). Yellow, although never reaching the saturation of other hues, obtains maximum saturation at a higher level of illumination than other colors (see also figure 8.1). Beyond the point of maximal saturation, further increases in intensity make the color appear white. Thus, colored stimuli appear achromatic at both high and low luminance levels.

Luminance interacts with size in the discrimination and perception of surface color. Thus, the Bezold-Brucke and Abney effects are both affected by stimulus size. Consistent with the neurophysiology (see table 2.2), the threshold for color discrimination without luminance contrast decreases monotonically as spatial frequency is decreased (Hilz, Huppman, and Cavonius, 1974). However, when luminance contrast is introduced, wavelength sensitivity reaches a maximum at an intermediate spatial frequency. Hue discrimination is especially great when gratings with a spatial frequency of about 3 cycles/degree have a luminance contrast of 10 percent. Luminance contrast has little effect on hue discrimination for objects larger than 2 degrees.

Luminance-chromatic interactions must result from a system with a considerable range of spatial resolution. The properties of a spatially scaled feature-contour system could predict these interactions (Grossberg, 1987a). They are unlikely to be solely determined from only one of the three streams of Livingstone and Hubel (1987a), especially because perceived color also depends on temporal modulation (Van der Horst, 1969). A chromatic stimulus matched for luminance to an achromatic stimulus by the method of flicker photometry does not look equally bright (Helmholtz-Kohlrausch effect) when stationary lights are compared. The discrepancy is particularly marked at the extremes of the spectrum, where the luminance may have to be reduced by a factor of three or more to obtain a brightness match.

The most well known attempt to integrate the effects of luminance into the perception of color, comes from Land in his Retinex model (1977). Land claims that the color appearance of surfaces can be derived from three separate channels that compare lightness on the basis of cone characteristics. However, there is considerable evidence against the view that neurons in the visual cortex have the character of retinal mechanisms. There are other good solutions, besides that of Land, to the color appearances found in his demonstrations (Judd, 1960; Wyszecki, 1986). Land, nevertheless, correctly assesses the importance of lightness differences between different areas of a scene in producing color constancy at a surface. He maintains that lightness differences across the scene are more important for color constancy than the wavelength of incident illumination. In one of Land's demonstrations, two different black-and-white slides of the same colored scene are projected so that they coincide on a screen. Each slide is illuminated by a different monochromatic light, yet Land has shown that it is possible to recreate the original colors in the scene. Moreover, this is achieved by some surprising combinations of monochromatic lights. For example, black-and-white slides illuminated by two slightly different yellow light sources can result in the recreation of a colored scene with a very broad range of colors, including blue and red.

6.2.6 Motion and Perceived Surface Color
There is some dispute about whether apparent motion is the same as, and uses the same neural mechanisms as, real motion (Anstis, 1980). Nevertheless, whether derived from stabilized retinal images (Kolers and Pomerantz, 1971) or in the normal way by a sequence of light flashes separated by the appropriate spatial and temporal parameters, an object's apparent motion is unaffected by the color of its surface (Kolers and Green, 1984). Surface color changes during apparent motion do not alter its speed (Kolers and von Grunau, 1976) or the perceived direction of motion (Ramachandran and Anstis, 1983). Indeed, the change of color during apparent motion seems to be controlled from the boundary change. Shape changes during apparent

movement may appear to be gradual, but color changes are all-or-none (Kolers and von Grunau, 1976) and occur *after* the shape change. Another effect of motion, known as *fluttering hearts*, concerns not the perceived color of a surface but the cohesion of surface color and its boundary. Under dim illumination, a red figure oscillated perpendicularly to the line of sight appears to become dislodged and moves out of synchrony to a green background. The phenomenon is known as fluttering hearts because the original demonstration was with a red heart-shaped figure. The different temporal response thresholds of the three cone types have been held responsible (von Grunau, 1975a, b), but the effect occurs only for the dark-adapted eye, suggesting a rod-cone interaction. The different response thresholds of the cone types may, however, be the cause of colors produced by achromatic pattern flicker (Pieron, 1931). These effects, of which the most well known is the Benham Top, are of considerable antiquity (see Cohen and Gordon, 1949), but their origin is still unclear.

6.2.7 Perceived Depth and Surface Color
Refraction in the optical system causes blue light to strike the retina more nasally than red light. Presumably from experience, surface colors can be interpreted to be at distances compatible with differences that can be caused by optical refraction (Egusa, 1983). However, because the photoreceptors themselves are directionally selective (Stiles-Crawford effect), there can be a complete negation of the effects of refraction. The effects of perceived depth on the appearance of surface colors are, therefore, very variable across subjects.

6.3 Apperceptive Visual Disorders: Modular and Nonmodular
Accounts Compared

Disorders of perception that, in general, support the modular against nonmodular accounts of the pictorial register were described in chapters 3 and 5. However, a network in which chromatic input differentially contributes to boundary and surface production would also provide a satisfactory explanation of the dissociations. There are other neuropsychological data that would support both types of account but perhaps more the nonmodular. These data concern impaired early stages of object perception.

Compared with the sophistication of models in artificial intelligence, diagrams drawn by neuropsychologists to describe object recognition are computationally primitive; however, they are empirically defensible. Neuropsychological models, following the classic paper of Lissauer (1890; Shallice and Jackson, 1988), essentially fractionate object recognition into two stages. Lissauer made the distinction between apperception and association. *Apperception* refers to the perceptual processes required to form a temporary representation and association to the activation of stored object knowledge. In more recent times, disorders of apperception have sometimes been called "apperceptive agnosia," which makes no sense. Agnosia is the current term—coined by Freud (1891/1935)—that replaced the earlier term *mind-blindness.* Agnosia means "without knowledge," but that is exactly what apperception must be. It would be preferable to talk of apperceptive or associative visual disorders. Most disorders of object recognition are of the apperceptive type and may not be as rare as commonly thought. Poppelreuter (in Lange, 1936/1989) showed, from observations on a large sample, that apperceptive disorders could be shown in most cases of occipital lobe damage if the patient was put under time pressure.

Without a clear definition, it is no surprise to find concern about the variety of symptoms taken to demonstrate an apperceptive disorder. Poetzl (1928 in Levine, 1978), for example, described Lissauer's case as if it were an attentional problem: "Details that are normally irrelevant command attention, whereas the important details—those which form the nucleus for correct identification—often recede into the background or momentarily disappear. . . . What Wertheimer called the centre of gravity of the Gestalt . . . is no longer stable . . . but at different moments, different complexes of parts emerge as the centre of gravity." However, there is one commonly used criterion for an apperceptive disorder. It is normally required that patients should have reasonable acuity but cannot copy what is in front of them (Benson and Greenberg, 1969). For those patients for whom copying is possible, it must be achieved in a slavish point-by-point fashion.

Recent neuropsychological research (for review, see Ellis and Young, 1988) has tried to make clearer the different processing disorders that are present in disturbed apperception (Charnallet, Carbonnel, and Pellat, 1986). It has been helped by drawing on ideas formulated in both modular (Marr, 1982) and nonmodular (Grossberg and Minolla, 1985) models of computer vision. If Lissauer's scheme is transposed to Marr's theory of object recognition, apperceptive disorders include failures up to and including the formation of a three-dimensional temporary representation. Therefore, testing ought to examine the formation of a three-dimensional model (Warrington and James, 1986) that could be impaired by many factors, including sensory loss (Campion, 1987), disorders of stereoscopic vision (Riddoch, 1917), and spatial transform processes (Warrington and Taylor, 1973; Humphreys and Riddoch, 1984). Apperceptive disorders should also cover the incorrect match of the intact three-dimensional model to intact representations in long-term storage.

Warrington and Taylor (1973) found that patients with right parietal lesions were particularly impaired in object recognition tasks. The patients had difficulty in recognizing objects from what they called an "unusual" view but not from "usual" views. There are several interpretations of their patients' disorders that might highlight disordered apperception rather than impairments of long-term storage (but see also chapter 7). For example, the formation of a three-dimensional representation could be impaired. The effect of right parietal lesions could be to allow the formation of only those representations that retain the main axis. Alternatively, these patients may have failed to recognize an object from a particular view because of the omission of a salient feature from the representation at the pictorial register (Warrington and James, 1986). The problem could also be (see Riddoch and Humphreys, 1987a) impaired access to representations in long-term storage.

Temporary representations contain both local and global features; it is reasonable to presume that access to the permanent representations might proceed from either (Humphreys and Riddoch, 1987). In the normal person there is preferential access from global features or, in the terms of the Grossberg and Mingolla (1985) model, large-scale boundary contours. Thus, a brain-damaged patient has been reported who was able to categorize objects from boundary information (Riddoch and Humphreys, 1987a) but was unable to integrate the detail sufficiently with the outline in order to achieve within-category recognition. Internal object detail hindered the patient in his attempt to recognize an object, and, unlike normals, he found silhouettes easier than line drawings. Riddoch and Humphreys argue that the patient's recognition difficulties were probably due to his inability to access the descriptions in long-term memory. However, since he could draw quite well from memory, the permanent storage of visual knowledge was probably intact.

6.4 Summary and Progression to Object Recognition

In the nonmodular account, the formation of the temporary representation does not require an isolated color input. Color as a functional module (see chapter 8) is a mental construction from the surface qualities held within a boundary at the temporary representation. The appearance of these surface qualities results from a complex interaction of luminance and chromatic (wavelength-based) information. Color also plays a part in boundary formation by virtue of chromatic contrast. It has even been suggested to be its main role (Bertulis and Glezer, 1984), but, on evolutionary grounds, that is not likely. Our visual system would not have evolved for the purpose of detecting equiluminant boundaries, because they are rare in nature; they are mainly to be found in well-controlled laboratory conditions. However, as the boundary-contour system is fed by chromatic contrast, it is very useful when the luminance-controlled parts are under strain. Such conditions would arise under "dappled" lighting, such as that present when one is trying to find a fruit among the leaves of a tree.

The formation of boundaries does not require object knowledge. Comparisons made directly at the pictorial register (see chapter 7) are not affected by how frequently the object's name has been encountered (Wingfield, 1968) or how typical the object is of a category (Rosch, 1975a). However, attentional resources are not allocated to the pictorial register simply by increasing or decreasing the spotlight diameter; rather, they are allocated on the basis of boundary segmentation (Rock and Gutman, 1981; Duncan, 1984). Thus, it is easier to select two attributes of the same boundaried surface than two attributes from different boundaries (Duncan, 1984) and, where integration of attributes is required for successful completion of a task, it helps to represent them within a common boundary (Wickens and Andre, 1990). Two objects may be overlapping, as in the classic clinical test of Poppelreuter (see figure 6.3), but normals have no difficulty in directing attention to a particular boundary; indeed, attention paid to one of

Figure 6.3
Overlapping objects as in the test devised by Poppelreuter. Some patients have problems directing their attention to the individual objects.

two overlapping shapes results in superior recognition for that shape (Rock and Gutman, 1981).

Selection from the pictorial register by boundary segmentation has considerable implications for the allocation of attention. It is a short but very important step to allow selection to occur as a result of the meaning of those boundaries—that is to say, by reference to descriptions in long-term storage (meaningful objects) that correspond to those boundaries. Selection from the pictorial register by objects is described as "late" (Deutsch and Deutsch, 1963; Norman, 1968) as opposed to the modular input selection of Broadbent and Treisman, which is described as "early." The argument between the two approaches has been fierce, but it would now appear that attention is directed in a search for objects rather than for feature (modular) attributes (Driver and Baylis, 1989). Attention is captured by an "exogenous" (see section 5.2.3) aspect of the display such as color (Williams, 1966) because an *object* of that color is important for further action (Allport, 1987; Styles and Allport, 1986). Indeed, there is neurological evidence in support of object-based attention (Posner and Rothbart, 1989) that implicates the cingulate gyrus of the frontal lobes (see figures 3.1b and 2.1). Thus, the importance of boundary-based attention leads to a consideration of the nature of object representations, which is the subject of the next chapter.

Chapter 7
Object Knowledge

7.1 In Normals

7.1.1 Entry Level Representations

We are not born with the mental structures that categorize visual stimuli as objects but must acquire them from experience (see Neisser, 1987, for further discussion.) Early in the first year of life, children rely on uncategorized information at the pictorial register rather than permanent representations to drive action (Piaget, 1926). Only as permanent storage is acquired does the child have the possibility to change from being dominated by sensory processes. Lange (1936/1989) put it thus: "(as) the accent moves increasingly in the direction of action and speech—perceptions and conceptions lose sensory content in order to be increasingly ready for the extraction of meaning." If responses to objects are to be governed by meaning, uncategorized representations at the pictorial register must have easy access to stored knowledge. It is proposed that access occurs at the part of stored knowledge concerned with object recognition. The representation that allows object recognition will have access to many networks (knowledge structures concerning objects) but not necessarily at the same strength. A camel, for example, will differentially access networks for animal objects, transportation objects, or brown objects. The organization of these networks will be considered later. The procedures and representations for making within-category classifications will be only briefly considered; the primary concern is to consider knowledge (and naming, see chapter 10) for a camel, not that for particular camels.

Object recognition is a classification problem that has been tackled by researchers from two main directions. Some are more concerned with the perceptual problems, and others by the place of object recognition in cognition. Computer-vision theorists are mostly in the former category; they try to solve problems of edge extraction and resolving stereoscopic images rather than those of modeling human object recognition. Thus, with some exceptions (see Ullman, 1984,

1989), current algorithms for object recognition concentrate on the formation of the initial representations at the pictorial register. Nevertheless, computer vision models must propose some sort of template against which the temporary representation is matched. Whether or not the template contains information about color will be considered in the next chapter. The primary and most difficult task is to achieve categorization. The permanent representation of an object (template) must be in such a form that temporary representations differing widely in their sensory components are recognized (categorized) as coming from the same object. The difficulties in giving a proper account of equivalence in object recognition have been recognized for some time (Hoeffding, 1891): Neisser (1967) called it the "Hoeffding step."

Researchers concerned with more general cognitive functions are more interested in the place of the object template within the rest of stored knowledge. Rosch (1975a), for example, has suggested that the first contact point for the temporary representation is also the first stored knowledge evoked by the object's name. She calls the first contact point a *basic-level* representation. Access to information concerning all object properties flows from the basic level. In Rosch's model, some basic-level representations (e.g., bird) are quite general; for other objects (e.g., cow), they are more specific (Rosch et al., 1976). The basic level was seen as a prototype (Rosch, 1975a), but the notion of a prototype requires elaboration (Armstrong, Gleitman, and Gleitman, 1983). It is possible to conceive of a prototypical mammal or triangle; it is much harder for a vegetable or a tool (see Roth and Frisby, 1986). Therefore, the basic visual categorization for these objects must be somewhat more specific. Jolicoeur, Gluck, and Kosslyn (1984) suggest replacing basic level with the term *entry level*. The entry level for any object would be that which would require the least perceptual analysis to build a detailed representation. The entry level for a robin would be that of a bird, as Rosch suggested; however, certain atypical-looking birds (e.g., penguin), might have their entry level directly at the subordinate form. Thus, the entry level becomes specified in terms more similar to those approaching the problems of object recognition from the computer vision perspective.

The entry level representation must be determined by spatial and/ or visual coordinates, because there are certain views of objects that are harder and that some patients find impossible (see section 6.3) to recognize. Palmer, Rosch, and Chase (1981) have therefore suggested that entry level representations are in what they call a "canonical" form. The canonical representation is a visual prototype, of which there are several versions (Marr, 1982; Biederman, 1987). In Marr's terminology, the prototype is a heirarchically organized object-centered view based on generalized cone shapes. Recent network models (McClelland and Rumelhart, 1981) for word recognition propose what may be a similar hierarchy. The network, which has priority of output at the categorial level from a "hidden" unit, results from the building up of weights between connections in the network. The entry level representation could, therefore, consist of multiple spatial (possibly viewer-centered) representations organized on connectionist principles (Humphreys and Bruce, 1989). The different weights on the connections would be responsible for the favored recognition from "usual" views. The connectionist networks do not require special representations for prototypes. Nevertheless, it is important to be clear that even if the categorial aspect of the entry level representation is hidden, it is functionally present. Its effect is seen in any task that requires categorization. Furthermore, entry level representations can be uniquely attached to verbal labels.

One consequence of entry level activation is the better maintenance of the temporary representation. The phenomenon is known as the "object superiority effect" because of the superior recognition for parts of objects over parts of nonobjects. Recognizing part of a familiar object (e.g., the mouth presented in a face) can even be as accurate as recognizing the part presented by itself (Homa, Haver, and Schwartz, 1976); this is not the case for nonobjects. Object superiority is not achieved simply by selection of different spatial scales. Nonobjects can be constructed from object parts with the same spatial scales as objects, but they do not produce object superiority effects. There must be an extant entry level representation to produce an object superiority effect. Thus, the whole object has processing priority over its parts only if the temporary representation can be matched as a whole at the entry level (Davidoff and Donnelly, 1990). An unsuccessful match to the stored representations still allows detail to fill-in inside the boundaries held at the pictorial register (see section 6.1), but it means that the object parts, each defined by boundaries, cannot be integrated. Therefore, in cases where brain damage prevents proper object classification, recognition must proceed in a laborious, part-by-part, manner. Such piecemeal recognition procedures are commonly observed in patients with object-(and word-) recognition disorders (see section 6.3).

In the following sections, only stimuli that fully activate an entry level representation are referred to as objects. Stimuli that do not activate an entry level representation remain as boundaried surfaces at the pictorial register. Entry level representations, therefore, serve to divide the visual world into objects. The dramatic difference that is found once a stored representation can organize the material in the pictorial register is seen in the perception of ambiguous figures. Once an ambiguous display has been successfully categorized, it is more easily done a second time and much easier to remember (Wiseman and Neisser, 1974).

One relatively straightforward approach to the investigation of entry level representations is simply to demand categorization of a stimulus as an object or nonobject (Kroll and Potter, 1984; Riddoch and Humphreys, 1987b). In these studies, nonobjects were constructed from random shapes or from parts of real objects (a wolf's head on a sheep's body would be categorized as a nonobject). Kroll and Potter found that object decisions were made easier by the prior presentation of a related object, which suggested that entry level representations are in some way organized. Nonreplications (Lupker, 1988) of the Kroll and Potter priming effect may result from task demands that encourage independent responses to each presentation. Activation of stored knowledge also helps to resolve information at the entry level when the visual input is unclear and contains little detail or no good outline information (Gregory, 1970). However, the long time span over which the benefits of Gregory's "hypothesis testing" operate make unclear the mechanisms by which these ambiguities at the entry level are resolved. It could be from name priming, since names may bias the selection of entry level information (Carmichael, Hogan and Walter, 1932; Lupker and Katz, 1981). Kolers and Brison (1984) point out that a line drawing of a banana might be a gourd, a canoe, a partly eaten pear, a hammock or—we take their word for it—a cesta for a game of jai alai. Recognition will be biased in accordance with whatever label is given.

7.1.2 Multiple Storage
Fodor's (1983) argument concerning modularity had two parts. He first proposed that input systems are modular (see chapters 2 to 5). The critical property of modularity (see section 1.2) is information encapsulation (Davidoff, 1986a; Shallice, 1988a). Second, Fodor (1983) argued that, because of information encapsulation, the central systems (rules for thought) must operate on different (i.e., nonmodular) principles. The isolation of input modules from each other would prevent the integration necessary for general thought processes. The present concern is not rules for thought themselves but our representations of knowledge upon which the general rules must operate. For these representations, a modified form of modularity is proposed because there is substantial evidence (see Shallice, 1988a; Ellis and Young, 1988; Roth and Frisby, 1986) that the organization of stored knowledge is not equipotential but rather that different types of knowledge have

separate storage. In most texts on cognitive psychology, stored knowledge is usually called *semantic*. To avoid confusion with knowledge of a logical nature, the term *object knowledge* is preferred. It is hoped that, by changing the terminology, some important distinctions can be made and some confusion avoided.

There has been considerable debate (Paivio, 1971; Pylyshyn, 1973; Anderson, 1978; Snodgrass, 1984) as to whether object knowledge is stored in one or two (pictorial versus verbal) semantic systems. The debate has also concerned whether pictures are remembered better than words (Nelson, Reed, and Walling, 1976) and whether memory is better for physical or functional characteristics of stimuli (Intraub and Nicklos, 1985). Paivio (1975) believes that there must be dual coding for the representation of knowledge. Some judgments, such as size, are performed more quickly from pictures than from words, which suggests that the relevant object knowledge is stored in a pictorial code. Storage in a verbal code is demonstrated when judgments of associated relatedness are made more quickly from words (Te Linde, 1982) and when the congenitally blind display some knowledge concerning the visual properties of objects (Wyke and Holgate, 1973).

These experimental results could also be interpreted from a unitary system for knowledge representation. Knowledge could be coded in a propositional form (Anderson, 1978) capable of realization in either a pictorial or a verbal output. Paivio's and other similar results are seen as a consequence of different entry systems for pictures and words to stored knowledge (Seymour, 1979; Morton, 1985). For example, the faster categorization from pictures than from words (Potter and Faulconer, 1975) does not necessarily argue for a visual store of knowledge. The extent of the picture-over-word advantage may depend on the amount of visual processing required (Pellegrino et al., 1977; Snodgrass, 1984; Snodgrass and McCullough, 1986). Furthermore, priming studies also indicate facilitation at the entry level rather than at the semantic system. Very little priming is shown between words and pictures in a categorization task (Smith and Magee, 1980; Guenther, Klatzky, and Putnam, 1980) or a naming task (Sperber et al., 1979; Carr et al., 1982), and object identification is not influenced by prior presentation of the object's name but by a different picture of an object that is given the same name (Warren and Morton, 1982). Therefore, it can be argued that priming advantages arise at the entry level rather than at a more central representation (Kroll and Potter, 1984).

Object knowledge may be divided in other ways besides that of verbal versus visual. The knowledge of sensory aspects of an object— for example, its color, size, and emitted noise—is different in kind from that for other object properties. For example, it is unlikely that a decision could be made about whether a penguin has a big bill from the knowledge either that it lives in the Antarctic or that it is a favorite attraction at the zoo. Sensory properties of an object can therefore be contrasted with its associated and functional properties. Associated properties for bread are, for example, that it goes with butter or that it is made from wheat grown in North America. Functional properties are those that link objects conceptually. For example, butter is linked to water in a functional sense because both are a cooking medium. Although an object's associative and functional properties are logically distinct, there is in our everyday experience a considerable overlap between them. Butter and water, for example, are both found in a kitchen. Some of the best evidence for storage distinctions based on sensory versus functional properties comes from neuropsychological investigations. Their history can be traced to the study of disorders of object recognition reported by Lissauer (1890; Shallice and Jackson, 1988).

7.2 After Brain Damage

7.2.1 Agnosic Disorders of Object Recognition
Visual agnosia refers to a loss of knowledge from vision compared with that derived from touch and other modalities. By definition, the disorder does not involve problems with verbal comprehension (Rubens and Benson, 1971; Hecaen et al., 1974), and patients with word-comprehension difficulties—transcortical sensory aphasia—are not necessarily agnosic for visual stimuli (Benson, 1979; Warrington and McCarthy, 1983). However, there is a doubt about the preservation of reading in visual agnosia. Some patients can read normally (Newcombe and Ratcliff, 1974; Albert, Reches, and Silverberg, 1975), but most cannot. In an inventive procedure using the same stimuli as letters or objects, Levine (1978) found that his patient demonstrated the same recognition level for both verbal and nonverbal stimuli. Levine argued that reports of preserved reading are due to the less-detailed specification usually required for letter compared with object recognition. Alternatively, the remarkably preserved reading shown by the patient of Newcombe and Ratcliff (1974) indicates a discrete entry level system for verbal material (also see section 11.3).

The term visual agnosia requires a considerable amount of unpacking (Humphreys and Riddoch, 1987), even after taking into account the classic division of Lissauer. He distinguished (see section 6.3) between apperceptive disorders of object recognition and those based on impairments of association. Apperceptive disorders can be considered inabilities to form temporary representations. The diagnosis of an associative visual disorder assumes intact temporary representations but damage to or problems in accessing stored object knowledge. It is necessary to discuss further whether the impairment arises from damaged entry level systems and/or associated stored knowledge.

Damaged entry level representation would prevent recognition from the intact integration of boundary contours with feature contours (Grossberg and Mingolla, 1985). Thus, disorders at the entry level are probably involved in the poor object recognition of many cases that have been described as visual agnosia (Adler, 1944; Davidoff and Wilson, 1985; Sartori and Job, 1988). These patients could provide quite detailed nonvisual information from a question but showed that they had no detailed knowledge of what objects looked like. The patient of Davidoff and Wilson, for example, could count the number of legs in a picture, but if the legs were not shown, the patient could not give the correct answer. A swan pictured swimming on a pond was said to have no legs visible but "four legs, I think below the water." In a less extreme case, the patient of Schwartz, Marin, and Saffran (1979) no longer knew the visual difference between a dog and a cat. Depending on the amount of detail that was required to differentiate objects at the entry level, most of these patients could be assessed to have intact semantics but impaired entry level representations. Impairments at or near the entry level descriptions could also be the reason some patients show markedly abnormal face recognition. Most of these patients show pronounced feature-by-feature matching for both faces and other objects (Ellis and Young, 1988), which could be due to their problems with integrating object parts.

Despite the difficulty in accessing the entry level representations, enough information might trickle through to make possible some judgments from other knowledge structures. There seems to be no other way of explaining the successful matching of visually dissimilar pictures—according to the functions of the object—by patients with apperceptive disorders (Warrington and James, 1988). In fact, the amount of information that needs to be extracted to perform what appear to be complex visual tasks may be quite small. Marin, Glenn, and Rafal (1983) described a patient with very impaired picture recognition who was able to drive around and function moderately well in familiar surroundings; Bub et al. (1988) described an alexic patient who was able to retrieve enough verbal information from a word to be able to match it to a picture.

The theory of the existence of visual agnosia,—that is, disorder of recognition without apperceptive disorder—was controversial at the time of Lissauer (Mauthner, 1881; Simerling, 1890; quoted in Levine, 1978), and those doubts have persisted (Bay, 1953; Campion, 1987). Visual agnosia implies a dual representation of stored knowledge that is to some theorists (see section 7.1.2) unsatisfactory. To avoid proposing dual coding for knowledge representations, it is necessary to argue (Riddoch and Humphreys, 1987a) that studies that show separate impairments of stored knowledge for pictures and words (Warrington, 1975) are contaminated by differences at their respective entry level. Such arguments are often persuasive. However, the proposal for multiple and against unitary storage does not rest entirely or even mainly on visual agnosia. It is at least equally supported by a parallel line of neuropsychological research showing highly specific semantic impairments.

7.2.2 Category-Specific Impairments
The loss of object knowledge found after brain damage can be fitted easily into Paivio's model for the dual representations of knowledge. There have been other similar schemes based on data in neuropsychology. The organization of semantic memory has, for example, often contrasted abstract with concrete aspects of objects (Goldstein, 1948; Marshall and Newcombe, 1973; Warrington, 1975). In a classic case, the patient AB (Warrington, 1975) showed poor comprehension of simple concrete words but understood reasonably complex abstract words. Therefore, it was supposed that the differential loss of knowledge arose because one type of stored knowledge was unavailable. However, the concrete/abstract dimension does not fully reflect the full varieties of loss that can arise after brain damage. In particular, the loss of object knowledge that has been subsequently studied by Warrington requires a different division for the modules of stored knowledge.

Warrington's theoretical approach (see Shallice, 1988a) requires that superordinate information be less susceptible to brain damage than subordinate information (but see Rapp and Caramazza, 1989). The superordinate information emerges, according to Shallice, from networks (McClelland and Rumelhart, 1985) that are more likely, when damaged, to lose attribute information. These neural networks would be the neurophysiological basis for the prediction that knowledge can be lost for specific categories of objects. Shallice's recent proposal bears a resemblance to Lissauer's concept of associative visual disorder in which items become differentially associated with particular input-output pathways. Many such disorders and preserved islands of knowledge have now been reported. They include disorders for inanimate objects (Nielsen, 1946; Hecaen and Ajuriaguerra, 1956), animate objects (Warrington and Shallice, 1984; Hart, Berndt, and Caramazza, 1985), indoor objects (Yamadori and Albert, 1973), and body parts (Goodglass et al., 1966; Dennis, 1976; Ogden, 1985). Perhaps most remarkable of all was the preservation of information concerning countries in the absence of much other information for objects (McKenna and Warrington, 1978). Konorski (1967) extrapolated from these dissociations to distinguish nine "gnostic fields" of object knowledge. It will be argued that these fields of knowledge might be further, or alternatively, divided into their sensory and functional properties.

The first division of stored knowledge that Warrington proposed was that between living and nonliving objects. The evidence came from a stroke victim (VER) who was able to show more verbal comprehension of living than nonliving objects (Warrington and McCarthy, 1983). Warrington and Shallice (1984) showed an opposite pattern of performance in four patients with herpes simplex encephalitis. These patients were impaired in their ability to give information about living objects when presented as words or pictures. However, Warrington and McCarthy (1987) argued that the impairments of another patient (YOT) were not completely encompassed by the living/ nonliving dichotomy. Despite being generally better at retrieving information concerning living than nonliving objects, the patient retained knowledge about fabrics but not about body parts. An opposite discrepancy was noted in Warrington and Shallice. A more exact description of the patients' disordered stored knowledge would be to contrast sensory and functional attributes of objects. Fabrics, though nonliving, are distinguished by their sensory properties; conversely, body parts are primarily distinguished by their function. Warrington and McCarthy (1983) propose the following explanation of the deficit shown by VER: "Consider differentiating between two types of item: a wallet and a purse compared with a cabbage and a cauliflower. In the first case, sensory attributes are relatively unimportant (wallets can be of very different shapes, colors and sizes) whereas in the second it is these very sensory attributes which are crucial." Therefore, cognitive structures that subserve tight functional differentiation are likely to have different properties than ones based on sensory features. It is therefore reasonable to have them differentially associated with the entry level representations.

The patient YOT also showed selective impairment for knowledge concerning common manipulable objects compared with that for large outdoor objects. This further loss of knowledge shown in another of Konorski's gnostic fields made Warrington and McCarthy (1987) reject the sensory versus functional modification of the living/nonliving dichotomy. However, it may not be necessary. To account for YOT's poor performance with manipulable objects, it may be sufficient to have the stored sensory knowledge for objects represented in accordance with the appropriate sensory experience. Small objects would, unlike large objects, have many kinesthetic associations. A similar proposal (see figure 7.1) is given by Allport (1985) to show how the different "non linguistic" attributes could contribute to name production. Depending upon the category of object, different sensory modalities are important to distinguish between category members; color may be more important for fruit than for flowers, and smell more important for flowers than fruit. The distinction between knowledge based on appearance and that based on function gets further support from studies with "split-brain" patients (Levy and Trevarthen, 1976), divided visual field tests with normals (Landis, Assal, and Perret, 1979), and the consequences of unilateral cortical damage (Warrington and Taylor, 1978). The distinction forms a major part of the model proposed in this and subsequent chapters for object knowledge that incorporates knowledge concerning the colors of objects.

7.3 A Model for the Division of Object Knowledge

A model that emphasizes the divisions of knowledge described in the previous section is given in figure 7.2. Its critical aspects are as follows. Pictorial input is analyzed by a boundary-contour system and feature-contour system that are integrated at the pictorial register. The information in temporary storage then makes contact with stored representations. From the effects of masking, Potter (1976) assesses that

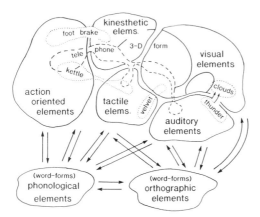

Figure 7.1
Allport's (1985) model for the access of object knowledge in word comprehension.

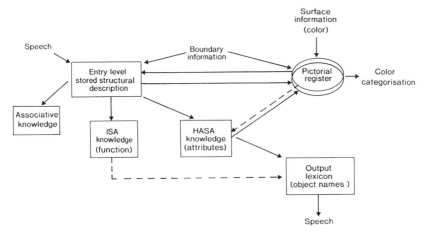

Figure 7.2
A model for object naming. Three types of knowledge are shown. Connections from associative knowledge to name output are not shown but would be as for ISA knowledge.

access to permanent storage takes several tenths of a second. The boundary-contour system, according to Grossberg and Mingolla (1985) and as shown in figure 7.2, also makes invisible contact with an entry (basic) level system, but that is not critical to the model. It would be equally acceptable if contact was made directly from the boundaries held at the pictorial register.

The entry level representation is defined spatially by boundaries; it is the information concerning size and shape for an object. The categorization of visual information takes place at the entry level representations prior to being named (Potter and Faulconer, 1975). Categorization may even be mandatory (Smith and Magee, 1980) but is, nevertheless, capacity limited (Biederman et al., 1988). Thus, access to stored knowledge is disrupted by conflicting information to an extent that depends on the amount of attention that has to be allocated to it (Loftus and Ginn, 1984; Loftus, Hanna, and Lester, 1988).

Associated stored knowledge for the object is activated via the entry level representations. There are two basic forms of stored knowledge, which are expressed by the linguistic terms *isa* and *hasa*. The hasa knowledge concerns sensory information. For example, an object may be furry, brown, and make a distinctive noise. Isa information concerns the functions of objects. Grapes, pears, and pineapples are, for example, connected in an isa network for fruit. (English usage of is and has does not always reflect their use in isa and hasa. Thus, it might be said that a car has a top speed of 90 miles per hour, that is, it "isa" (fast) means of transport. Similarly, one might say that an apple is red, by which is meant it "hasa" red color.) Thus, the distinction between isa and hasa is not determined by the use of "is" and "has." However, even as defined, it could be argued that the distinction between isa and hasa is often blurred. Some hasa properties might necessarily imply an isa status; for example, a jagged edge could imply a cutting tool. Alternatively, some isa knowledge might inevitably predict appearance. Flight, for example, might be possible for a bird only if it has two oval structures suspended on either side of its body, but that is doubtful. Such necessary connections between appearance and function are rare and will be ignored, though the same argument returns in another form (see chapter 10) when modality-specific naming disorders are considered.

Isa and hasa knowledge are, for no better reason than parsimony, each represented in figure 7.2 in an amodal form and not further divided as verbal or visual semantics. However, since the hasa knowledge, in particular, concerns sensory attributes of objects, some more direct visuo-spatial representation would not be unreasonable. Apart from hasa and isa knowledge, there is a further type of stored knowledge called "associative" with which the model is less concerned. Associative knowledge concerns the experiential episodes that link entry level representations.

The activation of the entry level facilitates recognition of the identical object (Homa et al., 1976; Davidoff, 1986b; Davidoff and Donnelly, 1990) and of those that would be given the same name (Warren and Morton, 1982; Kroll and Potter, 1984). Activating the entry level by the object's name also facilitates physical identity matching. However, such priming must be given sufficiently far in advance to allow the construction of representations at the pictorial register (Rosch et al., 1976). Identity matches at the pictorial register are not affected by frequency (Wingfield, 1968), typicality (Rosch, 1975a, experiment 5), or priming with a superordinate name (Rosch et al., 1976, experiment 6). The pictorial register thus plays a dual role in the processing of an object. It is a temporary buffer store at which all visual stimuli form representations and it can also be part of the object knowledge structures once the entry level is activated. For objects, only the information stored at the entry level directly interacts with the temporary representation at the pictorial register. Information at the hasa representations is available to the pictorial register only subsequent to access to the entry level descriptions. The part of stored knowledge that is temporarily activated and representable in a visual form is called the pictorial interface by Seymour (1979). However, here (but see chapter 9) it is identified as identical with the pictorial register.

The preceding arguments presume that the entry level representations do not contain information concerning object color. Thus, it is reasonable to ask the fate of unmediated color and other surface information held at the pictorial register. It will be argued (see chapter 9) that, after entry level activation by boundary information, a feedback loop allows the surface information to access the associated hasa knowledge directly from the pictorial register. The entry level representations simultaneously activate that and other hasa knowledge. The effect is to somewhat facilitate object naming (see chapter 9).

7.4 Relationships to Other Models

The model is similar to many others, but there are some differences that might help clarify both normal and impaired functions of object knowledge structures. The model resembles that of Rosch et al. (1976), since the entry level description, like their basic level representation, is the key that unlocks the stored knowledge concerning an object. However, the initial categorization also activates separate knowledge stores not contained at the entry level. The model in figure 7.2 would also, like that of Rosch, have primable connections between object representations within isa networks. Stored information within an associative or (isa) network can, if activated, lower the threshold for other categorially related material (Bruce, 1983). Thus, a living/nonliving (isa) decision is helped by a picture prime from the same category (Guenther, Klatsky, and Putnam, 1980). Rosch (1975a) has argued that the benefit found from activation of stored information, unlike decisions based at the base level (Smith, Balzano, and Walker, 1977), depends on the typicality of the item to be categorized. Humphreys, Riddoch, and Quinlan (1988) wish to make a qualification. They believe that typicality is important only for items from visually (structurally) similar categories. Typicality may, therefore, also have an effect at the entry level representations.

The model in figure 7.2 less resembles the spreading activation model of Collins and Loftus (1975), because that places greater emphasis on the superordinate (fruit, furniture), that is, isa knowledge, than on entry level representations (apple, chair). In their model, a network of activation, by combining information about objects, allows information at the superordinate (isa) level to become available more readily than that at the basic level (Shallice, 1988a; McClelland and Rumelhart, 1985). The present model (see also Rapp and Caramazza,

1989) places less emphasis on isa nodes in knowledge networks, especially in the production of object names.

In all models of cognitive organization, presentation of an object activates not only the representation for that particular object but also connected representations. Therefore, models require an inhibition system to prevent chaos. McClelland (1979) suggested that inhibitory connections need not have stabilized activity at one level of the network before information is passed on to the next. The passage of information through the network was said to be in a "cascade." Humphreys, Riddoch, and Quinlan (1988) have used the McClelland cascade to model object naming. They suggest that activation of earlier accessed representations need not be complete before semantic (or in the present terminology, isa and associative) representations are activated. Activation of names can begin before the system has stabilized at the isa representations. Humphreys et al. can thereby explain why a picture of a common animal (cow) is not named more quickly than that of an uncommon animal (gorilla), as one might expect on the basis of frequency. They found that frequency is important only for structurally distinct categories. Structurally similar category items are held up, in their model, prior to the access of isa information, and the arrival of information at the lexical entries is delayed. Somehow, during this delay a lexical entry is decided upon without the effect of frequency being shown.

Humphreys, Riddoch, and Quinlan argue that structurally distinct category items require little perceptual elaboration, reach name output earlier, and are affected by word frequency. Furthermore, in a categorization task, structurally distinct items are not affected by the typicality of their category membership. Structurally similar items are delayed at a stage where typicality is important; structurally distinct items are not. However, the variables by which Humphreys, Riddoch, and Quinlan define structural similarity are visually based; this is also true of typicality (Riddoch and Humphreys, 1987c). Thus, although the cascade of their model is shown going through the isa representations, in fact it needs to consider only hasa representations. Their version of the McClelland's cascade model might only apply to the relationships between entry level categorization, hasa representations, and name output.

The model proposed in figure 7.2 also has similarities to those proposed (see Humphreys and Riddoch, 1987) for the loss of object knowledge from the visual modality (visual agnosia). For models of visual agnosia, the central issue is the intact status of the entry level representations. Riddoch and Humphreys (1987a) argue that the apparent loss of isa information concerning a specific category (Hart,

Berndt, and Caramazza, 1985) is really because items from some categories (e.g., fruit) are structurally similar. They contend that the supposed category-specific disorders arise from compromised entry level structures that cause problems that are mistakenly interpreted to arise at a more semantic level. Careful reading of case histories of visual agnosia might, therefore, warrant a reinterpretation as impairments at the entry level that cause (cascade) interference in the rest of stored knowledge. For example, the interesting case of Albert, Reches, and Silverberg (1975) reported as associative agnosia with preserved reading (section 7.2) may not be so completely free from entry level problems as stated.

Shallice (1988a) denies that entry level representations are impaired in visual agnosia. He argues that visually agnosic patients are able to recognize objects from unusual views, which runs counter to an entry level impairment. However, it is not necessarily so. Preserved recognition could be achieved from preserved feature recognition rather than intact entry level representations. The findings of Warrington and McCarthy (1983, 1987) pose more difficulty for Riddoch and Humphreys. Warrington and McCarthy found patients with better-preserved knowledge for living objects, which tend to be structurally similar, than for nonliving objects. Better performance on a category with visually confusable items would be difficult to accommodate in the Riddoch and Humphreys (1987a) belief that the cause of category-specific impairments is a visual confusion between similar entry level representations. The category-specific disorders reported by Warrington and McCarthy provide less difficulty for the model proposed in figure 7.2, since the route from entry level representations to hasa representations is not necessarily determined by structural similarity. However, it must be admitted that the organization of hasa representations is somewhat underspecified. Allport's (1985) suggestion (see figure 7.1) that there are modality-specific object representations is, nevertheless, able to accommodate certain category-specific disorders within a model that explicitly represents hasa properties.

Visual agnosia becomes a less contentious issue when knowledge is represented as both hasa and isa object properties. Knowledge of detailed appearance, function, and associations are all activated from an entry level categorization. Visual agnosia could, therefore, arise from a disorder at the entry level that also prevents the activation of detailed visual hasa representations. These representations would still be accessible by routes to them from other modalities. Information loss concerning object categories differentiated by function would require isa information to be unavailable. In such a scheme, it would be perfectly possible to retain all isa knowledge yet have no idea what an object looked like. It would also be possible to lose only the knowledge concerning visual properties contained at the hasa representations (see chapter 9). However, it does not seem possible—at least, no case has been yet recorded—to retain all hasa information for an object and have no knowledge of its function.

Chapter 8
Colors without Objects

8.1.1 Selection at the Pictorial Register
This chapter considers the procedures and mental structures by which color modularity is achieved from a nonmodular pictorial register. It would appear that modular selection (readout) *is* possible from information held at the pictorial register despite its being held in the form of surfaces within two- or three-dimensional boundaries. Studies show that color can be extracted independently of locus (Clark, 1969) and that color and shape can be selected independently of each other (Gottwald and Garner, 1972; Handel and Imai, 1972). Garner (1974) calls shape and color *separable* dimensions because of these demonstrations of *functional modularity.*

There are certain limitations to the functional modularity for color. First, the extraction of color and shape information from the pictorial register is not totally modular. To a limited extent, the addition of color affects size and shape judgments (Egeth and Pachella, 1969; Williams, 1974; Gamer, 1983), especially if the discrimination is difficult (Morgan and Alluisi, 1967). Williams (1974) found that the presence of an irrelevant color affected a same/different judgment; it was easier to say that two shapes were the same if the colors were the same and also easier to say that the shapes were different if the colors were different. One interpretation of these asymmetric results favoring color is that a color decision is arrived at first, thereby delaying a shape judgment. Color would, in that case, be immune from shape interference (Geller, 1977). However, Overmyer and Simon (1985) found that the interference of shape on color judgments operated in a fashion similar to that of color on shape.

Second, the modular extraction of color does not readily extend to its submodules (hue, saturation, and lightness). The three components of color interact in categorization tasks (Garner and Felfoldy, 1970; Felfoldy and Garner, 1971); for that reason, Garner (1974) calls them *integral*. To the adult observer—though apparently less so for children (Ward and Vela, 1986)—it would seem that a colored surface is first seen as a whole or, as Lockhead (1972) puts it, a blob. Thus, even though it is possible to break down colors into subcomponents, they resist separation. The separation of surface color into its components (hue, saturation, and lightness) can be achieved, with more or less success, according to task demands (Garner, 1988), individual differences (Ward, Foley, and Cole, 1986; Stalmeier and DeWeert, 1988), and training (Foard and Kemler-Nelson, 1984), but it is difficult even for color experts (Burns and Shepp, 1988). Indeed, an informal experiment in which the brightnesses of three color guns of a television monitor are independently controlled is sufficient to show the difficulty in predicting how much or even which gun has to be altered to match a given color. The difficulty found in separating hue from lightness is to be expected given their complicated neurophysiological relationship, but it still comes as a surprise, since the standard systems in use for color coding are based on exactly that separation.

The most commonly used color scaling system is that first published by Munsell in 1905. Munsell selected colored samples and asked his subjects, who were all in some way color experts, to rate the perceptual difference between subsets of highly similar colors. In that way, colors with subjectively equal intervals can be produced across three dimensions. These dimensions are hue, saturation, and lightness. The last two are known as *chroma* and *value* in the Munsell notation and are not completely independent for nonexperts (Davidoff, 1974). The color solid produced is a highly distorted sphere (see figure 8.1). The vertical axis of the sphere is lightness; it has white at one end and black at the other. The midpoint gives samples whose luminous reflectance is roughly 20 percent. The horizontal axis is saturation, and around the central circumference the various hues are systematically arranged. Distortions to the color solid occur because hues have maximum saturation at different lightnesses. For example, in the yellow region and in no other, light colors can be very saturated. Indow (1988) recently reviewed the studies that have contributed to the settings of the color solid. He found that the surface of the color solid is not perfectly smooth, especially in the blue region.

The ease with which color, compared with other information, might be extracted from the pictorial register (see the discussion in chapter 5 on prior entry) is an important consideration. For normals, preferential extraction depends on the importance of aspects of the display. Any item from a list that attracts attention because it is in some way special is learned faster than the rest of the list (Von Restorff, 1933). However, extraction also appears to depend on interesting individual

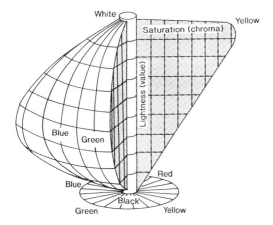

Figure 8.1
The Munsell color space. Colors increase in saturation as they approach the surface of the solid.

predispositions to select certain types of information. Young children, for example, usually prefer to select by color rather than shape (Brian and Goodenough, 1929; Suchman and Trabasso, 1966; Tomikawa and Dodd, 1980). The same appears to be true for those with brain damage (Meador, 1984; Grewal, Haward, and Davies, 1987; Huang and Borter, 1987). Therefore, teaching the brain-damaged associations via color is highly successful. Goldstein and Oakley (1986) found that a color discrimination was achieved much more easily by the brain-damaged than an orientation discrimination, even though the opposite was true for normals.

8.1.2 The Internal Color Space
The processes by which separate categorial storage for the boundary and surface qualities of the temporary representation is achieved are not yet fully understood. Somehow, modular storage is established from nonmodular representations. In the model (see figure 8.2) the modular store for the surface quality of color is labeled the internal color space. It is the memory "palette" from which color categorization proceeds. Individual items in the palette represent particular combinations of hue, saturation, and brightness; they could be compared with the viewer-centered stored descriptions of objects. These individual items are organized into regions (categories) of colors (red, green, etc.); they could correspond to stored object-centered descriptions. Representations at the internal color space are normally acti-

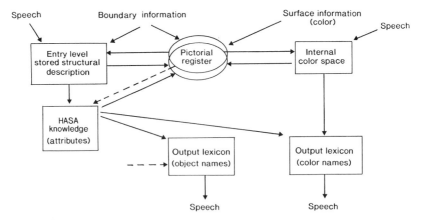

Figure 8.2
A model for color naming that extends that for object naming given in 7.2.

vated by instructions to select a category (e.g., red, green) rather than particular items. Thus, the internal color space plays a pivotal role in color cognition; its role for color is equivalent to the entry level for objects. It is important to stress that the internal color space is not coded for shape, nor is it directly concerned with the colors associated with objects (hasa color). Those associations are connected to the entry level descriptions and are considered in chapter 9.

Color names and other associations (see chapters 9 and 10) become attached to items and regions of the internal color space. In each part of the color space, Rosch (Heider) found that it was easier to form associations with certain colors; these were called *focal* or *landmark* colors. Focal colors appear to be salient for children as young as four months of age (Bornstein, 1975) and are important in the establishment of color-name labels (Mervis, Catlin, and Rosch, 1975). Children are more likely to point to a focal color when asked simply to "point to a color," and they use focal hues to represent the basic color names. Thus, the organization of the color space does not simply reflect the number of discriminable hues, nor do all colors play an equal role. Heider and Olivier (1972) argue that the internal color space is the same worldwide. They showed that the Dani of New Guinea catego-rized colors in much the same way as North Americans despite having only the terms *mili* and *mola* for all colors. Similarly, the Quechi Indians categorize blue and green differently even though they use the same word for them (Zollinger, 1988). The universality of the color space suggests that its organization has a neurophysiological basis. That basis is presumably derived from the opponent processes at the lateral geniculate nucleus and V1, which give distinct properties to red, yellow, green, and blue surfaces. However, the final organization of the internal color space does not correspond to the neurophysiology of color vision; at the internal color space, red is not necessarily paired with green, nor yellow with blue. Moreover, to some extent, the organization of the internal color space is flexible and alterable by experience. For example, with training (see section 8.1.1), colored surfaces may be organized by lightness or saturation.

According to Dixon (1960, 1981), the effects of unconscious activation of stored knowledge by colored stimuli are not attributable to opponent-process neurophysiology (see sections 2.1.6 and 6.1 for other considerations of unconscious awareness of color). Dixon (1960) used a complicated technique to show the unconscious effects of color. He presented the word *cancer,* colored red (or green), subliminally to one eye and to the other eye red and green light sources that could be adjusted to create an achromatic appearance. The threshold for the mixture to be seen as "going red (green)" was affected but not that for "going green (red)." Dixon therefore argued that a central representation for color had been activated. These effects implicate the internal color space. Presumably there is an unconscious activation of the representation for redness (greenness) that acts to prevent recognition of stimuli that are so colored.

The parallel between the internal color space and the entry level representations extends to their evocation by imagery. For example, it takes around half a second to generate a color, which is about the same time required to create a shape image. The similarity may not be accidental, given the impossibility of color without shape at the pictorial register (see section 3.2). Nevertheless, there is a disagreement about whether imagery is affected by the organization of the internal color space (Rosch, 1975b; Neumann and D'Agostino, 1981). For objects, it will be remembered (see section 7.3), identity matches at the pictorial register are not affected by frequency (Wingfield, 1968), typicality (Rosch 1975a, experiment 5), or priming with a superordinate name (Rosch et al., 1976, experiment 6) but are facilitated by a basic-level name prime. The effect of priming with a color name was somewhat different; focal colors were matched more easily and nonfocal colors less easily (Rosch, 1975b). The focal color acted as the pivot in the network of colors generated by the color name. The farther from the pivot—the more atypical the color—the harder it was to generate the color. However, Neumann and D'Agostino (1981) failed to find a decrease in priming with typicality. The Rosch (1975b) result was confirmed only by priming with a pictorial example of a focal color. It would appear that either the varieties of a color generated by the color name are readily altered by the experimental context, or a color name—but not a color patch—generates all examples of the category (Neumann and D'Agostino, 1981; D'Agostino, 1982).

8.1.3 Remembering Colors

Colors can be remembered with considerable accuracy for up to thirty seconds (Nilsson and Nelson, 1981; Uchikawa and Ikeda, 1981). At longer intervals, there are small errors in the remembered hue, but they are not greater at sixty-five hours than at fifteen minutes (Hamwi and Landis, 1955). The precision with which colors can be recognized suggests that they can be maintained in a pictorial code; this is also indicated by the unimportance of color names in the short-term memory for colors. Brown and Lenneberg (1954) found that a Zuni observer, despite having no names to differentiate yellow from orange, could reliably remember a specific color in that range for up to seven seconds. There was also evidence for pictorial coding in an experiment concerned with surface texture (Siple and Springer, 1983). Subjects were asked to remember the colors of stimuli presented with and without texture. Providing surface texture in a colored picture did not improve retrieval of the color if the texture was not provided at recognition. When texture was added to color, the object was immediately recognized as that seen previously. Thus, color and texture properties interacted facilitatively at recognition, which suggests that their coding was pictorial. However, the stimuli to be remembered were objects, so there was the possibility that these results also reflected the storage of color and texture hasa properties (see chapter 9) rather than memory of surface colors.

More persuasive evidence for pictorial coding comes from a study in which colors had to be recognized from similar alternatives; recognition was impaired by visual but not by verbal interference (Davidoff and Ostergaard, 1984). However, it is by no means clear from these experiments that modular storage is involved in the recognition; the colored shapes could be maintained in exactly the same form as at the pictorial register. Evidence that the rehearsal mechanisms, or neurophysiological substrate by which a pictorial code is maintained, distinguish between boundary and surface information comes from another part of that study. Davidoff and Ostergaard (1984) reported a patient who had quite normal short-term memory for shapes but whose short-term color memory was very poor despite his good ability to discriminate between colors. There was some evidence of a similar condition in the patient of Mohr et al. (1971). Further support comes from research with normals. Generally, the colors of shapes appear harder to retrieve than other attributes. The arbitrarily colored surface of an object was recalled no better than it would have been by chance (Park and Mason, 1982; Stefurak and Boynton, 1986), but in accord with its special status (see chapter 5), recall of location made almost no demands on memory (Park and Mason, 1982).

It may be normal for all young children to remember colors pictorially, because their memory for a color patch is not affected by giving it a color name (Svinicki, Meier, and Svinicki, 1976). However, in adults the recognition of color information is often mediated by the organization of the internal color space. There are two consequences: namely, superior recognition for focal colors and a likelihood of verbal coding. Focal colors are generally easier to remember than nonfocal colors (Ridley, 1985; Garro, 1986) except under special circumstances. With a widely spaced set of colors and hence no possibility of name confusion, focality is less important (Lucy and Shweder, 1979; D'Agostino, 1982), but its influence does not disappear (Garro, 1988). With widely spaced colors, a useful strategy for remembering samples is to remember the color names associated with them. Thus, the superior recognition for focal colors can be eliminated by casual experimentation, which allows incidental conversation and hence interference to take place (Lucy and Shweder, 1988). Verbal coding must be commonly employed because color recognition is commonly susceptible to verbal rather than visual interference (Davidoff and Ostergaard, 1984; Allen, 1984) and is affected by the label given at presentation (Hendrick, Wallace, and Tappenbeck, 1968; Bornstein, 1976; Loftus, 1977). Verbal coding is, therefore, likely to play an important role in color memory (see chapter 10).

8.1.4 Disorders of the Internal Color Space
Intervening between the pictorial register and the lexicon for color names (see figure 8.2) a stage is posited (the internal color space) at which colors are categorized. Some part of this space may derive from the categorial output of opponent process mechanisms (Mullen and Kulikowski, 1990) at the pictorial register; other parts of the space must be the result of experience. Selective damage within the route to the color lexicon could spare the internal color space; that is to say, there ought to be patients who cannot name colors but who can nevertheless categorize them (e.g., into reds, blues, and browns). Sittig (1921) made exactly that claim and drew a distinction between Farbenagnosie and Farbennamenamnesie. Sittig's use of the term color agnosia (Farbenagnosie) was more precise than that of many who have used the term since his day. In his terminology, a pure agnosia for color meant an inability to categorize colors and was not necessarily

accompanied by an impairment in the memory of object color nor a loss of color names (Farbennammenamnesie). Sittig (quoted in De Renzi et al., 1972a) reported that one of the three patients in his study who had difficulty naming colors should really be considered color agnosic. Other similar cases have been reported (Stengel, 1948; Beauvois and Saillant, 1985, case MP). The dissociation is supported by cases of visual agnosia in which there is preserved ability to categorize colors with (Kertesz, 1979; Beauvois and Saillant, 1985, case RV) and without (Levine, 1978) the ability to name colors. The further dissociation between color agnosia and the memory for object color (considered in detail in chapter 9) is predictable because the extraction of color information from the pictorial register does not rely on an input from the stored knowledge of objects; the dissociation has been confirmed in only a few cases (Kinsbourne and Warrington, 1964; Beauvois and Saillant, 1985) because color categorization is so infrequently examined.

The case for a discrete stage of color categorization seems clearly made from the preceding studies of brain damage. However, Gelb and Goldstein (quoted in DeRenzi et al., 1972a) claimed that it was part of a more general loss of abstract attitude (Goldstein, 1948). They questioned the diagnosis of normal color categorization in the presence of other language impairments. The claims that patients had normal performance on the Holmgren wool test—which is the one most commonly used for the assessment of impaired color categorization—were, in particular, considered suspect. The Holmgren test requires that patients sort nonidentical skeins of wool into color categories. A large-scale investigation of the Holmgren test was carried out by De Renzi et al. (1972a). The results did not support Goldstein's suggestion. They found that performance was affected by both left hemisphere and right hemisphere damage. The impairment of the group with right hemisphere damage was related to their ability to discriminate colors, supporting the hypothesis (see section 3.1.4) of hemispheric specialization. De Renzi et al. could not pinpoint the disturbed mechanism in those with left hemisphere damage. Poor performance by left-brain-damaged patients on the Holmgren test was not related to general tests of language or, contrary to Gelb and Goldstein, conceptual thinking. There must, therefore, be a specific deficit of color categorization related to left hemisphere function.

Color categorization has recently been investigated, by techniques capable of more precision, in two patients who successfully passed the Ishihara color blindness test but had difficulty naming colors (Fukuzawa et al., 1988). Fukuzawa et al. employed a multidimensional scaling procedure in which objects reliably associated with a color (e.g., in Japan this would mean an apple for red and a persimmon for orange) were presented in three separate studies. The objects were presented as color patches, color names, and as line drawings. The subjects' task was to select, from three stimuli, the two colors, color names, or imagined colors of objects that were the most similar. From these data, the researchers plotted a color space for their patients. The results of the multidimensional scaling were compared with tasks similar to the Holmgren wool test. In these, the patients were asked for a binary categorization of colored patches (green versus yellow, yellow versus red, and purple versus blue) and to sort seventy colors into as many color groups as desired. Case 1 showed that his color space was normal on all the tests despite having some difficulty, though not as much as case 2, with color naming. Case 2's mental color space was abnormal; the multidimensional scaling clustered colors into a general bluish or reddish space, there was an unusual cutoff point for green versus yellow, and in the larger-scale categorization, there were confusions in the green/yellow and blue/green areas. Case 2 showed that color categorization can be impaired for only part of the color space.

The Fukuzawa et al. technique for investigating color space is considerably more sophisticated than those used in previous studies. However, it may not be an effective way of recovering the color space for all subjects. It is less likely to be effective if judgments are requested from disparate areas of the color space. Some subjects, without good access to an internal space that arranges colors in the conventional circle (see figure 8.1), would find such similarity judgments hard to comprehend. Red, yellow, and green would be distinct colors to them, and it might make no sense whatsoever to say that one of them was more different from the other two.

8.2 Associations with Color

8.2.1 Synesthesia
The separate extraction of surface information from the pictorial register allows it to become associated to other stimuli independently of shape. One particularly remarkable type of association is called *synesthesia*, which is the sensation of color produced by a different modality, usually sound. Synesthesia has a long recorded history that, despite being more anecdotal than scientific, merits serious consideration. Synesthetic subjects have included many famous composers. Liszt, Scriabin, Rimsky-Korsakov, and Messiaen all reported seeing colors on hearing music. A direct perception of color has also been reported

from other stimuli. Galton (1883), for example, recorded that some people associated colors with numbers, days of the week, and with other ordered categories. Recently, Baron-Cohen, Wyke, and Binnie (1987) investigated a similar synesthetic individual who claimed that words instantly evoked a color experience. They tested her with the same 103 words at two sessions separated by a ten-week interval. She reported seeing the words in exactly the same color combinations on both occasions. However, the combinations of colors bore no relationship to the meaning or sound of the words. Their results closely paralleled those for the association of color with musical notes (Rizzo and Eslinger, 1989). The associations with individual notes and chords were extremely consistent, but the color of chords did not reliably relate to the colors of the component notes.

Reports of synesthesia are often dismissed by the scientific community, probably because those who do not have these color associations find them incomprehensible (Shanon, 1982). Indeed, there are aspects of synesthesia that are obscure. For example, for no obvious reason, it appears helpful to have perfect pitch (Cuddy, 1985), though this was not the case for the subject tested by Rizzo and Eslinger (1989). However, despite the paucity of firm data, there have been attempts to give a theoretical account of synesthesia. These explanations place different weights on the role of experience. The most nativist of the explanations (Cytowic and Wood, 1982) suggests a link between sensory reception areas. Cytowic and Wood propose that cross-modal connections are present early in development of some individuals but subsequently disappear, leaving behind the ability of sound to produce colors. Their hypothesis of a direct link between sensory reception areas is not supported by electrophysiological investigations (Rizzo and Eslinger, 1989); the anatomical locus is more likely to be subcortical. Both the parietal cortex (where system) and temporal cortex (what system) send connections (see figure 2.1) to subcortical regions (the amygdala and hippocampus), which are concerned with learning and the transfer of information from short- to long-term memory (Scoville and Milner, 1957; Mishkin, 1978; but see Brown, Wilson, and Riches, 1987). These subcortical structures would play a part in the association of color with other modalities. Research with nonhuman primates suggests that the amygdala, in particular, plays a role in learning cross-modal associations (Murray and Mishkin, 1985). In another account (Shanon, 1982), synesthetic associations must be acquired fairly late in development. Shanon found that the colors synesthetically associated with numbers are those that have the most frequent names in the individual's language. Therefore, the establishment of color synesthesia would need to be mediated through color-name categorization and not result from connections made to uncategorized information at the pictorial register. However, an explanation based on late experience must find its rarity a problem. A weak form of synesthesia in which cross-modal associations do not require the visualization of sounds in color is more commonly found. For example, white is often associated with high-pitch tones, and black with low-pitch tones (Marks, 1975). The combination of these "synesthetic" stimuli from different modalities reduces response latencies. Facilitation of the subjects' response latencies when white is paired with a high tone may be mediated by controlled or automatic processing strategies (Schneider and Shiffrin, 1977), depending on the strategy employed (Melara, 1989).

8.2.2 The Meaning of Colors
The interest in color far outweighs its significance in many tasks. Color is useful in vigilance tasks (Pfendler and Widdel, 1986) and segmentation (see chapter 5) but (see chapter 9) surprisingly redundant in many others. However, despite being remarkably inaccurate about its effectiveness, people prefer to work from colored instrument-panel displays (Narborough-Hall, 1985; Greenstein and Fleming, 1964; Tullis, 1981). Therefore, it is unwise to unthinkingly accept people's convictions concerning color. In particular, one ought to be cautious about the widely held belief that different parts of the color space are necessarily associated with particular emotions.

There are particularly strongly held beliefs about the emotional responses to "warm" and "cold" colors. Warm (the "red" end of the spectrum) and cold ("blue" end of the spectrum) colors have been found to differentially alter both physiological and emotional states (Lewinski, 1938; Goldstein, 1942; Dixon, 1960; Wilson, 1966). The arousal value of red colors, it is said, accelerates the passage of time (Smets, 1969), makes you feel warmer, and increases your grip strength (O'Connell, Harper, and McAndrew, 1985). Color is also believed to produce a direct effect on the endocrine system via the pituitary gland; its action is to increase aggressive behavior under long-wave (red) light and reduce it under short-wave (blue/violet) light. There is a subtle shade (Baker-Miller pink) that is purported (see Schauss, 1985) to reduce aggression and violence and has had mixed to dramatic success in this respect in police detention cells.

The preceding results should be treated with caution. There are only a few well-documented effects of color on behavior; these are in the treatment of jaundice and the production of epileptic seizures (see Kaiser, 1984). They are accompanied by labyrinthian (i.e., incomprehensible) justifications for the use of color as therapy in almost any disease state (Amber, 1983) and premature conclusions based on poor experimentation. Indeed, most of the studies that purport to show effects of color on mood and behavior are not well controlled. For example, none of the studies that showed changed physiological arousal from different colored lights properly controlled brightness (Kaiser, 1984). Therefore, the findings that color alone can change heart rate, EEG, and the like are not to be believed. Proper stimulus control shows that time does not pass faster in "red" light (Caldwell and Jones, 1985), and wall colors do not affect perceived temperature (Fanger, Breum, and Jerking, 1977; Greene and Bell, 1980). The effects of color in producing changes in mood state are artifacts of poor experimental design and demand characteristics. Not surprisingly, then, the effect of Baker-Miller pink is spurious (Piggins and Nichols, 1982), and muscle strength is not affected by the color of the ambient illumination (Greene, Bell, and Boyer, 1983; Ingram and Lieberman, 1985). The conclusion must be that it is subjective measures (response bias) not objective measures that are, in general, altered by changing the color of one's surroundings (Goodfellow and Smith, 1973; Kunishima and Yanase, 1985).

Explanations for the association of emotions with colors stress either innate or learned causation. The alternative explanations are associated with different parts of the model given in figure 8.2. The first is associated with the internal color space and the second the hasa representations. The internal color space is important for color memory (Ridley, 1987; Garro, 1986) and would, of course, assist in the ready formation of associations. Because the internal color space is universal, these associations with mood could be innate and could arise from links to subcortical structures. The argument is supported from ethological evidence. Color is an important warning signal for many subhuman species (Tinbergen, 1951); it could be that some remnant of our evolution is lodged in the human subcortical networks. Thus, it could be innately determined that Goethe's "warm" colors have a somewhat different arousal value than the "cold" colors. These links from the internal color space to mood are distinct from those gained by experience to color names; the independence is shown by their dissociation after brain damage (Damasio, McKee, and Damasio, 1979).

Given that the evidence for an effect of color on emotional state is so weak, it may seem more worthwhile to pursue an explanation based on experience. Another part of the model in figure 8.2 that could supply an association of color with mood from experience is the hasa associations with objects. The hasa representations, considered at greater length in chapter 9, do not represent modular colors. There-

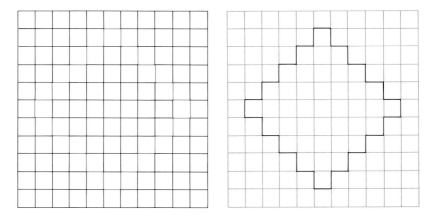

Plate 1 (chapter 6)
The two figures have identical spatial arrangements. In (a) a blue diamond line pattern is surrounded by a black crossed grating. In (b) the colors are reversed (taken from Van Tuijl, 1975).

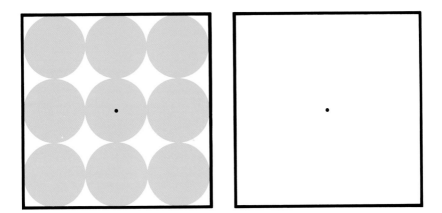

Plate 2 (chapter 6)
The reader should fixate on the yellow circles (fixation dot provided) and after ten seconds transfer gaze to the clear white square. The afterimage may not be as expected. To obtain the normal color opponent afterimage, make a hole in a white card sufficient to allow only inspection of one yellow circle. After inspection of twenty seconds, transfer gaze to the clear white square (taken from Albers, 1971).

Plate 3 (chapter 9)
Examples of the inappropriate coloring performance shown by the patient discussed in Davidoff and Ostergaard 1984.

Plate 4 (chapter 11)
Stimulus to produce Stroop interference. The written word interferes with attempts to say the name of the ink color.

fore, emotional associations are not directly modular; the associations would be with particular objects. Because there is a considerable overlap of colors with objects, it is not surprising that the meaning of a color is often arbitrary. There are, of course, exceptions. A limited cross-cultural consistency in color meaning could be expected, because many naturally occurring objects and events have the same colors in different cultures. The seasons of the year would be one such exception, as they produce reliable associations of particular colors with appropriate words (Seymour, 1980). However, anthropological evidence clearly requires us to put restrictions on the meaning of particular colors (Varley, 1980). Even associations with red, which might, because of its connection to fire, danger, and blood, seem automatic, are not completely universal (Courtney, 1986). Indeed, Wright and Rainwater (1962) found that very little mood was attributed to color (hue) if presented as isolated patches; any emotional connotation came mainly from their lightness and saturation. Kunishima and Yanase (1985) reported much the same for Japanese subjects. Lightness (perhaps associated with daylight) and saturation (perhaps associated with ripe fruit) of colors are much more likely to be reliably connected to positive affect than are hues that can apply to many objects. There is even good cross-cultural correspondence for the emotional connotations of lightness and saturation. Osgood (1960) reported considerable agreement between Navajos and Caucasians for the emotional tone of lightness and saturation but quite considerable variation in that for hue. Lighter colors were judged more favorably, and saturated colors more potent. The hasa account is also somewhat supported by neuropsychological evidence from a patient with preserved emotional associations to color (Ferro and Santos, 1984). Their patient, with a severe visual recognition impairment, could not categorize or name colors but could recall the colors of objects.

8.2.3 Color Preference

In his book on the experimental study of aesthetics, Fechner (1876) proposed that the relative pleasantness of a set of objects could be assessed from forced-choice decisions between the objects taken in pairs. The empirical validation of Fechner's method was first attempted by Cohn (1894), who measured the aesthetic preferences for certain parts of the color space. Three major questions have been tackled by subsequent research. First, do the mechanisms controlling the organization of colors within the color space contribute toward these aesthetic preferences? Second, are there individual differences in the preferences exhibited, and third, are these color preferences related to their associations with objects?

Martindale and Moore (1988) tackled the first of these questions concerning aesthetic preference. They have had the courage, or perhaps temerity, to attempt a reductionist account of aesthetic preference for colors. Martindale and Moore directly relate aesthetic judgments concerning colors to the structure of a color space. In their model, colors are coded in a network of connections used in perceptual and cognitive judgments. The units (nodes) of the network are organized from a prototypical unit (Rosch, 1975a,b). Aesthetic pleasure is computed in the same set of units as the perceptual and cognitive processes. In essence, their model relates the amount of pleasure elicited by a colored stimulus to the activation of the internal representations coding that color (see figure 8.3).

In their study, Martindale and Moore used five colors in each of eight regions of the color space. The eight prototypical and most nonprototypical colors (Munsell patches) were taken from Rosch (1975b). The three intermediate steps were taken from Neumann and D'Agostino (1981). A monotonic increase in preference was found related to the typicality of the examplar. The results therefore showed that typicality (cognitive distance from the prototype) of the color within the network was an important variable in determining aesthetic preference. However, while typicality accounted for a significant proportion (23 percent) of the variance, color (e.g., red versus blue) was a much more important determinant of liking, explaining 62 percent of the variance.

In the Martindale and Moore network model, the excitatory state of the units and, therefore, the aesthetic preference is alterable by the

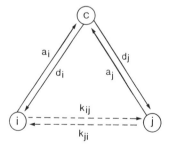

Figure 8.3
Excitatory (unbroken) and inhibitory (dashed line) connections between examplars (i and j) of the superordinate color category unit (c). Each examplar is connected to the superordinate unit by ascending (a) and descending (d) connections. Within-level connections are denoted by k. Connections (inhibitory) from atypical examplars to typical examplars are weak compared with those in the opposite direction. (Taken from Martindale and Moore, 1988.)

activation of units elsewhere in the network. In a less formal sense, Fechner proposed a similar mechanism in his laws of hedonic contrast. Fechner (1876) proposed that when a stimulus is preceded (or accompanied) by a more pleasant stimulus, its pleasantness decreases. Martindale and Moore (1988) make more complicated predictions. They propose that the units of the color space act in a way similar to those in the network model of McClelland and Rumelhart (1981). Units are connected to each other in two ways: directly and indirectly via the prototype. Direct connections between examplars of a prototype are inhibitory, but those between the prototype and the examplars are excitatory. Thus, the activation of a color unit both inhibits and excites other examplars of the same color category. Whether aesthetic preference increases or decreases depends on the resultant effect of the two opposing forces. Martindale and Moore (1988) found that the effect of most color primes was to reduce aesthetic preference. There was only one condition in which aesthetic preference increased; that was for a highly typical color when it was preceded by a moderately nontypical color of the same category. To accommodate these findings, constraints needed to be placed upon the strengths of inhibitory connections. Inhibition was said to be inversely proportional to the typicality of the examplar. Thus, inhibition from nontypical category examplars on typical examplars was much weaker than the reciprocal inhibition from typical examplars. A study with category-name priming (Martindale and Moore, 1988, experiment 5) reinforced these findings of asymmetrical connections between units. Echoing the study of Rosch (1975b) on identity matching (see section 8.1.3), a category-name prime increased preference for typical examplars but decreased preference for nontypical examplars. It was argued that the category name activated units for all examplars, which then proceeded to inhibit each other. As the inhibition of the nontypical unit on the typical was weak, it was less than the excitatory activation from the prototype. Inhibition of the typical unit on the atypical was strong; therefore, preference increased only for typical examplars.

The main concern of the Martindale and Moore model is to show how preference can vary because of an immediately preceding color. Fechner argued that stimuli had to be similar to alter preference, but he was contrasting intermodal with intramodal priming. The Martindale and Moore proposal for preference is even more restricted. They found that priming a blue stimulus with red stimulus, whatever its typicality, had no effect whatsoever on preference. Thus, aesthetic preference for color is constrained by the submodule of the internal color space. If color preference is so functionally modular, it ought to be the case that its contributions to preference should be independent of shape; that prediction has been confirmed (Ekehammar, Zuber, and Nilsson, 1987). However, it is unlikely that all color preference can be limited to the judgments of isolated colors. A model for aesthetic preference must also consider combinations of colors and color preferences in objects. This is clearly a substantial limitation to Martindale and Moore's proposal. Moreover, it does not explain the majority of the variance, even for the somewhat artificial conditions required to obtain their preference scores. Most of the variance in the Martindale and Moore study comes from the differential preferences shown for the eight colors.

The study of the more substantial differences in color preference (e.g., red versus blue) has had two main aims. The first is to attribute the differences to innate preferences for certain parts of the color space, and the second is to relate them to culturally acquired response patterns. Connected to both these approaches is the relation of color preference to personality. Innately determined preferences for one color over another have been attributed to some unspecified action of our neurophysiology. There is said to be, in general, a preference for blue and a dislike of yellow (McManus, Jones, and Cottrell, 1981). The same has even been reported to be true of monkeys (Humphrey, 1972). However, Pickford (1972) in his review of the research on cross-cultural and personality preferences for colors concludes that the lack of stimulus control in these studies makes it impossible to be adamant about the preference for blue. Also, as for the Martindale and Moore model, there are good reasons for doubting the generality of color preferences obtained from isolated samples. Preferences certainly will not be the same if there are surrounding colored surfaces (Granger, 1955), as one of the Bauhaus color theorists (Itten, 1961) stressed in the 1930s.

One cause of the considerable variation found in color preference could be that preference is influenced by personality (Eysenck, 1941). Different personalities are said to prefer different colors. Whether or not preference is innately determined would then depend on the origins of personality differences. However, the link between color preference and personality is not so assured (see Corbus and Nichols, 1963) as has been promised by the tests of Luscher (Scott, 1970) and Pfister (1951). These tests of personality are based simply on the preference for color patches, and their validity or, to be charitable, their precision, is questionable. For example, Holmes et al. (1985) found that the color preferences of psychiatric patients completely reflected those of the normal population; violet is not the color of madness (Holmes, Fouty, and Wurtz, 1985), as has been suggested elsewhere. Furthermore, given the difficulties in standardizing color printing, it is unlikely that the particular color shades used in the

Luscher test can be important. Replacing the color patches with color names would probably produce no difference in choice behavior. So, at most, it can be only a color category that is related to personality. Even that relationship is likely to be determined by different learning experiences and the current associations of objects with colors. Granted the remote possibility that these associations differentially interact with personality, the Luscher and other such tests might have a limited predictive value. But, if color preference can be so dictated by culture and fashion, then the tests can have no more than a passing validity.

For meaningless shapes, liking is relatively independent of color (Ekehammar et al., 1987), and where they are arbitrarily associated with shapes, the choice of colors is often irrelevant (Smith, 1962). However, there is definitely no reason to believe that the preference— or lack of preference—shown for the colors of isolated patches should generalize to that for object colors. Color preference is, for example, a different matter for cars (Saito, 1983) than it is for cheese (Scanlon, 1985); indeed, cheese is preferred in different colors by different nationalities, even though they cannot taste the difference (Scanlon, 1985). Thus, the association of colors with objects means that expression for the liking of colors may be implicitly or explicitly considering the objects to which they are related. A further implication is that, with respect to objects, color is stored as an appendage to the object; certainly, that is how it is shown in figures 7.2 and 8.2. The evidence for that aspect of the model is considered in the next chapter.

Chapter 9
The Colors of Objects

9.1 The Role of Color in Object Recognition

9.1.1 In Normals

Models of object recognition differ in the way they represent the storage of knowledge concerning color. In some accounts, greater emphasis is given to the formation of "surface-coded" descriptions. By surface-coded is meant the descriptions that code surface characteristics, including color, brightness, and texture. For example, the account popularized by Marr (1982) proposes that surface-coded descriptions provide a necessary constituent step in the recognition process. His two-and-a-half-dimensional sketch (a temporary representation) specifies depth and orientation details for the surfaces of objects. The three-dimensional model representation is constructed from the two-and-a-half-dimensional sketch in a serial sequence and contains representations for surface details. Surface detail is, therefore, constructed before recognition takes place. Alternative accounts have been put forward (Grossberg and Mingolla, 1985; Grossberg, 1987a,b; Pentland, 1986; Biederman, 1987). Grossberg and Mingolla propose that object recognition can operate directly from the boundary contours (edges) of objects derived from an initial computation at the gray level. Their account allows the invisible boundary contour (see section 6.1) to make contact with the entry level representation in permanent storage. In parallel, surface features fill in the spaces between the boundary contours to generate surface-coded descriptions. Biederman's model is more similar to Marr's except that storage consists of a finite number of edge-based primitives (object parts). In summary, edge-based accounts do not require that surface-coded representations constructed at the pictorial register be used for the initial recognition (categorization) of objects.

There are reasons for favoring an edge-based model. Selection of the appropriate entry level to match the temporary representation must require extensive computations. An evolutionary advantage could ensue from allowing only the fast pathways (see table 2.2) to play a central role in these computations. It is therefore no accident that patients with difficulties in performing tasks that require rapid spatio-temporal integration have recognition difficulties (Davidoff, 1989). Two further lines of experimental evidence support the view that entry level representations are not color coded. The first is indirect in that superiority effects operate from outline stimuli with very little surface detail (Homa et al., 1976; Davidoff and Donnelly, 1990), and the second is direct investigation of the role of color in recognition. If some degree of recognition can proceed from edge-based entry level representations without recourse to other stored information, a rather counterintuitive prediction can be made. It ought to follow that there will be no difference in the speed with which objects can be recognized from black-and-white and colored photographs. The counterintuitive prediction has turned out to be correct (Ostergaard and Davidoff, 1985; Biederman and Ju, 1988; Davidoff and Ostergaard, 1988). The effect of color was not altered by its specificity—(Biederman and Ju used the term "diagnosticity"—for the object; that is, it was true for both objects with and without a defining or typical color. It should follow that an inappropriate color should not, in general, affect object recognition; this even more counterintuitive prediction has also turned out to be true. The number of errors in tachistoscopic recognition (Mial et al., 1974) and speed of identification (Ostergaard and Davidoff, 1985) were identical for appropriately and inappropriately colored objects. Corroborating evidence comes from Cavanagh (1987; Cavanagh and Leclerc, 1989), who found that shadows, which play an important role in forming an object representation, can be any color without disturbing the perception of a three-dimensional shape.

The limited role for color in recognition and hence its absence at the entry level representation has been disputed by Price and Humphreys (1989). They argue that color may be required at the entry level to disambiguate objects from categories that are structurally similar. In terms of the model presented in chapter 7 (see figure 7.2), they imply that only recognition of items from structurally similar categories requires access to hasa representations. Therefore, facilitation in object naming from the addition of color should occur only with structurally similar items. Price and Humphreys (1989) obtained exactly that result and wondered whether studies (Ostergaard and Davidoff, 1985; Biederman and Ju, 1988; Davidoff and Ostergaard, 1988) that obtained no advantage in recognition and naming paradigms did so by using a rather restricted number of objects. It certainly must be admitted that there are some within-category discriminations for which recognition would be improved by the addition of color detail. For example, a photograph of an orange without size cues would be difficult to distinguish from a grapefruit unless color information was provided. However, the limited role for color in identification is not restricted to simple laboratory tasks. A review of identification performance from many varieties of color-coded displays (Christ, 1975) showed that color gave no advantage over achromatic stimuli unless the stimuli were degraded. Subsequent similar research has shown that color coding is not more helpful than achromatic coding for identifying the state of a component in an aircraft cockpit (Luder and Barber, 1984) or oil-refinery control display (Zwaga and Duijnhouwer, 1984). If considerable shape information needs to be highlighted in a display, it would appear that coloring the display is not the way to do it. Thus, experienced map users were not more accurate in judging whether a colored rather than achromatic contour map matched a three-dimensional surface (Eley, 1987), and experienced pilots did not find colored aircraft landing simulators easier to use that achromatic versions (Kellogg, Kennedy, and Woodruff, 1984). Color can even be harmful in retrieving identify information (MacDonald and Cole, 1988), but, most often, it is not because rapid search is generally important when using complex information displays.

Achromatic texture is essentially the same as chromatic texture in the Biederman (1987) model; neither should normally aid recognition. Biederman and Ju (1988) confirmed that there is no difference in the speed with which recognition takes place from line drawings and black-and-white photographs. However, they had to ensure that no important entry level information had been omitted from the line drawing. Luminance differences make up both texture and boundary information, so the comparison between a line drawing and a black-and-white photograph is fair only when all boundary information is retained. By omitting internal boundary details (e.g., wing feathers on a bird) and shadows, recognition may be harmed. It is therefore unlikely that the Biederman and Ju comparison would produce the same result if subtle discriminations were required. Within-category differentiation, such as telling one face from another, would certainly require access to detailed texture (internal boundary) information. Thus, line drawings of faces are not easier to recognize than photographs (Davies, Ellis, and Shepherd, 1978), even if they are cartoons that capture the "character" of the person (Ellis, 1981).

Color is represented (see figures 7.2 and 8.2) as part of the hasa properties of an object, but that information is not required for many categorial and recognition judgments. One such task could be size judgment, which Paivio (1975) has shown is quicker from a picture than from a word. Consistent with size comparisons being performed at the entry level representation, Davidoff and Ostergaard (1988) found that the introduction of color did not improve performance in that task. Nor did color help speed performance on a living versus nonliving categorization (Davidoff and Ostergaard). The Humphreys et al. (1988) model presumes the living versus nonliving comparison is made either at or at a stage close to the entry level. However, the objects used by Davidoff and Ostergaard were quite disparate in shape, and it might be more reasonable to suppose that the judgments were carried out using isa representations. If so, the information entering that system must not include color (see figure 7.2). It is perfectly reasonable that the isa system does not have a chromatic input; its conceptual role concerns function.

9.1.2 After Brain Damage

Recognition is normally achieved by categorization at the entry level. For more detailed discriminations, access to hasa representations may be required. For patients with apperceptive visual disorders the situation is quite different; they achieve recognition in a much more piecemeal fashion. Adler (1944) found that her patient used all details provided; these were then "added up" in a conscious effort to recognize the object. For her patient, therefore, the color present at the pictorial register could be useful for recognition. Activation of other hasa representations, either visual (Levine, 1978) or nonvisual (Botez, Serbanescu, and Vernea, 1964) has also been found to promote recognition. The slowness with which recognition takes place in patients with apperceptive and associative visual disorders makes stored knowledge of sensory properties (color, sound, etc.) useful in tasks that do not normally require them. The model proposed in figure 7.2 is, therefore, not contradicted from studies of brain-damaged populations that show that the addition of surface properties improves object recognition.

9.2 The Role of Object Knowledge in the Perception of Color

9.2.1 Introduction

Several lines of research indicate that object knowledge can affect the organization of colored shapes and the perception of color. The most controversial aspect of the research is the implication that "top-down" pathways can operate in advance of data-driven recognition processes.

A discussion of these effects follows. In figure 8.2 two top-down pathways are shown from stored knowledge to the pictorial register. The first of these routes is that from the internal color space, which was considered in chapter 8. The route allows priming for focal colors. The internal color space is not coded for shape, so it can be discounted with respect to object knowledge. An effect from the other route is more likely but is still unexpected, especially if the entry-level representations are not color coded.

9.2.2 The Organization of Colored Shapes

The pictorial register contains filled-in boundaries defining shapes; it is generally supposed that these boundary contours and their surface detail are constructed by automatic data-driven processing. Treisman defines the conjoining process as entirely data driven, that is, without any influence from stored knowledge (see chapter 5). However, there is the intriguing possibility that the route from the entry-level representations might organize the boundaried surfaces into object parts with consequent effects for the allocation of surface color. There are three phenomena that demonstrate that stored knowledge of object boundaries affects the allocation of surface color at the pictorial register. The first concerns illusory conjunctions (when surface color becomes associated with the wrong contour; see section 5.2.3), the second concerns neon spreading (see section 6.2.3), and the third the McCollough effect (see section 5.2.4); all are controversial.

When subjects are asked to rapidly process colored stimuli, surface color information can migrate to the wrong boundary, forming what Treisman and Schmidt (1982) call "illusory conjunctions." There are indications that these illusory conjunctions are more frequent for meaningful shapes (Prinzmetal and Millis-Wright, 1984; Prinzmetal and Keysar, 1989). Treisman prefers an alternative explanation. She holds that these illusory conjunctions are due to the subjects' response biases. Treisman points out that, apart from tachistoscopic experimentation, illusory conjunctions are rare. Even within the tachistoscopic experiment, subjects expecting to see a carrot are not likely to misperceive a green triangle as an orange triangle (carrot) when an orange color is presented elsewhere in the display. However, Prinzmetal and Keysar do not claim that the organization of color-shape boundaries by meaning is more important than data-driven organization; their proposal is more modest. They claim that illusory conjunctions are primarily produced by positional uncertainty (see section 4.2.4) of the color and shape borders. They draw a parallel to the loss of spatial information over time that can also result in the mislocation of features (Wolford, 1975). Nevertheless, as a secondary factor, Prinz-metal and Keysar claim that stored knowledge makes a contribution. They found that illusory conjunctions could be affected by the subjective organization determined by Gestalt laws of perceptual organization (Koffka, 1935) and by written language. Gestalt effects were shown because stimuli organized by rows made illusory conjunctions more likely within rows. Effects of linguistic organization were shown because exactly the same physical string of letters yielded a different pattern of illusory conjunctions, depending on the part of the string from which a word was inferred.

Prinzmetal and Keysar also showed that the spreading neon illusion (Van Tuijl, 1975; see section 5.2.5) is modifiable by linguistic constraints. They placed grids of colored lines over five gray horizontally arranged letters that could be divided into syllables. A neon spread was produced in each letter. Grids of different colors were placed over the two left-most and two right-most letters with a plaid of both colors over the central letter. The color of the illusory spreading for the central letter was modified by the linguistic organization of the letter string. These results, and those from the illusory conjunctions experiment, imply that the alteration in attention to color by varying spatial scales (Fuster, 1988; Spitzer et al., 1988; see section 5.2.3) can be influenced by meaning.

The production of surface colors contingent upon the orientation of boundary lines (McCollough effect) are usually produced with gratings (see section 5.2.4). The neurophysiological locus of the effect is generally given to be somewhere in V1 (but see section 5.2.5), yet, like illusory conjunctions, it appears modifiable by stored knowledge and Gestalt organization. However, the effects of Gestalt organization (Jenkins and Ross, 1977; Uhlarik, Pringle, and Brigell, 1977) have been disputed (Foreit and Ambler, 1978; Milewski, Iaccino, and Smith, 1980; Broerse and Crassini, 1986), as have the claims (Finke, 1981) that the McCollough effect can be produced by imagery (Broerse and Crassini, 1984). The more dramatic claim that the McCollough effect can be induced from the organization of the line stimuli as faces (Meyer and Phillips, 1980) or as words (Allan et al., 1989) would show, if substantiated, very strong entry level modification of colored surfaces at the pictorial register.

9.2.3 Color Perception and Matching

There is a much-discussed proposal (Gregory, 1980) that stored knowledge can have dramatic influences on perception and, for present purposes, on color perception in particular. It was Hering's belief (1878) that "all objects that are known to us from experience, or that we regard as familiar by their colour, we see through the spectacles of memory color." To affect perception in that manner, stored information would have to interact with and alter the color of the surfaces at the pictorial register. A few studies indicate that such effects are possible. Bruner and Postman (1949), for example, claim that a tachistoscopically presented red two-of-spades was seen as purple—the percept being a compromise between stored knowledge and the presented color. It is tempting to dismiss the Bruner and Postman findings as artifactual because they do not fit easily into models of object recognition. The artifact, however, is not obvious. Subjects' comments that water flavored with pineapple was said to taste of orange if so colored (Zollinger, 1988) could be due to biased reporting; that cannot be the explanation of a rare event such as a purple two-of-spades.

One ought not to expect color matching (see also section 11.3 on the Stroop effect) to be affected by object identity. In general, that is so, but there is one exception. Menaud-Bateau and Cavanagh (1984) found that subjects were slower to judge two identical blue shapes to be the same color if they looked like bananas rather than, say, books. Their result is difficult to accommodate within models for the representation of stored knowledge because color matching could be accomplished from the boundaried surfaces without contact with entry level representations, yet alone their hasa properties. Color comparisons made *directly* at the pictorial register should be fast and immune to differences in the richness of stored knowledge concerning objects. Unless one proposes that there are implicit task demands to select by shape, stored object knowledge should not influence a comparison of colored surfaces. Thus, the result of Menaud-Bateau and Cavanagh indicates that further research is needed into the role of hasa properties in color matching. Seymour (1979) suggests that it could be studied in a task where identity matches are primed by an object's name. Hasa color information would be activated (see figure 8.2) and would then affect the colored information at the pictorial register. Seymour wonders whether rare examples of an object's color act like poor examples of focal colors (see section 8.1.3) for matches at the pictorial register. In that case it would, for example, be easier to match two reds or two greens than two yellows after priming with the word apple. However, irrespective of the route by which knowledge affects color matching, its influence on the pictorial register ought to be confined to those occasions that allow sufficient time for the generation of images. The findings of Menaud-Bateau and Cavanagh do not require a warning interval and, therefore, warrant a different explanation.

9.3 The Recognition and Retrieval of Object Color

9.3.1 In Normals

Recognition of an object color takes place after the activated entry level representation has accessed hasa color knowledge. Retrieval of object color, whether by imagery or verbal recall, may use the same networks. The hypothesis that imagery and recognition share neural networks is not new. It has been attributed to Freud (1900/1938), but Charcot (1883) raised the issue somewhat earlier, explicitly tying the loss of imagery to the consequence of losing the representations used for object recognition. It receives its modern exposition in several accounts (Kosslyn, 1981; Farah, 1985). For example, in Kosslyn's model of imagery (1981, 1983), objects are stored as lists of spatial coordinates that can be recreated at a buffer store. Or, in terms of the model presented in figure 7.2, edge-based pictorial knowledge is stored as entry level information and recreated as an image at the pictorial register.

There is not complete agreement concerning the correspondence between imagery and recognition. One unresolved issue (see section 7.1.1) concerns the supposed prototypical nature of entry level representations. If their prototypical nature is granted, then imagery differs from recognition, because the part of stored knowledge activated by instructions to image appears to be concrete. Images are created from particular viewer-centered representations of an object, not from object-centered views (Pinker, 1985). Another issue that might distinguish imagery from recognition concerns the placement of color at the entry level or as part of the associated hasa representations (see section 9.1.1). If color plays little part in object recognition because information concerning object color is functionally more distant than object shape, then its imagery may operate differently than that of shape. The distinction was illustrated in an experiment by Intons-Peterson and Roskos-Ewoldsen (1989). They made the prediction that imagery for an object's weight or color (hasa properties) was less likely than other imagery to depend on the same pathways used when the stimulus is present; this prediction was upheld. Detection and imagery of an unfamiliar-colored stimulus were harder against a similarly colored background, but imagery for familiar-colored objects was easier if the background was the same color as the object. Thus, imagery requiring access to hasa properties is distinguished from that which does not. So, it is not too surprising that good imagery for object colors does not correlate with the ability to remember the colors of surfaces (Heuer, Fischman, and Reisberg, 1986). These differences between imagery and recognition could make it reasonable to give the networks activated in imagery a name other than the pictorial register. Seymour (1979), for example, uses the term *pictorial interface*. However, as shown in figure 8.2, they are represented here as identical or nearly so.

The memory for object colors differs somewhat from their recognition. In general, the remembered color is brighter, more saturated, and gravitates toward the color most typical for the object (Newhall, Burnham, and Clark, 1957; Siple and Springer, 1983). Thus, stored knowledge has some effect upon responses made at retrieval. Indeed, children as young as four know what colors objects should be and become confused by that knowledge when retrieving arbitrary associations of colors with objects (Perlmutter, 1980). There are two interpretations of such confusions. First, the confusion could arise because the object rather than the color was remembered. When asked to recall color about which they remember little, subjects would naturally elect for colors normally, though not necessarily correctly, associated with the object. Second, the arbitrary episodic color could actually be altered in memory to correspond more with the stored knowledge of object color. Distortions of color memory based upon object categorization were reported by Adams (1923), and there have been many subsequent replications (Duncker, 1939; Bruner, Postman, and Rodrigues, 1951; Herring and Bryden, 1970; White and Montgomery, 1976). Duncker even claimed that, to avoid being so influenced, it needed the special training of an artist. An important criticism (Ridley, 1987) of the second alternative proposes that it is the color name (see section 11.1.4) that produces the object color when retrieval is requested.

9.3.2 After Brain Damage

9.3.2.1 The Classic Study of Lewandowsky   The description at the entry level (see figure 7.2) is a shape-related representation for an object; object color is part of its associated hasa properties. Confirmation of their independence comes from the study of brain-damaged populations. The dissociated retrieval of object color and object shape in the brain-damaged was first described and explored at length by Lewandowsky (1908a,b). However, Lissauer (1890; Shallice and Jackson, 1989) had already made the pertinent observation that his patient with object recognition difficulties could not point to the color of a canary despite having normal color vision. Lissauer also made the observation, in passing, that his case would appear to go against the then currently held opinion that the inability to retrieve an object's color was an aphasic (linguistic) disturbance.

Lewandowsky was impressed that, in a normally color sighted individual, color and form could so readily "split-off" from each other. He wrote as follows (Davidoff and Fodor, 1989):

I would like today to briefly describe the symptom-complex of a cerebral disease which I believe to be new. It belongs to the category of disturbances which concern the color sense . . . the patient was not able to give the color of objects familiar to him, e.g. the color of a lemon, a leaf etc . . . . He gave color names at random, some of them being of a quite peculiar sort as, for example, bluish-red or such like. . . . When one placed a selection of colors, e.g. wool probes before the patient and asked him to indicate and pick out the color of blood, grass and a lemon, he failed in exactly the same way. He selected, if at all, entirely wrong colors and again without any regularity.

It should be noted in passing that in all respects our patient regarded black and white as colors, but despite that he was fully oriented to dark and light. He could not give the color of snow or coal but answered the question whether the night was dark or light with "DARK", when the moon shines with "LIGHT". When seeking out the color of a certain object he always took account of lightness but never the color itself. This should be of considerable significance for the psychology of color perception and its separation from brightness perception.

Of course we confirmed that on all trials the patient understood the meaning of all named objects for which he had to indicate the colors. For example, he answered the question whether he knew what blood is with, "naturally, that which flows everywhere in the body" and what leaves are with "that which grows on trees". Actually, it should be emphasised that his intelligence, as the word is commonly used, was quite unusually good. To entirely exclude the verbal expression of the examiner, we extended the test by giving the patient uncolored pictures of objects, for example a lemon, cigar or leaf which he recognised straight away. We even made the patient draw a leaf himself and then asked him to find the matching color and again he failed completely. It is thus out of the question that any form of language disorder could have a causal significance for this symptom complex.

We even went so far as to show the patient wrongly colored pictures and even here he was very uncertain; nonetheless, this condition provided the limit (of his poor performance). He frequently chose correctly when he saw the wrongly colored next to the correctly colored object, for example a green ox next to a brown ox. However, when he saw the pictures individually he was uncertain and sometimes declared that quite correctly colored objects, for example a green meadow, were wrong.

9.3.2.2 Loss of Abstract Attitude   Several group studies have followed up Lewandowsky's original observations. Group studies are possible because the inability to remember object colors seems to be a remarkably common accompaniment to language disorders. The tasks investigated have required patients to recall the colors of named objects, to fill in a line drawing of an object with an appropriate color, to match an uncolored drawing of an object with the appropriate color, and to choose which of several drawings has been colored correctly. Standardized versions of Lewandowsky's tasks have been developed by Lhermitte et al. (1969). Difficulty with the tasks is not confined to patients with comprehension problems (Wernicke's aphasia) (DeRenzi and Spinnler, 1967; DeRenzi et al., 1972b; Basso, Faglioni, and Spinnler, 1976), since patients with nonfluent speech but without comprehension difficulty (Broca's aphasia) are similarly impaired (Basso et al., 1985).

The inability to remember object color correlated with scores on, albeit substantially different, tests of conceptual thinking in Wernicke's and Broca's aphasia (Basso et al., 1985). The group studies therefore suggest more general deficits than that proposed by Lewandowsky, who said of his patient: "Colour vision was isolated; it led in this brain a life of its own and could not be connected or associated with the sense of brightness or form." However, the nature of the general deficits has not been easy to isolate. A simple relationship to language disturbance can be eliminated from case studies of object-recognition disorders. Such patients, perhaps not surprisingly, fail at Lewandowsky's visual tasks, but some do so without any general aphasic disturbance (Ferro and Santos, 1984; Beauvois and Saillant, 1985, case RV; Larrabee et al., 1985, case 1). Aural comprehension has also been ruled out from the results of another group study of aphasic patients (Varney, 1982). Cohen and Kelter (1979) suggested, following Goldstein (1948), a loss of abstract attitude (see section 8.1.4). The difficulties exhibited by left-brain-damaged patients, according to Goldstein, was not so much that knowledge was lost but that new categories cannot be formed. The study of Cohen and Kelter was in the Goldstein tradition and was a reaction to the remarks of Lewandowsky (1908a) concerning the difference between brightness and color. Cohen and Kelter compared the ability of aphasic patients to retrieve hue, brightness, and saturation of color patches. They found that their patients were impaired in memory for all three aspects of the color and concluded, reiterating Lange's opinion (1936/1989) of the problem for Lewandowsky's patient, that the inability to retrieve object color was due to a loss of abstract attitude. There is some justification for Lange's conclusion, because the patient was unable to sort colors into groups. Lewandowsky did not produce any counterevidence for the patient's ability to think abstractly except to remark on his intelligence (see preceding section) and to declare him free of his initial Wernicke's aphasia.

According to Lewandowsky, the difficulty for the patient was not in any general conceptual loss but rather in the integration of stored object color with object shape. There are two reasons for supporting his interpretation against that put forward by Cohen and Kelter. First, the three aspects of a color are integral (see section 8.1.1) and difficult to separate when the color is in view yet alone from memory. It is therefore not surprising that memory for lightness, saturation, and hue were all impaired. Second, and more directly, it has been shown that failure to recognize object colors need not be associated with a loss of abstract attitude (Kinsbourne and Warrington, 1964; Beauvois and Saillant, 1985, case RV). These case studies show (see tables 9.1 and 9.2), contrary to the group results (DeRenzi et al., 1972b), that failure on Lewandowsky's tasks can be combined with the preserved conceptual ability required to categorize colors.

9.3.2.3 Imagery Impairment   Beauvois and Saillant (1985) argue that retrieval of the appropriate visual semantics (pictorial hasa representations) is required for accurate color recall. Lewandowsky (1908a) thought likewise. He wrote: "It seems possible, that . . . in order to have "knowledge" of the color of an object, the respective color representation needs to be evoked." The inability to retrieve object color could, therefore, be a difficulty with image generation.

Tables 9.1, 9.2, and 9.3 give lists of case studies where patients with normal, except where noted, color vision have been asked to retrieve information about object color. Table 9.1 presents case studies of patients with disorders of visual recognition. In general, only those with limited visual problems (e.g., prosopagnosia) are able to imagine object colors, but there are exceptions (Levine, 1978). The amount of intact imagery could well depend on the extent to which the visual hasa representations were intact in each case. It may also depend on the task. Table 9.2 gives a list of case studies who were reported without visual recognition problems but who had difficulties naming objects. There may be doubts concerning the intact status of object recognition in some of these patients (see section 10.2.2) and also whether their apparent loss of color imagery is due to color-name

Table 9.1
Patients with object-recognition disorders

	Color categori- zation	Object-color			Color naming	Pointing to named colors
		Recognition	Imagery	Recall		
Adler (1944)	?	?	?	+	+	?
Ettlinger and Wyke (1961)[a]	?	?	−	+	−	−
Cole and Perez-Cruet (1964)[c]	?	?	?	+	−	−
Oxbury et al. case 1 (1969)	?	?	−	+	−	−
Rubens and Benson (1971)	?	?	?	+	−	−
Taylor and Warrington (1971)	?	?	−	?	−	−
Lhermitte et al. (1973)	?	−	−	+	−	?
Lhermitte and Pillon (1975)[b,c]	?	+	+	+	−/+	?
Mack and Boller (1977)	?	?	?	+/−	−	?
Levine (1978)	+	?	+	+	+	+
Wapner et al. (1978)	?	?	−	?	−	?
Kertesz (1979)	+	?	?	+/−	−	−
Pillon et al. (1981)[b]	+/−	−	−	+/−	−	?
Ferro and Santos (1984)	−	−	−	+	−	−
Beauvois and Saillant case RV (1985)	+	−	−	+	−	−
Larrabee et al. case 1 (1985)	?	?	−	+	−	?
McCarthy and Warrington (1986)[a]	?	?	?	−	−	−
Fukuzawa et al. case 1 (1988)[d]	+	?	+	+	−	−

a. No color vision testing reported.
b. Mild color vision loss.
c. Only prosopagnosia (face recognition disorder).
d. Only mild disorder of recognition.
+ Preserved function.
− Impaired function.
? Not tested.
−/+, +/− Impairment (intact status) uncertain.

Table 9.2
Patients with object-naming impairments

	Color categori-zation	Object-color			Color naming	Pointing to named colors
		Recognition	Imagery	Recall		
Kinsbourne and Warrington (1964)	+	+	−	−	−	−
Oxbury et al. case 2 (1969)	?	?	?	−	−	−
Lhermitte and Beauvois (1973)	?	−	−	+	−	−
Stachowiak and Poeck (1976)	?	?	?	+	−	?
Damasio et al. case 1 (1979)	?	+	−	+	−	−
Damasio et al. case 2 (1979)	?	−/+	−	+	−	−
Beauvois and Saillant case MP (1985)	−	+	+	+	−	−
Gil et al. (1985)	+	+	+	+	−	?
Larrabee et al. case 2 (1985)	?	?	+	+	−	?
Pena-Casanova et al. (1985)	?	?	?	+	−	−
Riddoch and Humphreys (1987c)	?	?	?	−	−	?
Basso et al. (1988)	?	?	−	?	?	?
Coslett and Saffran (1989)	?	+	?	+	−	−

+ Preserved function.
− Impaired function.
? Not tested.
−/+, +/− Impairment (intact status) uncertain.

Table 9.3
Patients without object-recognition and naming-impairments

	Color categori- zation	Object-color			Color naming	Pointing to named colors
		Recognition	Imagery	Recall		
Stengel case 1 (1948)	− [a]	+ +	−/+	−/+	−	−
Stengel case 2 (1948)	− [a]	?	?	−/+	−	?
Holmes (1950)[b]	?	?	?	+	−	−
Geschwind and Fusillo (1966)	+	?	+	+	−	−
Mohr et al. (1971)	?	?	?	+	−	+
Netley (1974)	?	?	−	−	−	−
Boucher et al. (1976)[a]	+	+	+	+	−	?
Varney and Digre (1983)	?	−	−	−	−	+
Farah et al. (1988)[b]	?	+	−	−	+	?
Fukuzawa et al. case 2 (1988)	−	?	−	−	−	−

a. No data given.
b. No color vision testing reported.
+ Preserved function.
− Impaired function.
? Not tested.
−/+ +/− Impairment (intact status) uncertain.

interference (see section 11.2.2.1). Table 9.3 gives data from patients without disorders of object recognition or object naming. The patients of table 9.3 are, no doubt, a biased sample; without a color-naming disorder or some other color-related problem it is unlikely that object-color retrieval would have been investigated.

Despite the fact that occipital lobe damage produces loss of both perceptual functions and visual imagery (Symonds and Mackenzie, 1957; Goldenberg et al., 1987), these functions cannot share completely identical processing networks. The most straightforward reason for making a distinction is that excellent drawing from memory may accompany impaired recognition (Riddoch and Humphreys, 1987a). Thus, there is a difference between the two visual tasks Lewandowsky used to test object-color retrieval. In the case where the patients are confronted with a wrongly colored object, Farah, Levine, and Calvanio (1988) argue that images do not have to be generated. They claim that imagery is required only when one is asked to point to the correct color of an object shown as an uncolored line drawing. Their patient could do the task that they claim does not require image generation but could not do the one that did. However, the two tasks were not matched for difficulty. When they were matched, Goldenberg and Artner (1991) found that left-posterior-damaged patients showed equal impairments. The difference between the tasks may, therefore, be a matter of degree. Nevertheless, the distinction Farah, Levine, and Calvanio make is required in some circumstances. When a discrepancy between stored knowledge and input is detected, clarification could take place using imagery. Some difference between imagery and recognition is surely reflected in the reports of patients who maintain that the colors of objects now "look different" (DeVreese, 1987). Thus, there is sufficient evidence to warrant separate listings, so in tables 9.1, 9.2, and 9.3 the two tasks are labeled object-color recognition and object-color imagery.

There are three interpretations of the patient's failure to recognize that an object is inappropriately colored. The first would be that the independent storage of object color from object shape adds another component to the task of visual imagery. The inability to integrate the information in the two stores would be at fault. In Lewandowsky's term, color is "split-off" from the other knowledge concerning the object. The patient reported in Davidoff and Ostergaard (1984) was of this type. Even after a successful verbal strategy prevented the repetition of his coloring errors (for examples see Plate 3), the patient never felt completely happy about his choices. When presented with a line drawing of a carrot, the patient's successful strategy was to ask himself "What color is a carrot?" to which he answered "Orange." He then looked for an orange color, which he could do successfully when provided with the color name, even though he could not name colors. The second interpretation is that the colored hasa object representations are permanently damaged. A variation on the second interpretation is given by Beauvois and Saillant (1985) for their patient RV. They suggest that impairments in retrieving object color from visual hasa representations result from an imperfect color input. They claimed that the patient RV, who had moderately impaired color vision, only made moderately wrong color errors. While that was generally so, there certainly were exceptions—for example, pink chickens and maroon straw. It is more likely that a problem with image generation results from an inability to use the information in permanent storage rather than faulty color input. The third interpretation, implicit in the results from Beauvois and Saillant (1985, case MP), is that object color and object shape are not stored separately. They would claim that a misapplied naming strategy (see section 11.2.2) causes the production of wrong object colors.

The neurological site for object-color storage is of considerable interest to models of knowledge storage. If anatomical distinctions can be found between areas associated with the imagery for object color and those for other stored knowledge, it adds support to the functional dissociations made in figure 7.2. Such evidence is available. It is clear, with respect to color perception, that there is no precise overlap in neural networks with those used for object-color imagery as claimed by Farah (1988). Unlike in dyschromatopsia, both case and group studies (DeRenzi et al., 1972b) confirm the remarkable fact that an inability to retrieve the color of an object is associated with a *left* hemisphere lesion. Therefore, support is given for the clear distinction made in figures 7.2 and 8.2 between the roles of colored surfaces and object color. The retrieval of object color must be based on relatively distinct neural networks, since impaired imagery for object color can accompany preserved imagery for object shape (Stengel, 1948; Riddoch and Humphreys, 1987a). Thus, it ought to be possible to distinguish object shape and object color neurologically and add support to the difference between entry level and hasa representations. Visual imagery impairments, in general, are associated with damage to the posterior left hemisphere (see Farah, 1984). The site has been confirmed in normals from regional cerebral blood flow patterns while judging the correctness of a sentence requiring visual imagery (Goldenberg et al., 1989). The neurological site for the impairment of object color retrieval is also associated with the left hemisphere, but Goldenberg and Artner (1991) have recently connected it to a different locus. They have shown, in a group study, that imagery for color is more reliably associated with damage to a different branch of the left posterior cerebral artery than impoverished imagery for shape. It is damage to the temporal-occipital branch rather than the occipital branch of the posterior artery that is associated with reduced color imagery.

The findings of Goldenberg and Artner suggest that a left temporal-occipital site is a separate store used for object colors. The impairment caused by damage to the site would arise from either degradation to the store of object colors or difficulty in integrating an intact entry level and hasa storage. An alternative role for the site could be that of a modular color "centre" (Lueck et al., 1989; see section 3.1.3), which was also found, by the regional blood flow method, to be more pronounced on the left and in much the same locus. However, the Goldenberg et al. study implies that the Lueck et al. results were contaminated by uncontrolled color imagery or implicit color naming (see section 11.2.2). It could be vice versa, but then one would have to admit the possibility of modular color input. In earlier chapters it was argued that the only possible type of color module is the internal color space. That store has plentiful connections (see figure 8.2) to hasa color representations and the lexicon of color names but is quite distinct from them (see double dissociations in the cases of Beauvois and Saillant, 1985). The internal color space is unlikely to be that functionally located at the left temporal-occipital site of Goldenberg and Artner (1990), since their tasks explicitly involved *object*-color imagery.

One might suppose that, if the retrieval of pictorial storage was a lateralized function, it would be to the other hemisphere. It is the right hemisphere that, if damaged, causes most problems in recognizing poor-quality drawings (Milner, 1958; Warrington and James, 1967), overlapping drawings (DeRenzi and Spinnler, 1966), and objects seen from unusual views or only partially illuminated (Warrington and Taylor, 1973). However, the function of the right hemisphere with respect to object recognition (see section 6.3) does not seem to be one that involves mental rotation (Mehta, Newcombe, and Ratcliff, 1988) or other processes requiring imagery but a failure to form (for theoretical alternatives see Humphreys and Riddoch, 1984; Warrington and James, 1986) an object-centered mental representation. So why is imagery a left hemisphere function? According to Farah et al. (1988), it is not because loss of visual image generation arises from a disconnection from language (Basso, Bisiach, and Luzzatti, 1980). Lewandowsky believed the same but was concerned that his patient had a unilateral left hemisphere lesion; it was the one serious difficulty he saw for his explanation of the patient's impairment in retrieving object color. With that lesion, it would be quite reasonable to explain the patient's performance by some disorder of language. Lewandowsky wondered why the intact right hemisphere could not be capable of integrating object color with object form. The question is still unanswered.

Chapter 10
Objects and Their Names

10.1 *The Role of Object Knowledge*

One particular response to an object—its name—has been the subject of much research. The result has been to give a role in object naming to processes that intervene between recognition and the articulation of the response. Naming, it is argued, is mediated by the "cognitive system" (Nelson, Reed, and Mackevoy, 1977; Morton, 1979). Most contemporary models for naming a visually presented object have, therefore, three stages: the first is the formation of a temporary structural representation, the second concerns the corresponding representations within the cognitive system, and the third or output stage is activation of a phonological description at a dictionary of lexical entries. The first stage was considered in chapters 5 and 6. The third stage is not dealt with in detail. In brief, the output lexicon has been shown to be functionally distinct from the entry level lexicon (Shallice, McLeod, and Lewis, 1985). To the output stage are attributed effects of name frequency (Oldfield and Wingfield, 1965), age of acquisition of lexical entries (Carroll and White, 1973), and the effect of alternative names on the speed of name production (Lachman, 1973), and the effect of alternative names on the speed of name production (Lachman, 1973). These frequency effects are said not to involve the cognitive system. Thus, effects of name frequency are not affected by priming from an associated object (Huttenlocher and Kubicek, 1983; Humphreys et al., 1988), and they still occur in word naming if given several seconds to prepare a response (Balota and Chumley, 1985). However, frequency effects disappear when object names are arbitrarily associated with shapes (Bartram, 1973), which suggests a more complicated relationship. One proposal (see section 7.4) is to favor a cascade of information that also depends on recognition difficulty (McClelland, 1979; Humphreys, Riddoch, and Quinlan 1988).

The organization of the second ("cognitive stage") was considered in chapter 7; the contribution of that stage to object naming is the main subject of this chapter. Most nameable objects have a wealth of associated isa and hasa properties; an important question concerns whether the activation of these is mandatory in the production of the object's name. Certainly, it cannot be the case that all stored knowledge is activated before a name is given. Indeed, some nameable stimuli have little associated information to activate. Random shapes, for example, have little or no isa or hasa information, but these shapes can be given names. In these cases, an episodically formed representation is the determining factor in name production. Thus, it will be argued that visual object (entry level) categorization is the primary link to the object name. Whereas name facilitation occurs for only a short while after associated "semantic" information is presented, activation of entry level representations shortens naming times for as much as six weeks (Mitchell and Brown, 1988). Indeed, the boundary-segmentation processes operating to form the parts (leg, arm, foot, and so forth) of the entry level representations may even be causal in the acquisition of particular object names (Jackendoff, 1987).

In figure 7.2 the hasa representations are shown on the main route from the entry level representation to name output. Therefore, at least some hasa knowledge is very likely to be activated before name output. In support, it has been found that the presentation of an object color (e.g., the red or green of an apple) plays a significant part in reducing the time to name the object (Ostergaard and Davidoff, 1985; Davidoff and Ostergaard, 1988). The facilitation occurs only with colors appropriate to the object (Ostergaard and Davidoff, 1985), because only those are contained in hasa knowledge. There is no inhibition from inappropriate surface colors, because these cannot activate hasa representations. However, the contribution from hasa mediation should not be overstated; the absolute reduction in naming latency is fairly small, though it might be more important for young children (Funnell, 1987). It usually contributes less to naming latencies than sorting out either the appropriate entry level representation or the correct output phonology. Furthermore, color is only one, and almost certainly not always the most important, hasa property of an object.

Hasa facilitation in object naming could have two sources; one likely and one unlikely. The unlikely source is from categorizing the colored surface at the internal color space. Information could be then fed into stored object knowledge with subsequent access to name phonology; however, on that proposal, all hasa knowledge with the same color name would be activated. It is more likely that the surface color has direct access to the hasa representation. On an edge-based account (see section 9.3.1), direct access could occur only after top-down activation of the pictorial register from the entry level (see figures 7.2 and 8.2).

Naming is sometimes discussed (Miller and Johnson-Laird, 1976) as if it necessarily arises after contact with the isa representations. But naming an object is not the same as naming the object's function. It is the hasa representations that contain the more important information for discriminating between objects within most categories (but see preceding comments by Warrington and McCarthy, 1983). Therefore, the output from hasa representations form the main input to the dictionary of phonological entries for object names. When confronted with an object, far from being the main input, isa representations are regarded here as secondary in finding the name. However, Miller and Johnson-Laird claim that it is not possible to name an object through a perceptual description alone. They argue that it is necessary to know what a table does to call an object a table; in some circumstances, it is claimed, a tree stump is a table. It is not so. Given a clear, detailed picture it would be called a tree stump. The most one might say, given the appropriate context, is that it was a tree stump being used as a table.

The model shown in figure 7.2 has an important difference from that given elsewhere for naming objects (Morton, 1979) and faces (Bruce and Young, 1986). In figure 7.2 isa and associative knowledge contribute only weakly to name production. Thus, priming with an entry level name facilitates picture naming of a related object more than priming with a category (isa) name (Rosch et al., 1976; Murphy and Smith, 1982) because a category name will activate too many unwanted exemplars. Other models argue for a specific contribution of isa knowledge to object naming from the results of Potter and Faulconer (1975). These models base their argument on the critical finding that isa categorizations of objects take place faster than the naming of the same stimuli. A similar result is obtained with faces (Young, Hay, and Ellis, 1986). Priming experiments also indicate that isa knowledge plays a part in the production of an object name (Sperber et al., 1979; Carr et al., 1982; Kelter et al., 1984). An interpretation of these studies is that an isa categorization stage intervenes between forming a structural description (entry level categorization) and name production. However, categorization by function or association cannot always be quicker than object naming. It must depend on the precision required for the categorization task. Deciding whether an individual was from Alabama or Arkansas might well take longer than giving their name; deciding whether they were American or Soviet might well be quicker. The route from the entry level representations clearly does not activate all isa knowledge before name output. Nevertheless,

it is acknowledged that access to the lexical entry from isa representations may be important, especially if there is a blockage on the hasa
route.

Neuropsychological evidence supports the view that naming is possible without access to isa information (Warrington and Taylor, 1978).
The reasoning that explained naming in left-brain-damaged patients
ran as follows. Perceptual categorization can be accomplished by an
intact right hemisphere (but see Serjent and Lorber, 1983). Therefore,
object naming would require only preserved connections to the name
output system held in an undamaged part of the left hemisphere. The
claim for the unavailability of isa information was not properly tested,
but such naming would be possible in both the Warrington and Taylor
model and that given in figure 7.2. Even more dramatic claims have
been made from neuropsychological case studies concerning access to
knowledge in picture naming; however, these fit less well. A few cases
have been reported in which patients perform "direct" naming without access to any "semantic" information (Heilman, Tucker, and Valenstein, 1976; Kremin, 1986). Such naming requires a direct route from
entry level representations to output phonology, bypassing semantics.
But, entry level representations *are* part of stored knowledge; in that
sense, semantics cannot be bypassed. The question is rather what
other stored knowledge contributes to object naming. The model in
figure 7.2 would predict that intact naming without retrieval of some
hasa and perhaps isa knowledge would be impossible to demonstrate.

10.2 Object Knowledge and the Retrieval of Object Names in Aphasia

10.2.1 Introduction
Disorders of naming are associated with all types of language disturbance of a central origin (aphasia). However, some aphasic patients
have more problems naming objects than carrying out other language
functions. The disorder is usually present whatever the input modality. For these patients, the most common reason for a clinically significant impairment of naming, when confronted with a picture, is the
inability to access the output phonology (Goodglass, Barton, and Kaplan, 1968; Stemberger, 1984; Kay and Ellis, 1987). It is not primarily a
disorder of comprehension. Goodglass (1980) found, when comparing
performance in aphasia for a range of stimuli, that objects were most
frequently hardest to name but the easiest to understand. Indeed,
effects of stored object knowledge have been specifically ruled out in
facilitating name retrieval (Corlew and Nation, 1975; Hatfield et al.,
1977). The same is true of name-finding difficulties in normals. When,

as commonly happens, a name cannot be put to an object or face, common experience tells us that our knowledge of function and appearance is intact. The problem that we have is in accessing the phonology; it is, as we say, on the "tip of the tongue." Nevertheless, if sensory properties such as color facilitate naming in normals, they might also give a little help to anomic patients in name retrieval. It is therefore worth reconsidering the evidence for the relative contributions of isa and hasa knowledge to naming. The result of that appraisal is to reinforce the distinctions between the two types of knowledge and their relative contribution to name retrieval.

10.2.2 Modality-Specific Aphasia

There is a particular rare type of confrontation naming impairment in which naming is impaired only from a single modality. Naming from verbal descriptions are intact. Three types of modality-specific naming disorders have been documented. First, there is an impairment through vision called *optic aphasia*. The term optic aphasia was introduced by Freund (1889) and implied a much greater disturbance of language than simply of object naming, though that is how it is often interpreted (Lhermitte and Beauvois, 1973; Lhermitte, Chedru, and Chain, 1973; Hecaen et al., 1974; Riddoch and Humphreys, 1987c). The term optic anomia (Beauvois, 1982; Poeck, 1984) would be more appropriate for today's usage. Second, there is an inability to name by touch (Beauvois et al. 1978), and third, by sound (Denes and Semenza, 1975). The importance of modality-specific aphasia for models of naming comes from the claim that certain parts of object knowledge are intact (Beauvois, 1982). Models that have a common semantic system intervening between entry level and response must dispute the existence of modality-specific aphasias. Riddoch and Humphreys (1987b), for example, claim that optic aphasia arises from an inability to sort out visually similar structural descriptions. They deny the implication from optic aphasia that object knowledge has dual representations (see section 7.1.2). However, modality-specific aphasias are highly compatible with models like that in figure 7.2, which have divisions within the semantic system. The divisions suggested by Beauvois (1982) do not completely overlap with the hasa versus isa distinction. She divides the semantic system into two types: visual and verbal. The output to phonology is only from the verbal system. Optic aphasia, in her model, results when visual semantics are disconnected from verbal semantics and not because the stored knowledge is degraded.

An intact semantic system is verified in patients with optic aphasia by showing that they comprehend objects that they cannot name.

Comprehension is often tested (Spreen, Benton, and Van Allen, 1966) by asking the patient to mime the use of the object, though this might not distinguish some objects—for example, a shoe from a sock. Opinions differ on the functional locus of the intact knowledge necessary to perform the mime. It has been placed either at the entry level structural representations (Riddoch and Humphreys, 1987b) or at the semantic representations (Lhermitte and Beauvois, 1973; Shallice, 1988a). Even broad category judgments, such as living versus nonliving, which ostensibly require access to semantics, Riddoch and Humphreys (1987c) argue are achievable from the entry level representations. Riddoch et al. (1988) propose that there is a link between stored structural descriptions and learned action routines that would allow a person to gesture the action of an object without being in other ways able to express its function. Thus, action is not dependent on "visual semantics"; its shape "affords" action (Gibson, 1979). However, even if a living versus nonliving judgment could be performed by visual similarity without access to isa information, it does not seem reasonable that it could for judgments of dangerous versus not dangerous. An unknown animal would be judged to be dangerous because of its visual similarity to other *dangerous* animals. To say that the shape "affords" danger begs the question. Furthermore, as Shallice (1988b) points out, it is impossible to tell from its shape that the primary use for a vase is to exhibit flowers. From its shape, it could equally be for drinking from or to pour with. To properly categorize the object, knowledge about its function is required. Shallice (1988a) argues that visual (isa) semantics must be intact in optic aphasia, because patients can demonstrate that visually distinct objects (a zipper and a button) can perform the same function.

    The different explanations offered for optic aphasia could result from the discrepancy in particular patients' preserved visual processing ability. For example, the patient of Riddoch and Humphreys was more impaired than that of Lhermitte and Beauvois; therefore, it would be easier to assume a visual cause for the disorder. However, both optic aphasic patients can be accommodated in figure 7.2. In both patients the disturbed route is from the entry level via hasa representations to name output. Naming to definition is unimpaired because of the intact link from isa representations to the phonological output. In naming a visually presented object that route is only weakly used, but when activated by precise verbal (nonhasa) definitions, it can produce an adequate response. The argument over the functional locus of the intact gesturing is unimportant, since even if it is at semantics, the connection from isa representations to object naming is weak and only relevant to priming or naming to functional description.

10.2.3 The Contribution of "Isa" Knowledge

It follows from the model given in figure 7.2 that impairments in confrontation naming should not arise solely from damaged isa representations. Nevertheless, there are apparently contradictory findings in studies of aphasia and dementia. Poor object naming in aphasia has been attributed to an altered and more concrete organization of lexical knowledge (Zurif et al., 1974). The more structured the representations, in their case predominantly of the isa type, the more objects' names can be differentiated. It has also been shown that some aphasic patients find it difficult to assign object boundaries according to functional category (Whitehouse, Caramazza, and Zurif, 1978; Caramazza, Berndt, and Brownell, 1982). However, it is unlikely that the difficulty found in deciding whether a line drawing was of a cup or a bowl had much to do with their impaired confrontation naming for everyday objects.

The role that impaired isa representations play in the anomia associated with the rather loosely defined neuropsychological category of dementia is also uncertain. It appears that the more hasa and isa information that is available, the more likely it is that a picture can be named (Martin, 1987). However, both visual (Rochford, 1971) and semantic (Huff, Corkin, and Growdon, 1986) explanations have been proposed as the main cause of naming impairment in dementia. It is quite reasonable to expect that conceptual confusion would affect confrontation naming in dementia, especially for those patients who cannot access phonology via other routes. Those patients would have no alternative but to use the pathway to phonology from the isa representations, and there could be faulty information associated with that route. The role of the route from isa representations to name output is, therefore, similar to the one suggested for it by Newcombe and Marshall (1980) in deep dyslexia. They propose that the route from the semantic system is inherently unstable and requires other routes for its output to be secure. The model in figure 7.2 differs from that suggested by Newcombe and Marshall in regarding the route from the isa representations as secondary *because* of its imprecision.

10.2.4 The Contribution of "Hasa" Knowledge

Quite a few studies, with both aphasics (Bisiach, 1966; Benton, Smith, and Lang, 1972; Damasio et al., 1979) and dements (Rochford, 1971; Kirshner, Webb, and Kelly, 1984) show positive effects in confrontation naming by the addition of visual detail to the displays. In most of the studies that find facilitation a comparison is made between objects and drawings. Color is, therefore, only one of the additions responsible for the better naming performance. Indeed, only one (Bisiach, 1966) of the three studies that have directly addressed the issue of object color in facilitating name retrieval in aphasia reached a positive conclusion. However, the negative studies (Wyke and Holgate, 1973; Towne and Banick, 1989) are somewhat suspect. The Wyke and Holgate study can be discounted because it made an unfair comparison: "banana" was the correct answer to the achromatic stimulus, but the subject had to say "yellow banana" to be credited with a correct answer to the chromatic. The Towne and Banick study came to what must be considered a conservative decision considering that nine out of eleven of their aphasics gave more correct names to colored stimuli, which led to a significance value of $p<0.07$. Therefore, it is not unreasonable to propose that the more and different hasa representations active, the more likely it is for the name to be produced. Damasio et al. (1979) have made a similar suggestion. Conversely, objects that have representations in only a few modalities could be especially vulnerable to naming loss (Gardner, 1973). A similar prediction would come from the distributed memory model of Allport (1985) (see figure 7.1). It would also follow that the two most common types of category-specific naming loss would be color (primarily visual representations) and body parts (primarily kinesthetic representations), since these would be more likely to be lost in an all-or-none fashion if hasa storage had a somewhat submodular organization.

10.3 Conclusions

Results of both normal and impaired populations have led to the conclusion that there are several important stages in object recognition and object naming. Perhaps most critical is the activation of the entry level representation. Only after categorization at the entry level representation can naming occur. The entry level activates both hasa and isa networks. Both isa and hasa information have access to name phonology, but the output from the hasa representations constitutes the major pathway in confrontation naming. Therefore, activation of the object-color representation (a hasa property) makes a contribution to object naming; however, that contribution is not large.

Chapter 11
Color Naming

11.1.1 A Model for Color Naming and Object-Color Naming
A distinction needs to be made between naming colors and naming the colors of objects. Both types of naming may require color categorization at the internal color space (see chapter 8), but it is achieved by different routes. With the color present, categorization proceeds directly from the pictorial register. To name the color of an object in the absence of sufficient colored visual information at the pictorial register there has to be access to stored hasa knowledge. In figures 7.2 and 8.2 the hasa information concerning color is stored separately from the entry level representations. Access to color-name phonologies from hasa storage occurs by two routes. First, hasa storage is connected to the internal color space by generating an image at the pictorial register. Second, there is a direct verbal association with the color lexicon.

Categorization at the internal color space means that many different shades of color are associated with the same color name. Color names can, like base level object names (see section 7.3), promote representations at the pictorial register. The effects of priming by a color name on identity matches at the pictorial register were considered in section 8.1.3. The effect of priming on a same-name (color category) task (are both stimuli red?) shows two major differences. First, priming affects all colors within a named category, that is, there is a facilitation throughout the category, not just for focal colors. Second, making a prime simultaneous with a stimulus does not completely remove facilitation for name comparisons as it does for identity matches (Rosch, 1975b, experiments 3 and 4). The effect of priming with a color name on the hasa representations is quite different. Color names do not directly access stored color hasa representations. Therefore, the command "Give as many objects as you can that are yellow" is one that subjects find difficult. Normal subjects may well take up to a minute to come up with four objects (DeVreese, 1988).

To some extent, the blind can give the colors associated with objects (Wyke and Holgate, 1973). Therefore, hasa properties of objects need not be stored in a pictorial form. Though Beauvois and Saillant (1985) argue that the extent of verbal color retrieval is limited, this must be doubted. Indeed, retrieval of an object color name (the hasa color name) is an exception to the general rule that it is quicker to retrieve object properties from pictures than from words (Te Linde and Paivio, 1979). Therefore, a direct link is posited from hasa representations to the output color lexicon for color names (see figure 8.2). The existence of two routes from hasa representations to the color lexicon does not necessarily imply dual storage (see section 7.1.2). Each route could be activated by different retrieval procedures upon an amodal storage system, just as a computer's stored information can be displayed in either a verbal or graphic output according to command. Instead of proposing that verbal storage is stronger or more plentiful for colors than for other object properties, the amodal explanation of the results from Te Linde and Paivio is that retrieval by the verbal route is easier.

Color naming requires that the categorized input (from the pictorial register or hasa representations) be associated with items in the color lexicon. The color lexicon is a separate part (Bills, 1931) of the larger lexicon that includes both object and category names. There is also the need to form a phonological representation to produce the word. It is these output stages rather than stored knowledge concerning objects that is generally defective in aphasia (see section 10.2.1); this might also be the case with developmental disorders of color naming. Poor color naming is associated with developmental dyslexia (Denckla, 1972), but so too is poor object naming (Katz, 1986). Both of these naming problems may have more to do with the inability to form a phonological representation than any impairment to stored object knowledge (Snowling, van Wagtendonk, and Stafford, 1988).

11.1.2 The Development of Color Naming

Putting the correct name to a color is difficult for young children. Many tasks of categorization cause children difficulty, but the surprise for color naming is that unlike, say, object naming, the perceptual basis is so early established and apparently simple. Color naming cannot be delayed because the visual system is not sufficiently well developed to perceive color. There is evidence that young infants have excellent color vision. Even week-old children show reliable discrimination between chromatic stimuli if the stimuli are large and the color separation considerable (Adams, 1989). The color-opponent channels are operating by three months of age (Brown and Teller, 1989), by which time children are able to discriminate and categorize spectral wavelengths into the four basic opponent-process categories. These groupings closely match those made by adults (Teller and Bornstein, 1985; Bornstein, Kessen, and Weiskopf, 1976). Color constancy is somewhat more delayed but is present well before the first coherent words are spoken (Maurer and Adams, 1987). Although very young infants cannot distinguish changes in the illuminant from changes in the surface color (Dannemiller, 1989b), color constancy can be demonstrated in children as young as four months old (Dannemiller and Hanko, 1987). There is even evidence (Heider, 1971; Mervis, Catlin, and Rosch, 1975) that children have a properly organized internal color space before they can name colors.

In the normal course of language development the vocabulary at age two is 500 words, but that includes no color words. The number of words for shapes remains greater than the number of color words up to the age of five (Modreski and Goss, 1969). Therefore, it appears to be more important to learn appropriate names to the entry level representations than to the internal color space. Indeed, even after having developed a color lexicon, children still have difficulty in producing the appropriate color-name response. Children behave like the blind in knowing which words are color names but being unable to link them to visual stimulation. At first, children use one of the four opponent-color names (red, green, yellow, blue) to stand for all colors. The remaining three names are then acquired before any others but in a variable order. However, Bartlett (1977) found that before children possessed all four color names, they did not use them accurately. The ontogeny of color naming therefore reflects, to a large degree, the underlying opponent-process neurophysiology, as Aubert, Mach, and Hering claimed in the nineteenth century (Miller and Johnson-Laird, 1976).

The poor performance of today's children with color names is nothing compared with that of previous generations. Bornstein (1985), in a historical review of research on the development of color naming from the nineteenth century to today, points to the remarkable difficulty that children used to have in acquiring color names. Darwin (1877) at first even mistakenly thought that his children were color blind because of the inability to learn color names despite his attempts to train them. Children, in Nagel's (1906) phrase, were said to show "farbendummheit": color stupidly. At this time, Binet put naming the four basic colors as a median achievement for an eight year old, though it was quickly changed to the performance expected of an average seven year old. The age for reliable basic color naming has gradually dropped throughout the century; it was five by 1950 (Bornstein, 1985), and now nobody would be surprised if four- or three-and-a-half-year-old children could do as well.

There has been speculation that the child has difficulty with color naming because color is an inherent part of an object (Lewandowsky, 1908b; Werner, 1940). Macnamara (1972) similarly argued that it is more important to be able to learn the names of objects than colors; therefore, shape cues are more salient to the young child. A color is identified as that associated with a particular object, so color naming takes second place to object naming. In support of the precedence of the object-based route, Menaud-Bateau and Cavanagh (1984) found that naming the color of a visually presented object was performed faster than naming the same color of a random shape (but note the contradictory finding of Ostergaard and Davidoff, 1985). The difficulty in explaining why color matching was influenced by hasa representations (Menaud-Bateau and Cavanagh, 1984) was discussed in section 9.2.3; the precedence for color naming is much easier to understand. It is a matter of preferential selection from the pictorial register of the object (entry level) over the color (internal color space) route. Nevertheless, it is not easy to account for all the preferences shown in development. One still has to explain why school-age children prefer to sort relatively meaningless objects by color rather than by shape (see section 8.1.2). The answer might lie in developmental fluctuations of attentional priority. In very young infants, there is a preference of attention to shapes over colors (Fantz, 1961); this could change developmentally. The modern preschool child is surrounded by a multitude of colored shapes, symbols, crayons, and other manufactured objects which would encourage color categorization. The dramatic decrease in the age at which colors can be named certainly implies that our society directs more attention to colors.

11.1.3 The Color Ontogeny of Languages
Languages, like children, have problems with color names. The development of color naming in the child shows a remarkable correspondence to a hierarchy of color names proposed for the world's languages (Berlin and Kay, 1969). Developing and extending an idea from Woodworth in 1910 (Miller and Johnson-Laird, 1976), Berlin and Kay proposed that there are eleven basic color names and that languages can be organized to the extent that they possess them. The organization that Berlin and Kay proposed is a cumulative addition in which the progression of names reflects an increased sophistication in color vocabulary. They studied color vocabularies in almost a hundred languages; naming tests were carried out in twenty lan-

guages, and evaluation of linguistic publications in seventy-eight others. The simplest lexicons consist of words for dark and light. If the color lexicon contains three words, one for red is added. The fourth word is an expression for green, yellow, or blue/green. Languages with five color terms have words for white, black, red, green (including blue), and yellow. Those with six have a term for blue; next comes brown and finally, in an irregular sequence, pink, purple, orange, and gray. Therefore, the *basic* color names, which, by definition, are not related to the colors of specific objects, are the four opponent-process colors (red, green, yellow, and blue), four other chromatic terms (brown, orange, pink, and purple), plus three achromatic terms (black, white, and gray).

The progression in the Berlin and Kay taxonomy of language names could be determined by the neurophysiology of the visual system (Ratliff, 1976; Kay and McDaniel, 1978). The predominance of light/dark terms in the world's languages would reflect the need to comment on the change in ambient light level. Their origin would be in the categorized output of a somewhat neurophysiologically distinct luminance pathway (chapter 2). The luminance "stream" also helps determine the brightness of surfaces, but that would seem less likely a reason for favoring light/dark terms over color terms. The neurophysiological action of the chromatic "stream" (i.e., the output of opponent process mechanisms) could also constrain color naming. Observations made at threshold show that discrimination between spectral sources is categorial. Thus, discrimination between stimuli is easy if they lie on either side of the category boundary (Mullen and Kulikowski, 1990). Furthermore, the position (wavelength) of each stimulus within its category is largely irrelevant to the discrimination. Categorization of suprathreshold stimuli may be different, but these differences in discrimination could be the reason why the color space becomes constructed around the focal red, green, yellow, and blue that Rosch (see section 8.1.2) found to have significance irrespective of whether the language contained words for them. According to Zollinger (1988), these four color names are different in kind from the later acquired names. He found that name frequency usage for these opponent-process colors, unlike "brown" (see p. 153), was not affected by moving to a different culture. Quinn, Rosano, and Wooten (1988) now discount their earlier idea that brown is a color irreducible to any other (Fuld, Werner, and Wooten, 1983). Brown is a color name that is given to surface colors that are called yellow when placed against other backgrounds.

The order of acquisition of the less-frequent basic color names is less clear. The explanation offered by Sun (1983), for what he calls the third wave of the Berlin and Kay taxonomy, capitalized on Rosch's theory of focal colors. The first two waves contain the terms for light/ dark and the primary colors. Sun proposed that the third wave (other focal colors: grey, brown, orange etc.) are constructed to be as perceptually close as possible to the established foci. He further suggests that the addition of color names to a language after the four primary color names will be in accord with their closeness to the center of the color space that contains the four focal colors. Sun considers the Munsell color space (see figure 8.1). Gray is in the middle of the Munsell color solid. Therefore, Sun argues that gray will be the next color to appear in the Berlin and Kay taxonomy after the first two waves have been established. After gray should come brown, followed by orange and pink. Purple should appear last in language color-name lexicons. Unfortunately for the Sun hypothesis, the evidence from the Berlin and Kay study gives only partial support. Purple, in particular, does not fit, because it is not a less-common color name than orange or pink. The argument by Sun is false because it is the *internal* color space that has to be established, which need not have a one-to-one correspondence with the Munsell color space.

Some anthropologists believe that modification to the plan of Berlin and Kay may be necessary (Sun, 1983); others, (see Saunders and van Brakel, 1988) that the edifice needs considerable revision. Their argument against basic color terms relies, in part, on inconsistencies that have been ignored in the Berlin and Kay review. Russian, for example, has two basic terms for what in English is called blue, and Hungarian has two basic terms for red. There is also a language (Shuswap from the northwest Pacific Coast) that has a word that crosses the yellow-green category (MacLaury, 1987). Perhaps, more importantly, it is not clear that when a color name is used in a language it covers the total color range to the same extent as in European languages. The words can be much more tied to specific objects and so are not really basic color terms. The reliance on object names as a label for color names is found in most languages when differentiation within the basic color categories is required (e.g., lemon or mustard in English) but is more extreme in languages with a paucity of color names. One such language is that of the Uzbeks of the southern USSR. One of the Uzbeks said to Luria (1976): "For us Uzbeks, a sewing machine is called a 'machine,' and a tractor also a 'machine.' It's the same with colors. Men don't know colors and call them all 'blue.'" Uneducated Uzbeks give colors the name of objects (for example, "pig dung" or "decayed teeth"). For that reason, they found it very difficult to sort colors into categories. They would say: "It can't be done"; "this is like calf's dung, and this is like a peach; you can't put them together." However, the rapid penetration of Western-style color words into more "primitive" languages certainly suggests that the basis for an accurate verbal code for color is present in every language. It requires only the need to associate focal colors with unique lexical entries.

Certain aspects of the Berlin and Kay structure for languages clearly differ from the developmental ontogeny for color naming. In many cultures, perhaps because of its association with fire and blood, red seems to have acquired a special significance. It is, with blue, the color most often produced in response to the command "Name a color" (Battig and Montague, 1969). Red seems to be more important linguistically than other colors. One can, in English, whiten, blacken, or redden, but -en is not added to other colors. The term for blue is rather rarer in the world's languages than might have been predicted from English or neurophysiology. Although the sky and sea are spoken of as blue, they are rarely good examples of what we would call blue elsewhere. In fact, blue is rare in nature, which might account for its relative scarcity as a color term. The proposal that at least part of color-name acquisition is based on cultural needs gains support from languages that favor names, such as turquoise, that are rare in other similar languages. Thus, the number of color names within a section of color space reflects not only our ability to discriminate between colors but also our experience (see Boynton, 1988). A more direct demonstration of the effect of experience in altering color naming is given by Zollinger (1988). He showed that the relatively rare term for brown in the speech of rural Japanese increased in frequency as people migrated from a small town to Tokyo and increased even further, to correspond to Western use, when they lived in Germany.

11.1.4 Effects of Color Names on Color Perception and Memory
The proposal, revived by Whorf (1956), that the possession of color names affects our perception of color (see also section 9.2.2) is part of a more general hypothesis called *linguistic relativism*. In its extreme form, linguistic relativism holds that the structure of a language fully determines the world view of those who speak it. World view is taken to include both perception and thought. However, the supporters of linguistic relativism do not propose that this leads to considerable variability in world view, because languages have similar underlying structures. In Sapir's (1921) words "When it comes to linguistic form, Plato walks with the Macedonian swineherd"; therefore, one should expect considerable similarity in their perception and thought. In fact, experimental tests of the dependence of world view on language are never contemplated (Kay and Kempton, 1984). More modest investi-

gations are undertaken, and variations in color judgments have been the most common sort of evidence put forward to substantiate them.

In the extreme form of the Whorf hypothesis, which has its historical roots in the writings of Boas and Sapir (Kay and Kempton, 1984), it is held that the semantic systems of languages are not constrained by any biological determination. Thus, it is held that nonlinguistic cognitive judgments such as those for color will vary according to an individual's language structure. However, the experimental evidence given as support for the claim needs to be considered carefully. It is necessary to ask at which functional stage in the model of color matching and naming an individual's language is supposed to act. With respect to color discrimination at the pictorial register, little credence should be attached to the Whorf hypothesis. Brown and Lenneberg (1954) found that Zuni Indians with a paucity of color names for the yellow-orange region of the spectrum had the same difficulty in making discriminations within that color range as English speakers. There are, therefore, some constraints on color judgments that are biological rather than linguistic. The biological constraints cannot be of the dramatic sort proposed by Rivers (1901), who suggested that "the Murray Islander differs from the Englishman: he is more pigmented, and his insensitiveness to blue may be . . . a function of . . . his pigmentation." For Rivers, the absence of the color name *blue* reflected the insensitivity to that part of the spectrum because of the yellow macular (foveal) pigmentation in dark-skinned people. However, there is no more than a partial correlation between skin color and possession of a word for blue. The biological constraints that determine color naming (see section 11.1.3) are those from basic visual neurophysiology, which emphasize similarities rather than differences between people.

The strongest form of the Whorf-Sapir hypothesis, which suggests that linguistic constraints are the *only* determinants of perception, is not upheld. A weaker version might admit that biological constraints determine color discrimination but still maintain that linguistic constraints affect the classification of colors. Thus, categorization of surface qualities at the pictorial register could depend upon the available lexical entries. Kay and Kempton (1984) investigated this possibility. They compared speakers of the Tarahumara language of northern Mexico with English speakers on tasks that investigated their internal color space. The Tarahumara language does not have words to differentiate blue from green. Therefore, it was argued that decisions about colors that spanned the lexical category boundary in English would be dealt with differently by the two subject groups.

Kay and Kempton used a multidimensional scaling procedure to obtain the subjective distance between samples. In their experiment, three Munsell items (called a triad) were presented to the subjects for them to determine which sample was most different from the other two. All possible triads from the total number were presented, which, for the eight samples of the study, gave fifty-six triads. They then computed the psychological distances between the Munsell samples and compared those with the known discrimination difficulty. Kay and Kempton found that English speakers exaggerated differences between samples that were on either side of the lexical boundary dividing green from blue. However, it is interesting to note that the subjects denied that they consciously employed the name strategy. They maintained that they judged colors simply to the extent they "looked different." Tarahumara speakers showed categorization much more consistent with the discrimination difficulty, though for them, too, there was a hint that they mentally pushed apart items that spanned the English lexical boundary. A second experiment showed that it was having to use the lexical boundary that produced the altered color space for the English speakers. Exactly the same stimuli were used, but the task was different. In the second experiment the subjects had to say to what extent an item on the lexical boundary was greener (or bluer) than an item distant from the boundary. For these instructions both groups of subjects ordered samples in proportion to their discriminability differences.

Tasks that require organization of stimuli according to the available color terms are bound to disadvantage languages with limited lexical entries. With only a name strategy available, the memory for colors will be in line with the Whorf-Sapir hypothesis and related to the ease with which they can be verbally communicated (Brown and Lenneberg, 1954; Lantz and Stefflre, 1964). For example, samples within the orange-yellow range will be harder to remember beyond the time span of pictorial memory if the language has a limited color-name vocabulary for that range (Brown and Lenneberg, 1954). Such demonstrations of the Whorf-Sapir hypothesis are somewhat obvious. It would be more interesting if it could be shown that people with languages that emphasize different aspects of color (see section 11.1.3) perform better on appropriately "ecological valid" tasks. Kuschel and Monberg (1974), for example, found that people from the Polynesian island of Bellona make finer differentiations than might be expected from their classification by Berlin and Kay. Their language has proper color words only for light, dark, and red, and the Bellona appear uninterested in color. Clothes, for example, are preferred for their patterns rather than their color, which is considered of little importance. When discussing fish names given in English as yellow-and-blue sea perch or purple-spotted bullseye, the Bellona claimed that it did not make any difference to them whether the pictures shown to them were colored or not. "Identification seemed equally certain when using colored or black and white pictures." However, they very commonly use specific words, as we occasionally do in English (e.g., brunette), for showing the color state of a particular object. These words often denote the change in surface appearance (including color) that foretell a change in the usefulness of the object. Though these words do not have the general abstract quality of "red" or "green," they do sometimes apply to several disparate objects. Thus, a better test of whether the Bellona peoples' world view is dictated by language would be an appropriately ecologically valid task where items would have to be grouped or remembered to the extent that they were, for example, "becoming brown."

11.2 Disorders of Color Naming

11.2.1 Color Anomia
Color anomia is here defined to be a naming impairment specific to part of the modular route from the pictorial register to the lexicon of color names via the internal color space. Color anomia does not refer to those sections of figure 8.2 that concern hasa representations. An inability to name the color of an object is a separate disorder, even though there is overlap with the pathways impaired in color anomia. One of the two routes for object-color naming (see section 11.1.1) has considerable overlap, and both routes converge on the same color lexicon. The existence of the modular route for color naming via the internal color space is supported by evidence from two patients with object-recognition disorders who managed to name colors (Adler, 1944; Levine, 1978); Levine's patient could even match an object to its correct color. It must be assumed that any impairments, at or to the pictorial register, responsible for poor shape recognition need not be so severe that color naming cannot proceed via the internal color space. To summarize: a pure case of color anomia would have no disturbance to the stores of knowledge concerning the colors of objects, nor color agnosia (see section 8.1.4) or other naming problems. Thus, in the model given in figure 8.2 it would be represented as a disconnection after color categorization and before or at the color lexicon.

Historical reports of patients with particular difficulties in producing color names are rare (see DeRenzi and Spinnler, 1967), although Wilbrand reported a case as long ago as 1887 that is referred to by Lewandowsky (1908a,b; Davidoff and Fodor, 1989). In more recent times, Goodglass et al. (1966) isolated color anomia as one of the more common forms of the rare category-specific naming disturbances. However, because it is relatively uncommon to test for color agnosia, there are few detailed reported cases fulfilling all the necessary conditions for color anomia. Of these few cases, the purest example of a color-naming deficit (see table 5) was probably that reported by Geschwind and Fusillo (1966), though DeRenzi and Spinnler (1967) briefly mention what would appear to be a similar case reported by Adler in 1890. Fukuzawa et al. (1988, case 1) discuss a similar case (see table 9.1) except for a mild object-naming impairment perhaps derived from a mild object-recognition disorder, and Gil et al., (1985) discuss another with more pronounced naming impairments, namely, optic aphasia (see table 9.2). The explanations offered for color anomia mostly stress either difficulties of access, or damage, to a color lexicon. Reviving the hypotheses proposed by Freund (1889) for optic aphasia (see section 10.2.2) and by Dejerine (1892) for alexia without agraphia, Geschwind saw color anomia as a disconnection (access disorder). Destruction of the left calcarine area (see figure 3.1b), when coupled with a lesion to the splenium, disconnected the intact right calcarine area from the intact left hemisphere angular gyrus (see figure 3.1a), where visual and verbal information are combined. Thus, preserved color information in the right hemisphere cannot be transmitted to the intact language areas of the left hemisphere. Geschwind and Fusillo (1966) argue that the disconnection does not affect the naming of visually presented objects, because they evoke tactile associations that pass to the speech center via intact anterior callosal connections. Colors do not have somesthetic associations; they therefore cannot use these intact pathways.

In the disconnection syndrome proposed by Dejerine it was the spared angular gyrus that allowed the arousal of optic images necessary for writing and color naming. However, subsequent reports (Gloning, Gloning, and Hoff, 1968; Cumming, Hurwitz, and Perl, 1970; Mohr et al., 1971; Greenblatt, 1973; Michel et al., 1979; Damasio and Damasio, 1983) indicate that the two disorders have no necessary connection. Figure 11.1a from Damasio and Damasio shows the lesion site for the combined disorders of alexia and color anomia with a right homonymous hemianopia (complete right visual field loss in both eyes); figure 11.1 shows the lesion site without color anomia. Thus, by subtraction one can deduce a critical cortical site for color anomia to be in the region of the left lingual gyrus and hippocampus. Color anomia cannot be explained (Cumming et al., 1970) simply from the destruction of the splenial fibers carrying color information. The case of color anomia reported by Mohr et al. (1971) clearly did not have a splenial lesion and, moreover, could read. It is also unlikely that the

(a)

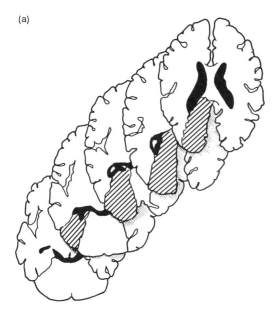

(b)

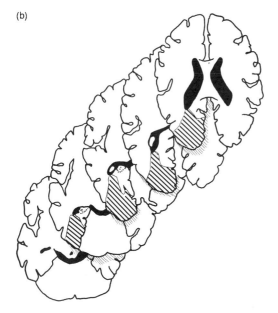

Figure 11.1
Diagram of slices of the brain that reveal the lesion sites for (a) color anomia combined
with alexia and a right visual field loss and (b) for alexia and right visual field loss
without color anomia. (Taken from Damasio and Damasio, 1980.)

late development of fibers connecting the two hemispheres causes the late development of color naming in children (see section 11.1.1)—an explanation proffered by Bornstein (1985). There would be no reason why color names could not become associated with input received directly by the left hemisphere.

The disconnection hypothesis is not satisfactory for all cases of color anomia. Moreover, it has difficulty explaining cases of color anomia that can point to a color if it is named to them (DeRenzi and Spinnler, 1967; Mohr et al., 1971; Denckla, 1972; Netley, 1974; Sasanuma, 1974; Basso, Faglioni, and Spinnler, 1976; Damasio et al., 1979; Davidoff and Ostergaard, 1984). In these cases the disconnection would have to be only partial or one way. Patients with weakened rather than total disconnection would be assisted—as are other types of naming disorders—by reducing the number of response alternatives. The explanation of a partial disconnection is not totally convincing, because in the usual testing of color names, there is only a limited list of alternatives; the patients might be expected to generate them without help. Another explanation of preserved pointing to colors in color anomia suggests that giving the color name ameliorates a much-reduced ability to maintain color at the pictorial register (Davidoff and Ostergaard, 1984). For yet other cases of color anomia (Kinsbourne and Warrington, 1964; Oxbury, Oxbury, and Humphrey, 1969, case 2), there may be no need whatsoever to propose a disconnection (access disorder). The problem in these cases could be a disturbance at the lexicon for color names. These patients found it difficult to learn paired associates with color names, suggesting a damaged store. However, a disconnection cannot be ruled out for the patient of Kinsbourne and Warrington (1964), according to DeVreese (1988), because responses were usually inappropriate color names. Damage to the lexicon would more likely, in his opinion, make the patient propose no color name to a color patch or a color name paraphasia such as reddish. In fact, it is difficult to distinguish between access disorders and other alternatives (see Shallice, 1988a), especially when there may be only partial damage to the color lexicon.

11.2.2 Impaired Retrieval of Object-Color Names

11.2.2.1 Routes for Retrieval There are two routes from hasa color knowledge to the color lexicon. Both of these, when damaged, would cause an inability to retrieve object-color names. However, damage to only one route might be difficult to spot. For example, the impaired ability to retrieve the color name of an imaged object may be unnoticed if the direct connection between hasa knowledge and the output lexicon (verbal route) is intact. Conversely, difficulties in using the verbal route could be hidden by generating an image and naming its color (visual route). Patients could successfully answer the question "What color is a strawberry?" with "red" by creating an image at the pictorial register and then extracting the color for naming.

One might look for evidence of a dissociation between the two routes in patients with impaired color input to the pictorial register (Hecaen et al., 1952; Meadows, 1974; Beyn and Knyazeva, 1962; Lhermitte and Pillon, 1975; Pearlman, Birch, and Meadows, 1979; Mollon et al., 1980; Heywood et al., 1987; Riddoch and Humphreys, 1987a), since they often have poor imagery. These patients can answer questions concerning object color, so they are probably using the verbal route. Indeed, impaired object-color imagery has been found accompanied by intact object-color recall in many studies (Ettlinger and Wyke, 1961; Oxbury et al., 1969, case 1; Lhermitte and Beauvois, 1973; Lhermitte et al., 1973; Damasio et al., 1979; Ferro and Santos, 1984; Beauvois and Saillant, 1985, case RV; Larrabee et al., 1985, case 1. However, there appear to be no reports of the reverse dissociation. The closest are the reports that object-color recognition, which may use the same pathways as imagery, remains possible despite the inability to retrieve the object's color from a spoken question (Stengel, 1948, case 1; Kinsbourne and Warrington, 1964; Farah et al., 1988).

The visual route has considerable overlap with that for naming colors, since it also requires color categorization (see figure 8.2). Therefore, neuropsychological research into impairments of the visual route for object-color name retrieval is very much concerned with making dissociations from color anomia. The separation of the hasa representations from the pure color-naming route is shown by both group (DeRenzi and Spinnler, 1967; Basso et al., 1976) and case studies (Stengel, 1948, case 1; Kinsbourne and Warrington, 1964; Geschwind and Fusillo, 1966; Damasio et al., 1979; Beauvois and Saillant, 1985, case MP; Gil et al., 1985; Larrabee et al., 1985, case 2; Farah et al., 1988; Fukuzawa et al. 1988, case 1; Coslett and Saffran, 1989), often of optic aphasia (see section 10.2.2). Nevertheless, the two impairments of impaired object-color imagery and color anomia often co-occur (Ettlinger and Wyke, 1961; Oxbury et al., 1969, case 1; Taylor and Warrington, 1971; Lhermitte et al., 1973; Lhermitte and Beauvois, 1973; Netley, 1974; Wapner, Judd, and Gardner, 1978; Pillon et al., 1981; Varney and Digre, 1983; Ferro and Santos, 1984; Beauvois and Saillant, 1985, case RV; Larrabee et al., 1985, case 1; Fukuzawa et al., 1988, case 2). Indeed, if both object-color recognition and object-color imagery were impaired, an associated color anomia has always been reported, though that might reflect nothing more than the extent of the brain damage.

The preceding studies show that there is a fairly common connection between the inability to retrieve object color from hasa storage via the visual route, and color anomia. However, the association may be spurious, because there is another explanation for their co-occurrence. There is evidence that the overt production of erroneous color names has a destabilizing effect on color-object integration [Poetzl (in Lange, 1936); Kinsbourne and Warrington, 1964; Geschwind and Fusillo, 1966; Damasio et al., 1979; Beauvois and Saillant, 1985]. Even if color naming was not necessary for the task, Kinsbourne and Warrington (1964) suggested that it could be used "out of habit." In support of their hypothesis, they found that object color was recognized only for those objects for which there was correct object-color recall; faulty recognition accompanied only faulty naming.

Two examples further illustrate the problem of color-name interference. The color-anomic patient of Davidoff and Ostergaard (1984) was asked to color a line drawing of a sailor in uniform. He started to color the sailor's uniform incorrectly, then changed to the correct color, but after naming the blue color red, returned to the earlier incorrect color. A more dramatic example is given in Boucher et al. (1976). The preserved ability to imagine and give the name of object colors either with the eyes shut or from a line drawing did not prevent their patient from making incorrect object-color name responses from a colored object or drawing. It is remarkable that the incorrect color label can misdirect proven correct retrieval.

In more-controlled experiments, Beauvois and Saillant (1985) directly showed that poor performance on object-color retrieval was reflecting a misapplied verbal retrieval strategy. Their patient MP made many errors in recalling object colors until manipulation of strategy, which included placing plaster over the mouth, promoted better performance (compare the task bias found for pictorial analysis in Guenther and Klatzky, 1977). The patient MP was then found to have intact hasa color knowledge whether retrieved from the visual or verbal route. Strategy manipulation had not been attempted previously, so there may be other patients in whom the hasa color representations are more intact than reported. Indeed, the implication is that color and form are not so "split-off" from each other as Lewandowsky proposed. However, in one important case study (Farah et al., 1988) object-color imagery was impaired without a color-naming problem.

The relationship between the verbal route and color naming has been considered in several studies (see tables 9.1, 9.2, and 9.3). Some patients fail at both tasks (Stengel, 1948; Kinsbourne and Warrington, 1964; Oxbury et al., 1969, case 2; Netley, 1974; Varney and Digre, 1983;

McCarthy and Warrington, 1986; Riddoch and Humphreys, 1987b; Fukuzawa et al., 1988, case 2) and, consequently, tell us little about any functional pathways. However, other studies are more informative. In many reports, an inability to name colors is accompanied by preserved ability to recall an object's color from a spoken question (Holmes, 1950; Ettlinger and Wyke, 1961; Geschwind and Fusillo, 1966; Oxbury, et al., 1969, case 1; Mohr et al., 1971; Rubens and Benson, 1971; Lhermitte and Beauvois, 1973; Lhermitte et al., 1973; Stachowiak and Poeck, 1975; Mack and Boller, 1977; Damasio et al., 1979; Ferro and Santos, 1984; Beauvois and Saillant, 1985; Gil et al., 1985; Larrabee et al., 1985; Pena-Casanova et al., 1985; Fukuzawa et al., 1988, case 1). These case studies provide further evidence that there is a route from hasa representations directly to the color lexicon. Extra, perhaps redundant, support that the verbal route is used comes from the inability of some of these patients to create a colored image at the pictorial register (Geschwind and Fusillo, 1966; Beauvois and Saillant, 1985, case MP; Gil et al., 1985; Larrabee et al., 1985, case 2; Fukuzawa et al., 1988, case 1. The reverse dissociation was found by Farah et al. (1988); their case could name colors but could not answer aural questions concerning names of object colors.

According to some authors (Pillon, Signoret, and Lhermitte, 1981; Beauvois and Saillant, 1985), the role of the direct link from color hasa associations to the color lexicon is limited. They propose that the verbal route is limited to strong associations (e.g., the color of blood) or to metaphors (e.g., green with envy). In the present model the latter would arrive at the color lexicon by interrogating a part of knowledge that this book does not address. However, verbal retrieval of object color names may not be so limited (see section 11.1.1), which might explain why it has been so difficult (see section 11.2.2) to find patients who can retrieve hasa color names from achromatic pictures of objects but not from verbal recall.

11.2.2.2 Achromatic Names Lewandowsky distinguished between brightness (luminous color) and surface color (see section 9.3.2.1), not between achromatic and chromatic surfaces. When trying to retrieve the names of surface detail, it would be possible to maintain a distinction for achromatic colors only if they were stored separately from other object colors. In everyday experience very few objects are completely achromatic, so the selective preservation of achromatic object-color names would be improbable. However, the preservation of the *names* for white and black has been reported several times in color anomia (Macrae and Trolle, 1956; Kriendler and Ionasescu, 1961; Kinsbourne and Warrington, 1964) with the addition of red (Macrae and

Trolle, 1956) and gray (Kinsbourne and Warrington, 1964). Moreover, contrary to the results of Lewandowsky (1908a, see section 1.1) and Lhermitte et al. (1973), the difficulty in recalling object colors from a spoken question has been found not to apply to achromatic responses (Kinsbourne and Warrington, 1964; Lhermitte et al., 1969). The latter result is possible only if some of the entries in the color lexicon are preserved or there is separate stored knowledge for achromatic hasa colors, perhaps in the form of hasa brightness. Indeed, DeVreese (1988) seems to imply that color names are inevitably accessed from knowledge of object brightness; however, that is not so. Only words such as *light* and *dark* would have mandatory access. Nevertheless, color knowledge for white and black objects may be difficult to establish separately from the knowledge that they are dark or light.

The differential retention of chromatic and achromatic color names may even depend on the language spoken. In German and English, black and white can be considered achromatic and contrasted to color; this is not so in Japanese, where black and white are considered color names. In Japanese, color photography is called natural photography; black-and-white photography is known as two-color photography. Japanese thus makes a clearer distinction than English between the surface properties that are categorized as colors. In English there is often confusion about the use of the word *black*. When we speak of coal being black we are referring to the surface reflectance, but when we say it was a black night, we mean that it was (very) dark.

11.3 Color Naming and Word Naming: Interference

In 1886 Cattell wrote: "Experiments I have made show that we can recognize a single color or picture in a slightly shorter time than a word or letter, but take longer to name it." Cattell was perhaps the first to make the insightful observation that we read print with a rapidity that is close to automaticity. Thus, the pathway for naming written color words must differ from those given in figure 8.2 for color and object-color naming. Unlike the other routes, the one connecting written words to their associated lexical entries appears to be "direct" (Potter and Faulconer, 1975). There are implications from the observation of Cattell (Cattell, 1886; Fraisse, 1969) for the situation where information in different routes is converging simultaneously on the common lexicon of color names. Considerable interference might be expected when the different routes demand output from different lexical entries.

Stroop (1935) found that the time it took to read a list of 100 color names printed in black was 41 seconds. Varying the print color pro-

duced no interference; there was only a nonsignificant 2-second increase in reading time. The color-naming route obviously had little
effect on progress of information through the "direct" reading route.
However, the opposite interference was very strong and is generally
referred to as the Stroop effect. Stroop found that naming the color of
a 100 patches took 63 seconds, but naming the ink color of 100 words
that read a different color name (see Plate 4) took 110 seconds. There
are three main contenders for the functional site of Stroop . The first
suggests that response interference occurs from preference shown at
the pictorial register (pictorial encoding hypothesis), the second delays
the interference until the output stage, and the third implicates the
routes from stored object knowledge.

The perceptual encoding hypothesis (Hock and Egeth, 1970) proposes that preferential attention is given to shape rather than color or
vice versa. If word information can be ignored, color comparisons
made directly at the pictorial register (see section 9.2.3) are immune
to word interference (Pritchatt, 1968; Egeth, Blecker, and Kamlet, 1969;
Harrison and Boese, 1976). Thus, the perceptual encoding hypothesis
successfully predicts that it makes no difference to a color discrimination between surface reds if they form the print color of potentially
distracting words such as chocolate (Harrison and Boese, 1976). However, if the word is read, there must be a selection for words and hence
the production of the Stroop effect. The perceptual encoding hypothesis predicts that the Stroop effect ought to be enhanced for particularly interesting words (Watts et al., 1986) and reduced if the normal
preference for reading can be overcome. MacKinnon, Geiselman, and
Woodward (1985) found that subjects could reduce the Stroop effect
but only with effort. The reduction in Stroop interference was accompanied by a poorer recall for the words in the list associated with
color—a result consonant with less attention having been paid to the
meaning of the words. If attention can be made even more selective
to color, then Stroop interference ought to be reduced further or even
removed (Dyer, 1973; Kahneman and Henik, 1981). A strong version
of the explanation based on selective attention even predicts that there
are circumstances where the color of the print affects reading the color
name (Treisman and Fearnley, 1969; Dyer, 1973; Morton and Chambers, 1973), but as Stroop (1935) found, it is not generally so. The
reverse Stroop, as it is called, will arise only if color selection takes
priority (see section 8.1.1) and a response in terms of the name of the
color is required. The fact that these conditions are hard to achieve
suggests that the priority for the direct reading route is very strong.

Stroop effects are commonly expressed as a race between competing
streams of information for limited response procedures (Keele, 1972;

Dyer, 1973; Morton and Chambers, 1973). The output race model is a useful analogy that, for example, neatly describes the increase in Stroop effects in the elderly (Cohn, Dussman, and Bradford, 1984). Color-naming latencies increase with age relative to reading times, so the word activated by the direct reading route is more likely to win the battle for response resources. The lack of resource allocation to color naming was shown by increasing the number of Stroop words; this affected color-naming latencies but not reading latencies (Williams, 1977). However, the lack of effect of set size on reading times (Williams, 1977) suggests to Glaser and Duengelhoff (1984) that race models are inappropriate. They argue that Stroop effects result from certain components of a task using automatic or inhibition immune systems; these are different for words than pictures. Word categorization is delayed by the presence of distracting pictures, whereas picture categorization (see also section 7.1.2) is immune to the presence of categorially related words (Smith and Magee, 1980). Thus, Stroop interference depends on whether the primary task is automatic. In the object-color naming task of Menaud-Bateau and Cavanagh (1984) object categorization is automatic (see sections 9.2.3 and 11.1.2), whereas in the normal Stroop task, reading is the automatic component. Training in one of the tasks does not affect performance on the other (Menaud-Bateau and Cavanagh, 1984). When experimental conditions alter the strength of the Stroop effect, this may be interpreted as altering the automatic nature of the task (Dunbar and MacLeod, 1984). For example, the reduction and reversal of the Stroop effect when words are made difficult to read (Gumenik and Glass, 1970) would be due to the impossibility of automatic reading. Alternatively put, the reduction in Stroop interference can be seen as the result of temporally contingent attentional processes affecting automatic procedures (Logan, 1980).

The second alternative for the site of Stroop interference places it solely at response output. The supporting evidence is not strong. It consists of the observation that simultaneous speech production, which is presumed to suppress inner speech, reduced Stroop interference in a silent reading task (Martin, 1978). Response competition at speech production is unlikely to be the major cause of Stroop interference. As Seymour (1979) points out, the word *blood* printed in red ink does not interfere with saying red; it might even cause facilitation. On a response competition model any word should interfere, but it does not. Interference only comes from a word that generates wrong color associations; it is not enough to potentially generate articulatory conflict. Thus, the speech competition model can be rejected. However, this does not leave attentional selection as the sole explanation of the Stroop effect. There is a third site that has been proposed for Stroop interference—that of stored knowledge.

Klein (1964) showed that Stroop effects arise not only form the names of colors but also from words associated with colors such as *grass* or *sky*. There was a "semantic" gradient of interference which corresponded to the degree to which the word was associated with the color name. One must assume that the written word activates the associated hasa knowledge to produce the output response "green." If the word *grass* is written in red ink, then the color name output "red" will be in conflict with that produced from object knowledge. Seymour (1979) argued that a considerable amount of interference can arise from associated knowledge rather than at name output. To show the effect of what he called overlapping conceptual nodes on color-name production, Seymour made use of the fact that seasons are associated in pairs (spring versus autumn, summer versus winter) and that a certain color is associated with each season (see section 8.2.2). Seymour (1977) asked people to name the color opposite to that associated with the written season word (e.g., brown to spring). He found that coloring the word *spring* in green facilitated the correct response. If the facilitation had been at the name output one might have predicted that coloring the word in brown would have been more helpful. However, it is important not to overstate the role of the route from hasa knowledge to name output in Stroop interference. The activation of hasa information might be important for Stroop interference from object words, but it is unlikely to be the major contributor for color words (see Naish, 1985).

The functional locus of Stroop interference is not known with certainty. The perceptual encoding hypothesis suggests an earlier site than does that of overlapping conceptual nodes. Neurophysiological research confirms the uncertainty. Results of evoked potentials research show Stroop effects to occur late in perceptual processing (Duncan-Johnson and Koppel, 1981) and to involve the frontal cortex (Posner and Rothbart, 1989), but enhanced early responses are found if attention is drawn to the colored or shape aspects of stimuli (Johnston and Venables, 1982). Neuropsychological research has been even less revealing. Stroop interference appears to be greater when words are presented to the left hemisphere (Dyer, 1973). Presumably, earlier arrival at the left hemisphere gives greater priority to that part of Stroop stimuli responsible for retarding the color name output. Unfortunately, for any clarification of Stroop interference, the left hemisphere is involved in all aspects of language, including color naming (Dimond and Beaumont, 1972) and stored knowledge of object color (see section 9.3.2.3). However, it has been argued that more might be learned from the processing of logographic scripts such as Chinese. Stroop interference is even greater in Chinese (Biederman and Tsao, 1979; Tsao, Wu, and Feustel, 1981) and in some forms of Japanese (Hatta, 1981), where color naming is more retarded when the words are presented to the right hemisphere. These findings suggest that there is a conflict of priorities between two right hemisphere systems, but it is not certain what they might be. It is possible that concrete nouns or aspects of logographic script (see Bryden and Allard, 1976), by being visually complex, are preferentially analyzed by the right hemisphere. There might also be a right hemisphere specialization for color vision, but that is, at most, only a relative effect for fine color discriminations (see section 3.1.4). These two processing systems could just possibly compete for selection of information at the pictorial register and cause greater conflict at perceptual encoding.

Chapter 12
Overview

An isolated color—what has been termed an input module for color—has played an important theoretical role in many contemporary accounts of information processing. In neurophysiology there are proposals for the independent analysis of color at the cell level and as a "stream" of information. In experimental psychology, whether as a feature map or as a domain, color has likewise been proposed as an independent building block for perception. These proposals were examined in depth. The result of that examination showed that neither of these research areas provided solid evidence for a color module; certainly, not as good as that from neuropsychology. For example, in acquired achromatopsia, color vision may be lost without much concomitant effect on other attributes of perception. However, even in neuropsychology, there is little evidence for preserved color discrimination with *completely* impaired form discrimination. Thus, brain damage produces effects compatible with what is perceptually possible. It is perfectly easy to imagine a crisp, clear world drained of color as in a black-and-white movie but difficult to conceive of the loss of a shape module (preserved color without any shape).

Although color and form may always be linked to some extent, there is no doubt that certain neurons and certain brain areas are more concerned with chromatic information than they are with other stimulus attributes. Therefore, an approach to the limited interactions between chromatic information and other attributes is to ignore them in the interests of parsimony. There is an advantage to that approach. It can be argued that the version of color and other input modules attacked in the opening chapters is one that nobody would seriously propose; it is a straw man. Furthermore, it can be argued that the weakness of the modular argument with respect to integration is no worse than the similar problem for the nonmodular approach. Once it has been admitted that parts of the brain concerned with visual input are not capable of dealing with all aspects of the input, then there is also a problem of integration for the nonmodular account. It is only resolved if all parts of the input system are in contact with each other. In chapter 6, as a resolution to the problem, surface detail was contrasted with boundary information. At a preattentive level, perhaps by using the largest spatial scale available, the detection of color can be largely independent of other attributes; however, it is never completely independent of the spatial scaling imposed on it from the boundary information.

Color can now be given a definition even if not yet explicit. It is derived from the phenomenal experience of surface information at the pictorial register. Color maintains a firm link to wavelength (chromatic) input since surface information is largely produced from the blob neurons. However, it is by no means only chromatic differences to which we apply the word *color*. Surface properties that involve texture differences (silver) and achromatic surfaces (grays) are equally color. Nevertheless, the chromatic differences are the most important. What we call color, as opposed to our phenomenal experience of surface qualities, is a construction at the internal color space. It is not, as some neurophysiologists believe, the reorganization of the input in a visual area specifically receptive to its chromatic aspects.

It may seem paradoxical that surfaces can be categorized as colors (red, blue etc.) when their input is inextricably linked with their shape. But, it is no more paradoxical than, say, for orientation. Boundaries can be categorized as vertical, horizontal etc. but it must be a boundary of a particular shape that is at a particular orientation. Storage of colors (and shapes) can, therefore, be functionally modular. However, the re-creation of a color by imagery is never as a "pure" color but is always, in some way, restricted by a boundary. For the imagery of object colors, it is clear what boundary contains the color; for the imagination of a "color", it is less so. Nevertheless, the evocation of color, without specifying an object, must at least be defined by the boundaries of the visual field.

Due to our neurophysiology, there will be regularities in surface qualities related to the chromatic aspects. These will be noted and are causal in the initial construction of the functional module of color. Red, green, yellow, and blue areas are the first to become consolidated in the internal color space, no doubt as a result of surface consistencies that result from opponent processes. Thus, these focal or landmark colors of the color space have been called universal. However, the categorization of colors into an internal color space is also connected with intellectual and linguistic development. So, some developmental and cross-cultural variabilty in color naming is inevitable. There will even be individual differences in the use of the term color since it is the overall name given to information constructed at the internal color space. Whatever the color space arrived at, it allows the association of modular colors to other stored knowledge. Thus, there will also be considerable cross-cultural variability in the meaning of color. Notwithstanding the real possibility that "red" and other wavelengths of electromagnetic radiation can have an innately different arousal, all color meanings are overlaid by their associations cultures determine for them. It was, therefore, argued in chapter 8 that the emotional tone of a color is predominantly arbitrary unless associated to an object.

Color is a property derived from surfaces, but conscious percepts are not predominantly of "boundaried surfaces"; it is of objects constructed at a pictorial register. Therefore, there must be an interaction between stored object knowledge and the pictorial register. Object knowledge is initially accessed by the boundary information at what, in the model introduced in chapter 7, is called the *entry level*. It is possible that the entry level representation does not contain surface detail. One of the arguments given for edge- (boundary-) based entry level representations was that surface attributes present in a display are largely irrelevant for certain tasks; another was the saving in neural storage. Contact with the entry level makes available three distinct types of knowledge. Only one of these concerns surface properties of objects and is known, along with other sensory information, as "hasa" knowledge. It is proposed that hasa color knowledge is laid down subsequent to the interaction of the entry level with the boundaried surfaces at the pictorial register. The coding of hasa information will often be as red, light red, or some form easily convertible to words. Perhaps for reasons of neural economy, hasa color will not be stored in pictorial form unless experience says it is necessary to make precise surface discriminations for that object.

The entry level is a visual categorization of the incoming information to which object-name labels become attached. Hasa information, therefore, can assist in the production of labels. The role of color, as one of these hasa properties, was discussed in chapters 9 and 10. The other two types of stored knowledge are function ("isa") and associative knowledge. Evidence was provided that these are functionally independent of hasa knowledge. The independence has some interesting consequences. First, the role of appearance and other hasa knowledge in object naming was contrasted with the limited role of function (isa knowledge). The distinctions between the types of object knowledge with respect to object naming provided a resolution to some of the controversy surrounding optic aphasia. Second, the distinction between knowledge of appearance and knowledge of function gave credence to the selective loss of object-color knowledge. These classic findings, which have been recently revived, were discussed and confirmed in chapter 9. The complications that arise for the model when object color is named were discussed in chapter 11.

The role of color in stored knowledge was not pursued except in respect to representations for recognition and naming. However, objects are not only stored in memory for purposes of identification; these representations play a part in our memories of scenes and events. The scripts (Schank and Abelson, 1977) in which these colored objects play a part would be unlikely to be revived by color alone, though it may be the case that a colored version of an object is a more potent cue to memory than an uncolored version. This book is not concerned with this aspect of cognition and restricted itself to the primary purpose of the visual system.

The primary function of the visual system is to categorize boundaried surfaces at the pictorial register as objects; that function takes precedence over the categorization of the surface color. Thus, it can be argued that changes in surface appearance first infer information about objects rather than colors. Primacy for object over color categorization implies a consequent primacy to the attached labels (names). Shapes are usually more rapidly named than colors. The particular shapes used to denote words, as discussed in chapter 11, are so rapidly named (read) that special automatic processing has been proposed. The consequence is that, when there is a race to produce a name, it is won by the word rather than the name of the surface color. It is, therefore, possible, that the slow development of color naming stems from the primacy of object categorization. Only recently has Western society commonly given color an abstract usage. It is difficult to believe now but, at the turn of the century, it was the norm for eight-year-old children to be able to name only four colors. Today, that performance could be expected of a three year old. Our species could have become more intelligent; more likely, the world has become more reliably colored.

References

Abney, W. W. (1913). *Researches in Color Vision and the Trichromatic Theory,* Chapter 8. London: Longman, Green and Co.

Adams, G. K. (1923). An experimental study of memory color and related phenomena. *American Journal of Psychology, 34,* 359–407.

Adams, R. J. (1989). Newborns' discrimination amid mid- and long-wavelength stimuli. *Journal of Experimental Child Psychology, 47,* 130–141.

Adler, A. (1944). Disintegration and restoration of optic recognition in visual agnosia. *Archives of Neurology and Psychiatry, 51,* 243–259.

Albers, J. (1971). *The Interaction of Color.* New Haven, Conn.: Yale University Press.

Albert, M. L., Reches, A.; and Silverberg, R. (1975), Associative visual agnosia without alexia. *Neurology, 25,* 322–326.

Allan, L. G.; Siegel, S.; Collins, J. C.; and MacQueen, G. M. (1989). Color aftereffect contingent on text. *Perception and Psychophysics, 46,* 105–113.

Allen, C. K. (1984). Short-term memory for colors and color names in the absence of vocalization. *Perceptual and Motor Skills, 59,* 263–266.

Allport, D. A. (1985). Distributed memory, modular systems and dysphasia. In S. K. Newman and R. Epstein (Eds.). *Current Perspectives in Dysphasia.* Edinburgh: Churchill Livingstone.

Allport, D.A. (1987). Selection for action: Some behavioral and neurophysiological considerations of attention and action. In H. Heuer and A. F. Sanders (Eds.). *Perspectives on Perception and Action.* Hillsdale, N.J.: Lawrence Erlbaum Associates.

Amber, R. B. (1983). *Color Therapy.* New York: Aurora Press.

Andersen, R. A. (1988). Visual and visual motor functions of the posterior parietal cortex. In P. Rakic and W. Singer (Eds.). *Neurobiology of Neocortex.* New York: Wiley.

Anderson, J. R. (1978). Arguments concerning representations for mental imagery. *Psychological Review, 85,* 249–277.

Anstis, S. M. (1980). The perception of apparent movement. *Philosophical Transactions of the Royal Society of London, Biol. 290,* 153–168.

Anstis, S. M. (1989). "Motion illusions from motion-defined edges." Paper presented at the Fifth International Symposium of the Northern Eye Institute. Bristol, U.K. July.

Arguin, M., and Cavanagh, P. (1988). Parallel processing of two disjunctive targets. *Perception and Psychophysics, 44,* 22–30.

Armstrong, S. L.; Gleitman, L. R.; and Gleitman, H. (1983). What some concepts might not be. *Cognition, 13,* 263–308.

Baddeley, A. D., and Hitch, G. (1974). Working memory. In G. Bower (Ed.) *The Psychology of Learning and Motivation. Attention and Performance V111.* New York: Academic Press.

174   References

Balota, D. A., and Chumley, J. I. (1985). The locus of word-frequency effects in the pronounciation task: Lexical access and/or production? *Journal of Memory and Language, 24*, 89–106.

Barbur, J. L., and Forsyth, P. M. (1990). The effective contrast of colored targets. In D. Brogan (Ed.). *Visual Search: Proceedings of the 1st International Conference on Visual Search*. London: Taylor and Francis.

Barbur, J. L.; Ruddock, K. H.; and Waterfield, V. A. (1980). Human visual responses in the absence of the geniculo-calcarine projection. *Brain, 103*, 905–928.

Baron-Cohen; S., Wyke, M. A.; and Binnie, C. (1987). Hearing words and seeing colors: An experimental investigation of a case of synaesthesia. *Perception, 16*, 761–767.

Barlow, H. B. (1953). Summation and inhibition in the frog's retina. *Journal of Physiology, 119*, 69–88.

Barlow, H. B. (1986). Why have multiple cortical areas? *Vision Research, 26*, 81–90.

Barlow, H. B.; Narasimhan, R.; and Rosenfeld, A. (1972). Visual pattern analysis in machines and animals. *Science, 177*, 567–575.

Barrow, H. G., and Tenenbaum, J. M. (1978). Recovering intrinsic scene characteristics from images. In A. Hanson & E. Riseman (Eds.) *Computer Vision Systems*. New York: Academic Press.

Bartlett, E. J. (1977). The acquisition of the meaning of color terms: A study of lexical development. In P. Smith and R. Campbell (Eds.). *Proceedings of the NATO Conference on the Psychology of Language*. New York: Plenum Press.

Bartley, S. H. (1951). The psychophysiology of vision. In S. S. Stevens (Ed.). *Handbook of Experimental Psychology*. New York: Wiley.

Bartram, D. J. (1973). The effects of familiarity and practice on naming pictures of objects. *Memory and Cognition, 1*, 101–105.

Basso, A.; Bisiach, E.; and Luzzatti, C. (1980). Loss of mental imagery: A case study. *Neuropsychologia, 18*, 435–442.

Basso, A.; Capitani, E.; Luzzatti, C.; Spinnler, H.; and Zanobio, M. E. (1985). Different basic components in the performance of Broca's and Wernicke's aphasics on the colour-figure matching test. *Neuropsychologia, 23*, 51–59.

Basso, A.; Capitani, E.; and Laiacona, M. (1988). Progressive language impairment without dementia: A case with isolated category specific semantic defect. *Journal of Neurology, Neurosurgery and Psychiatry, 51*, 1201–1207.

Basso, A.; Faglioni, P.; and Spinnler, H. (1976). Non verbal color impairment in aphasics. *Neuropsychologia, 14*, 183–192.

Battig, W. F., and Montague, W. E. (1969). Category norms for verbal items in 56 categories. *Journal of Experimental Psychology, 80*, Monograph, 1–45.

Bay, E. (1953). Disturbances of visual perception and their examination. *Brain, 76*, 515–550.

Baylis, G. C.; Rolls, E. T.; and Leonard, C. M. (1985). Selectivity between faces in the responses of a population of neurons in the superior temporal sulcus of the monkey. *Brain Research, 342*, 91–102.

Beauvois, M-F. (1982). Optic aphasia: A process of interaction between vision and language. *Philosophical Transactions of the Royal Society of London B, 298*, 35–47.

Beauvois, M-F., and Saillant, B. (1985). Optic aphasia for colours and colour agnosia: A distinction between visual and visuo-verbal impairments in the processing of colors. *Cognitive Neuropsychology, 2*, 1–48.

Beauvois, M-F.; Saillant, B.; Meininger, V.; and Lhermitte, F. (1978). Bilateral tactile aphasia: A tactoverbal dysfunction. *Brain, 101*, 381–401.

Beck, J. (1972). *Surface Color Perception*. Ithaca, N.Y.: Cornell University Press.

Beck, J. (1982). Textural segmentation. In J. Beck (Ed.). *Organization and Representation in Perception*. Hillsdale, NJ: Erlbaum.

Bender, M. B., and Krieger, H. P. (1951). Visual function in perimetrically blind fields. *Archives of Neurology and Psychiatry, 65,* 72–79.

Benson, D. F. (1979). *Aphasia, Alexia and Agraphia.* New York: Churchill Livingstone.

Benson, D. F., and Barton, M. I. (1970). Disturbances in constructional ability. *Cortex, 6,* 19–46.

Benson, D. F., and Greenberg, J. P. (1969). Visual form agnosia. *Archives of Neurology, 20,* 82–89.

Benton, A. L.; Smith, K. C.; and Lang, M. (1972). Stimulus characteristics and object naming in aphasic patients. *Journal of Communication Disorders, 5,* 19–24.

Benussi, V. (1902). Neber den Einfluss der Fabre and grosse der Zollnerschen Tauschung. *Zeitschfift fur Psychologie, 29,* 264–351, 385–433.

Berlin, B., and Kay, P. (1969). *Basic Color Terms: Their Universality and Evolution.* Berkeley: University of California Press.

Bertelson, P. (1961). Sequential redundancy and speed in a two-choice responding task. *Quarterly Journal of Experimental Psychology, 12,* 90–102.

Bertulis, A., and Glezer, V. (1984). Colour-spatial vision. *International Journal of Psychophysiology, 2,* 147–165.

Beyn, E. S., and Knyazeva, G. R. (1962). The problem of prosopagnosia. *Journal of Neurology, Neurosurgery and Psychiatry, 25,* 154–158.

Biederman, I. (1987). Recognition-by-components: A theory of human image understanding. *Psychological Review, 94,* 115–145.

Biederman, I.; Blickle, T. W.; Teitelbaum, R. C.; and Klatsky, G. J. (1988). Object search in nonsense displays. *Journal of Experimental Psychology: Learning, Memory and Cognition, 14,* 456–467.

Biederman, I., and Ju, G. (1988). Surface versus edge-based determinants of visual recognition. *Cognitive Psychology, 20,* 38–64.

Biederman, I., and Tsao, Y. (1979). On processing ideographs and English words: Some implications from Stroop-test results. *Cognitive Psychology, 11,* 125–132.

Bills, A. G. (1931). Blocking: A new principle of mental fatigue. *American Journal of Psychology, 43,* 230–245.

Birch, J.; Chisholm, I. A.; Kinnear, P.; Marre, M.; Pinckers, A. J. L. G.; Pokorny, J.; Smith, V. C.; and Verriest, G. (1979). Acquired color vision defects. In J. Pokorny, V. C. Smith, G. Verriest, and A. J. L. G. Pinckers (Eds.). *Congenital and Acquired Colour Vision Defects,* 243–348. New York: Grune & Stratton.

Bisiach, E. (1966). Perceptual factors in the pathogenesis of anomia. *Cortex, 2,* 90–95.

Blakemore, C., and Campbell, F. W. (1969). On the existence of neurons in the human visual system selectively sensitive to the orientation and size of retinal images. *Journal of Physiology, 187,* 727–750.

Blakemore, C.; Carpenter, R. H. S.; and Georgeson, M. A. (1970). Lateral inhibition between orientation detectors in the human visual system. *Nature, 228,* 37–39.

Blakemore, C., and Nachmias, J. (1971). The orientation specificity of two visual after effects. *Journal of Physiology, 213,* 157–174.

Blakemore, C., and Sutton, P. (1969). Size adaptation: A new after-effect. *Science, 166,* 245–247.

Blythe, I. M.; Kennard, C.; and Ruddock, K. H. (1987). Residual vision in patients with retrogeniculate lesions of the visual pathways. *Brain, 110,* 887–905.

Bornstein, M. H. (1975). Qualities of color vision in infancy. *Journal of Experimental Child Psychology, 19,* 401–419.

Bornstein, M. H. (1976). Name codes and color memory. *American Journal of Psychology, 89,* 269–279.

Bornstein, M. H. (1985). On the development of color naming in young children: Data and theory. *Brain and Language, 26,* 72–93.

Bornstein, M. H.; Kessen, W.; and Weiskopf, S. (1976). Color vision and hue categorization in young human infants. *Journal of Experimental Psychology: Human Perception and Performance, 2*, 115–129.

Botez, M. I.; Serbanescu, T.; and Vernea, I. (1964). Visual static agnosia with special reference to literal agnosic alexia. *Neurology, 14*, 1101–1111.

Boucher, M.; Kopp, N.; Michel, F.; Tommasi, M.; and Schott, B. (1976). Observation anatomo-clinique d'un cas d'alexie sans agraphie. *Revue Neurologique, 132*, 656–659.

Boynton, R. M. (1988). Color vision. *Annual Review of Psychology, 39*, 69–100.

Bradley, A.; Switkes, E.; and DeValois, K. (1988). Orientation and spatial frequency selectivity of adaptation to color and luminance gratings. *Vision Research, 28*, 841–856.

Breitmeyer, B. G., and Valberg, A. (1979). Local, foveal inhibitory effects of global peripheral excitation. *Science, 203*, 463–465.

Brian, C. R., and Goodenough, F. L. (1929). The relative potency of color and form perception at various ages. *Journal of Experimental Psychology, 12*, 197–213.

Briand, K. A., and Klein, R. M. (1987). Is Posner's "beam" the same as Treisman's "glue"? On the relation between visual orienting and feature integration theory. *Journal of Experimental Psychology: Human Perception and Performance, 13*, 228–241.

Brigner, W. L., and Gallagher, M. B. (1974). Subjective contour: Apparent depth or simultaneous brightness contrast. *Perceptual and Motor Skills, 38*, 1047–1053.

Broadbent, D. E. (1958). *Perception and Communication*. London: Pergamon.

Broadbent, D. E., and Broadbent, M. H. P. (1986). Encoding speed of visual features and the occurrence of illusory conjunctions. *Perception, 15*, 515–524.

Broerse, J., and Crassini, B. (1984). Investigations of perception and imagery using CAEs: The role of experimental design and psychophysical method. *Perception and Psychophysics, 35*, 155–164.

Broerse, J. & Crassini, B. (1986). Making ambiguous displays unambiguous: The influence of real colors and colored aftereffects on perceptual alternation. *Perception and Psychophysics, 39*, 105–116.

Brooks, L. R. (1968). Spatial and verbal components in the act of recall. *Canadian Journal of Psychology, 22*, 349–368.

Brown, A. M., and Teller, D. Y. (1989). Chromatic opponency in 3-month-old human infants. *Vision Research, 29*, 37–45.

Brown, M. W.; Wilson, F. A. W.; and Riches, I. P. (1987). Neuronal evidence that inferotemporal cortex is more important than hippocampus in certain processes underlying recognition memory. *Brain Research, 409*, 158–162.

Brown, R. W., and Lenneberg, E. H. (1954). A study in language and cognition. *Journal of Abnormal and Social Psychology, 49*, 454–462.

Bruce, M. and Foster, J. J. (1982). The visibility of colored characters on colored backgrounds on viewdata displays. *Visible Language, 16*, 382–390.

Bruce, V. (1983). Recognizing faces. *Philosophical Transactions of the Royal Society of London Series B, 302*, 423–436.

Bruce, V., and Young, A. W. (1986). Understanding face recognition. *British Journal of Psychology, 77*, 305–327.

Bruner, J. S., and Postman, L. (1949). On the perception of incongruity: A paradigm. *Journal of Personality, 18*, 206–223.

Bruner, J. S.; Postman, L.; and Rodrigues, J. (1951). Expectations and the perception of color. *American Journal of Psychology, 64*, 216–227.

Brussel, E. M.; Stober, S. R.; and Bodinger, D. M. (1977). Sensory information and subjective contour. *American Journal of Psychology, 90*, 145–156.

Bryden, M. P., and Allard, F. (1976). Visual hemifield differences depend on typeface. *Brain and Language, 3*, 191–200.

Bub, D. N.; Black, S.; Hampson, E.; and Kertesz, A. (1988). Semantic encoding of pictures and words: Some neuropsychological observations. *Cognitive Neuropsychology, 5*, 27–66.

Bundesen, C., and Pedersen, L. F. (1983). Color segregation and visual search. *Perception and Psychophysics, 33*, 487–493.

Burns, B., and Shepp, B. E. (1988). Dimensional interactions and the structure of psychological space: The representation of hue, saturation and brightness. *Perception and Psychophysics, 43*, 494–507.

Burns, S. A.; Elsner, A. E.; Pokorny, J.; and Smith, V. C. (1984). The Abney effect: Chromaticity coordinates of unique and other constant hues. *Vision Research, 24*, 479–489.

Caldwell, J. E., and Jones, G. E. (1985). The effects of exposure to red and blue light on physiological indices and time estimation. *Perception, 14*, 19–29.

Callaghan, T. C. (1984). Dimensional interaction of hue and brightness in preattentive field segmentation. *Perception and Psychophysics, 36*, 25–34.

Callaghan, T. C. (1989). Interference and dominance in texture segregation: Hue, geometric form, and line orientation. *Perception and Psychophysics, 46*, 299–311.

Callaghan, T. C. (1990). Early perception: Searching for textures and single elements. Paper presented at The Second International Conference on Visual Search, Durham, U.K., September.

Callaghan, T. C.; Lasaga, M. I.; and Garner, W. R. (1986). Visual texture based on orientation and hue. *Perception and Psychophysics, 39*, 32–38.

Campbell, F. W., and Maffei, L. (1981). The influence of spatial frequency and contrast on the perception of moving patterns. *Vision Research, 21*, 713–721.

Campion, J. (1987). Apperceptive agnosia: The specification and description of constructs. In G. W. Humphreys and M. J. Riddoch (Eds.). *Visual object processing: A cognitive neuropsychological approach.* London: Lawrence Erlbaum Associates.

Capitani, E.; Scotti, G.; and Spinnler, H. (1978). Colour imperception in patients with focal excisions of the cerebral hemispheres. *Neuropsychologia, 16*, 491–496.

Caramazza, A.; Berndt, R. S.; and Brownell, H. H. (1982). The semantic deficit hypothesis: Perceptual parsing and object classification by aphasic patients. *Brain and Language, 15*, 161–189.

Carmichael, L.; Hogan, H. P.; and Walter, A. A. (1932). An experimental study of the effect of language on the reproduction of visually perceived form. *Journal of Experimental Psychology, 15*, 73–86.

Carney, T.; Shadlen, M.; and Switkes, E. (1987). Parallel processing of motion and colour information. *Nature, 328*, 647–649.

Carr, T. H.; McCauley, C.; Sperber, R. D.; and Parmalee, C. M. (1982). Words, pictures and priming: On semantic activation, concious identification and the automaticity of information processing. *Journal of Experimental Psychology: Human Perception and Performance, 8*, 757–777.

Carroll, J. B., and White, M. N. (1973). Word frequency and age of acquisition as determiners of picture-naming latency. *Quarterly Journal of Experimental Psychology, 25*, 85–95.

Carter, R. C. (1982). Visual search with color. *Journal of Experimental Psychology: Human Perception and Performance, 8*, 127–136.

Cattell, J. McK. (1886). The time taken up by cerebral operations. *Mind, 11*, 524–538.

Cavanagh, P. (1987). Reconstructing the third dimension: Interactions between color, texture, motion, binocular disparity and shape. *Computer Vision, Graphics and Image Processing, 37*, 171–195.

Cavanagh, P. (1989). Multiple analyses of orientation in the visual system. In D. H. K. Lam and C. D. Gilbert (Eds.). *Neural Mechanisms of Visual Perception.* Houston: Gulf Publishing.

Cavanagh, P.; Arguin, M.; and von Grunau, M. (1989). Interattribute apparent motion. *Vision Research, 29,* 1197–1204.

Cavanagh, P.; Arguin, M.; and Treisman, A. (1990). Effects of stimulus domain on visual search for orientation and size features. *Journal of Experimental Psychology: Human Perception and Performance.* (In press).

Cavanagh, P., and Anstis, S. M. (1988). "Red/green opponent-color input for motion at low spatial frequencies." Paper presented at the Annual Meeting of the Society for Neurosciences, Toronto. Abstract 187.1.

Cavanagh, P.; Boeglin, J.; and Favreau, O. E. (1985). Perception of motion in equiluminous kinematograms. *Perception, 14,* 151–162.

Cavanagh, P., and Favreau, O. E. (1985). Color and luminance share a common motion pathway. *Vision Research, 25,* 1595–1601.

Cavanagh, P., and Leclerc, Y. G. (1989). Shape from shadows. *Journal of Experimental Psychology: Human Perception and Performance, 15,* 3–27.

Cavanagh, P.; MacLeod, D. A.; and Anstis, S. M. (1987). Equiluminance: Spatial and temporal factors and the contribution of the blue cones. *Journal of the Optical Society of America(A), 4,* 1428–1438.

Cavanagh, P.; Tyler, C. W.; and Favreau O. E. (1984). Perceived velocity of moving chromatic gratings. *Journal of the Optical Society of America(A), 1,* 893–899.

Charcot, J. M. (1883). Un cas de suppression brusque et isolée de la vision mentale des signes et des objets (formes et couleurs). *Progres Medical, 11,* 568–571.

Charnallet, A.; Carbonnel, S.; and Pellat, J. (1988). Right visual hemiagnosia: A single case report. *Cortex, 24,* 347–355.

Christ, R. E. (1975). Review and analysis of color coding research for visual displays. *Human Factors, 17,* 562–570.

Clark, S. E. (1969). Retrieval of colour information from perceptual memory. *Journal of Experimental Psychology, 82,* 263–266.

Cohen, J., and Gordon, D. A. (1949). The Prevost-Fechner-Benham subjective colors. *Psychological Bulletin, 46,* 97–136.

Cohen, R., and Kelter, S. (1979). Cognitive impairment of aphasics in a color-to-picture matching task. *Cortex, 15,* 235–245.

Cohn, J. (1894). Experimentelle Untersuchungen ueber die Gefuehlsbetonung der Farben, Helligkeiten, und ihre Combinationen. *Philosophische Studien, 10,* 562–603.

Cohn, N. B.; Dussman, R. E.; and Bradford, D. C. (1984). Age-related decrement in Stroop color test performance. *Journal of Clinical Psychology, 40,* 1244–1250.

Cole, M., and Perez-Cruet, J. (1964). Prosopagnosia. *Neuropsychologia, 2,* 233–246.

Collins, A. M., and Loftus, E. F. (1975). A spreading-activation theory of semantic processing. *Psychological Review, 82,* 407–428.

Coltheart, M. (1983). Iconic memory. *Philosophical Transactions of the Royal Society of London, B302,* 283–294.

Comerford, J. P. (1974). Stereopsis with chromatic contours. *Vision Research, 14,* 975–982.

Corbus, G., and Nichols, R. C. (1963). Personality variables and the response to color. *Psychological Bulletin, 60,* 566–575.

Corlew, M. M., and Nation, J. E. (1975). Characteristics of visual stimuli and naming performance in aphasic patients. *Cortex, 11,* 186–191.

Coslett, H. B., and Saffran, E. M. (1989). Preserved object recognition and reading comprehension in optic aphasia. *Brain, 112,* 1091–1110.

Courtney, A. J. (1986). Chinese population stereotypes: Color associations. *Human Factors, 28,* 97–99.

Cowey, A. (1979). Cortical maps and visual perception. *Quarterly Journal of Experimental Psychology, 31,* 1–17.

Cowey, A. (1985). Aspects of cortical organization related to selective attention impairments of visual perception. In M. I. Posner and O. S. M. Marin (Eds.). *Attention and Performance X1.* Hillsdale, N.J.: Lawrence Erlbaum Associates.

Cowey, A.; Stoerig, P.; and Perry, V. H. (1989). Transneuronal retrograde degeneration of retinal ganglion cells after damage to striate cortex in macaque monkeys: Selective loss of Pb cells. *Neuroscience, 29,* 65–80.

Crick, F. H. C. (1984). The function of the thalamic reticular spotlight: The searchlight hypothesis. *Proceedings of the National Academy of Sciences, USA, 81,* 4586–4590.

Critchley, M. (1965). Acquired anomalies of color perception of central origin. *Brain, 88,* 711–724.

Cuddy, L. L. (1985). The color of melody. *Music Perception, 2,* 345–360.

Cumming, W. J. K.; Hurwitz, L. J.; and Perl, N. T. (1970). A study of a patient who had alexia without agraphia. *Journal of Neurology, Neurosurgery and Psychiatry, 33,* 34–39.

Cytowic, R. E., and Wood, F. B. (1982). Synaesthesia: 1. A review of major theories and their brain basis. *Brain and Cognition, 1,* 23–35.

D'Agostino, P. R. (1982). Plasticity of mental color codes. *American Journal of Psychology, 95,* 3–12.

Dallenbach, K. M. (1923). Position versus intensity as a determinant of clearness. *American Journal of Psychology, 34,* 282–286.

Damasio, A. R., and Damasio, H. (1983). The anatomic basis of pure alexia. *Neurology, 33,* 1573–1584.

Damasio, A. R. and Damasio, H. (1986). Hemianopia, hemiachromatopsia and the mechanisms of alexia. *Cortex, 22,* 161–169.

Damasio, A. R.; Damasio, H.; and Van Hoesen, G. W. (1982). Prosopagnosia: Anatomical basis and behavioral mechanisms. *Neurology, 32,* 331–341.

Damasio, A. R.; McKee, J.; and Damasio, H. (1979). Determinants of performance in color anomia. *Brain and Language, 7,* 74–85.

Damasio, A. R.; Yamada, T.; Damasio, H.; Corbett, J.; and McKee, J. (1980). Central achromatopsia: Behavioral, anatomic and physiologic aspects. *Neurology, 30,* 1064–1071.

Dannemiller, J. L. (1989a). Computational approaches to color constancy: Adaptive and ontogenetic considerations. *Psychological Review, 96,* 255–266.

Dannemiller, J. L. (1989b). A test of color constancy in 9–20 week old human infants following simulated illuminant changes. *Developmental Psychology, 25,* 171–184.

Dannemiller, J. L., and Hanko, S. A. (1987). A test of color constancy in 4-month-old human infants. *Journal of Experimental Child Psychology, 44,* 255–267.

Darwin, C. H. (1877). A biographical sketch of a young infant. *Kosmos, 1,* 367–376.

Davidoff, J. B. (1974). The psychological relationship between lightness and saturation. *Perception and Psychophysics, 16,* 79–83.

Davidoff, J. B. (1975). Hemispheric differences in the perception of lightness. *Neuropsychologia, 13,* 121–124.

Davidoff, J. B. (1976). Hemispheric sensitivity differences in the perception of color. *Quarterly Journal of Experimental Psychology, 28,* 387–394.

Davidoff, J. B. (1982). Non verbal studies. In J. G. Beaumont (Ed.). *Divided Visual Field Studies of Cerebral Organization.* London: Academic Press.

Davidoff, J. B. (1986a). The specificity of face perception: Evidence from psychological investigations. In R. Bruyer (Ed.). *The Neuropsychology of Face Perception and Facial Expression.* Hillsdale, N.J.: Lawrence Erlbaum Associates.

Davidoff, J. B. (1986b). The mental representation of faces: Spatial and temporal factors. *Perception and Psychophysics*, 40, 391–400.

Davidoff, J. B. (1989). Prosopagnosia: A disorder of rapid spatial integration. In G. Denes, C. Semenza, and P. Bisiacchi (Eds.). *Perspectives on Cognitive Neuropsychology*. London: Lawrence Erlbaum Associates.

Davidoff, J. B., and Donnelly, N. (1990). Object superiority: A comparison of complete and part probes. *Acta Psychologica*, 73, 225–243.

Davidoff, J. B., and Fodor, G. (1989). An annotated translation of Lewandowsky (1908). *Cognitive Neuropsychology*, 6, 165–177.

Davidoff, J. B., and Ostergaard, A. L. (1984). Color anomia resulting from weakened short-term memory. *Brain*, 107, 415–431.

Davidoff, J. B., and Ostergaard, A. L. (1988). The role of colour in categorical judgments. *Quarterly Journal of Experimental Psychology*, 40A, 533–544.

Davidoff, J. B., and Wilson, B. (1985). A case of visual agnosia showing a disorder of pre-semantic visual classification. *Cortex*, 21, 121–134.

Davies, G. M.; Ellis, H. D.; and Shepherd, J. W. (1978). Face recognition as a function of mode of representation. *Journal of Applied Psychology*, 63, 180–187.

Daw, N. W. (1968). Color-coded ganglion cells in the goldfish retina: Extension of their receptive fields by means of new stimuli. *Journal of Physiology*, 197, 567–592.

Dean, P. (1979). Visual cortex ablation and thresholds for successively presented stimuli in rhesus monkeys. II. Hue. *Experimental Brain Research*, 35, 69–83.

DeHaan, E. H. F.; Young, A. W.; and Newcombe, F. (1987). Face recognition without awareness. *Cognitive Neuropsychology*, 4, 385–415.

Dejerine, J. (1892). Contribution à l'étude anatomo-pathologique et clinique des différentes variétés de cécité verbale. *Memoires de la Société de Biologie*, 4, 61–90.

DeMonasterio, F. M., and Gouras, P. (1975). Functional properties of ganglion cells of the rhesus monkey retina. *Journal of Physiology*, 251, 167–195.

Denckla, M. B. (1972). Color-naming defects in dyslexic boys. *Cortex*, 8, 164–176.

Denes, G., and Semenza, C. (1975). Auditory modality-specific anomia: Evidence from a case of pure word deafness. *Cortex*, 11, 401–411.

Dennis, M. (1976). Dissociated naming and locating of body parts after left anterior temporal lobe resection: An experimental case study. *Brain and Language*, 3, 147–163.

DeRenzi, E. (1982). *Disorders of Space Exploration and Cognition*. New York: Wiley.

DeRenzi, E. (1986). Prosopagnosia in two patients with CT scan evidence of damage confined to the right hemisphere. *Neuropsychologia*, 24, 385–389.

DeRenzi, E.; Faglioni, P.; Scotti, G.; and Spinnler, H. (1972a). Impairment of color sorting behavior after hemispheric damage: An experimental study with the Holmgren skein test. *Cortex*, 8, 147–163.

DeRenzi, E.; Faglioni, P.; Scotti, G., and Spinnler, H. (1972b). Impairment in associating colour to form concomitant with aphasia. *Brain*, 95, 293–304.

DeRenzi, E., and Spinnler, H. (1966). Visual recognition in patients with unilateral cerebral disease. *Journal of Mental and Nervous Disease*, 142, 515–525.

DeRenzi, E., and Spinnler, H. (1967). Impaired performance on color tasks in patients with hemispheric damage. *Cortex*, 3, 194–217.

Derrington, A. M., and Badcock, D. R. (1985). The low level motion system has both chromatic and luminance inputs. *Vision Research*, 25, 1874–1884.

Derrington, A. M.; Krauskopf, J.; and Lennie P. (1984). Chromatic mechanisms in lateral geniculate nucleus of macaque. *Journal of Physiology*, 357, 241–265.

Desimone, R.; Schein, S. J.; Moran, J.; and Ungerleider, L. G. (1985). Contour, color, and shape analysis beyond the striate cortex. *Vision Research*, 25, 441–452.

Deutsch, J. A., and Deutsch, D. (1963). Attention: Some theoretical considerations. *Psychological Review, 70,* 80–90.

DeValois, K. K. (1978). Interactions among spatial frequency channels in the human visual system. In J. S. Cool and E. L. Smith (Eds.). *Frontiers in Visual Science.* Berlin: Springer.

DeValois, K. K., and Switkes, E. (1983). Simultaneous masking interactions between chromatic and luminance gratings. *Journal of the Optical Society of America, 73,* 11–18.

DeValois, R. L.; Albrecht, D. G.; and Thorell, L. G. (1982). Spatial frequency selectivity of cells in macaque visual cortex. *Vision Research, 22,* 545–559.

DeValois, R. L.; Snodderly, D. M.; Yund, E. W.; and Hepler, N. K. (1977). Responses of macaque lateral geniculate cells to luminance and color figures. *Sensory Processes, 1,* 244–259.

DeVreese, L. P. (1987). Varieties of colour-naming defects associated with posterior brain damage: A neurolinguistic re-appraisal. *Functional Neurology, 2,* 111–112.

DeVreese, L. P. (1988). Category-specific versus modality-specific aphasia for colors: A review of the pioneer case studies. *International Journal of Neuroscience, 43,* 195–206.

De Weert, C. M. M., and Sadza, K. J. (1983). New data concerning the contribution of color differences to stereopsis. In J. D. Mollon and R. T. Sharpe (Eds.), 553–562. *Colour Vision: Physiology and Psychophysics.* New York: Academic Press.

DeYoe, E. A., and Van Essen, D. C. (1985). Segregation of efferent connections and receptive field properties in visual area V2 of the macaque. *Nature, 317,* 58–61.

DeYoe, E. A., and Van Essen, D. C. (1988). Concurrent processing streams in monkey visual cortex. *Trends in the Neurosciences, 11,* 219–226.

Dimond, S. J., and Beaumont, J. G. (1972). Hemispheric function and color naming. *Journal of Experimental Psychology, 46,* 87–92.

Dixon, N. F. (1960). Apparent changes in the visual threshold: Central or peripheral? *British Journal of Psychology, 51,* 297–309.

Dixon, N. F. (1981). *Preconscious Processing.* Chichester: Wiley.

Dobbins, A., Sucker, S. W., and Cynader, M. S. (1987). Endstopped neurons in the visual cortex as a substrate for calculating curvature. *Nature, 329,* 438–441.

Driver, J., and Baylis, G. C. (1989). Movement and visual attention: The spotlight metaphor breaks down. *Journal of Experimental Psychology: Human Perception and Performance, 15,* 448–456.

Dunbar, K., and MacLeod, C. M. (1984). A horse race of a different color: Stroop interference patterns with transformed words. *Journal of Experimental Psychology: Human Perception and Performance, 10,* 622–639.

Duncan, J. (1984). Selective attention and the organization of visual information. *Journal of Experimental Psychology: General, 113,* 501–517.

Duncan, J. (1988). Boundary conditions on parallel processing in human vision. *Perception, 18,* 457–469.

Duncan, J., and Humphreys, G. W. (1989). Visual search and stimulus similarity. *Psychological Review, 96,* 433–458.

Duncan-Johnson, C. C., and Koppel, B. S. (1981). The Stroop effect: Brain potentials localise the source of the interference. *Science, 214,* 938–940.

Duncker, K. (1939). The influence of past experience upon perceptual properties. *American Journal of Psychology, 52,* 255–265.

Dyer, F. N. (1973). Stroop-phenomenon and its use in the study of perceptual, cognitive and response processes. *Memory and Cognition, 1,* 106–120.

D'Zmura, M., and Lennie, P. (1986). Mechanisms of color constancy. *Journal of the Optical Society of America, 3A,* 1662–1672.

Eco, U. (1988). On Truth. A Fiction. In U. Eco, M. Santambrogio, and P. Violi (Eds.). *Meaning and Mental Representations*. Bloomington: Indiana University Press.

Egeth, H. E.; Blecker, D. L.; and Kamlet, A. S. (1969). Verbal interference in a perceptual comparison task. *Perception and Psychophysics, 6*, 355–356.

Egeth, H. E., and Pachella, R. (1969). Multidimensional stimulus identification. *Perception and Psychophysics, 5*, 341–346.

Egusa, H. (1983). Effects of brightness, hue, and saturation on perceived depth between adjacent regions in the visual field. *Perception, 12*, 167–175.

Ejima, Y., and Takahashi, S. (1988). Illusory contours induced by isoluminant chromatic patterns. *Vision Research, 28*, 1367–1377.

Ekehammar, B.; Zuber, I.; and Nilsson, I. (1987). A method for studying color-form reaction to visual stimuli. *Reports from the Psychology Dept. of the University of Stockholm. No. 661*. October.

Eisner, A., and MacLeod, I. A. (1980). Blue-sensitive cones do not contribute to luminance. *Journal of the Optical Society of America, 70*, 121–123.

Eley, M. G. (1987). Color-layering and the performance of the topographic map user. *Ergonomics, 30*, 655–663.

Elliot, J. (1780). *Philosophical Observations on the Senses: Vision and Hearing*. London: Murray.

Ellis, A. W., and Young, A. W. (1988). *Human Cognitive Neuropsychology*. London: Lawrence Erlbaum Associates.

Ellis, H. D. (1981). Theoretical aspects of face recognition. In G. Davies, H. D. Ellis, and J. Shepherd (Eds.). *Perceiving and Remembering Faces*. London: Academic Press.

Elsner, A. (1978). Hue difference contours can be used in processing orientation information. *Perception and Psychophysics, 24*, 451–456.

Eriksen, B., and Eriksen, C. W. (1974). Effect of noise letters upon the identification of a target letter in a nonsearch task. *Perception and Psychophysics, 16*, 143–149.

Eriksen, C. W. (1952). Location of objects in a visual display as a function of the number of dimensions on which the objects differ. *Journal of Experimental Psychology, 44*, 55–60.

Eriksen, C. W., and Murphy, T. D. (1987). Movement of attentional focus across the visual field: A critical look at the evidence. *Perception and Psychophysics, 42*, 299–305.

Eriksen, C. W., and Yeh, Y. (1985). Allocation of attention in the visual field. *Journal of Experimental Psychology: Human Perception and Performance, 11*, 583–597.

Ettlinger, G., and Wyke, M. (1961). Defects in visual identification in a patient with cerebrovascular disease. *Journal of Neurology, Neurosurgery and Psychiatry, 24*, 254–259.

Eysenck, H. J. (1941). A critical and experimental study of color preferences. *American Journal of Psychology, 54*, 385–394.

Fanger, P. O., Breum, N. O., and Jerking, E. (1977). Can color and noise influence man's thermal comfort? *Ergonomics, 20*, 11–18.

Fantz, R. L. (1961). The origin of form perception. *Scientific American, 204*, May, 66–87.

Farah, M. J. (1984). The neurological basis of mental imagery: A componential analysis. *Cognition, 18*, 245–272.

Farah, M. J. (1985). Psychophysical evidence for a shared representational medium for visual images and percepts. *Journal of Experimental Psychology: General, 114*, 93–105.

Farah, M. J. (1988). Is visual imagery really visual? Overlooked evidence from neuropsychology. *Psychological Review, 95*, 305–317.

Farah, M. J., Levine, D. N., and Calvanio, R. (1988). A case study of mental imagery deficit. *Brain and Cognition, 8*, 147–164.

Farell, B., and Krauskopf, J. (1989). Comparison of stereo and vernier offset thresholds for stimuli modulated chromatically and in luminance. *Investigative Ophthalmology and Visual Science, 30, Supplement,* 129.

Farmer, E. W., and Taylor, R. M. (1980). Visual search through color displays: Effects of target-background similarity and background uniformity. *Perception and Psychophysics, 27,* 267–272.

Favreau, O. E., and Cavanagh, P. (1981). Color and luminance: Independent frequency shifts. *Science, 212,* 831–832.

Favreau, O. E.; Emerson, V.; and Corballis, M. (1972). Motion perception: A color-contingent aftereffect. *Science, 176,* 78–79.

Fechner, G. (1876). *Vorschule der Aesthetik.* Leipzig: Breitkopf und Haertel.

Felfoldy, G. L., and Garner, W. R. (1971). The effects on speeded classification of implicit and explicit instructions regarding stimulus dimensions. *Perception and Psychophysics, 9,* 289–292.

Felsten, G.; Benevento, L. A.; and Burman, D. (1983). Opponent-colour responses in macaque extrageniculate visual pathways: The lateral pulvinar. *Brain Research, 288,* 363–367.

Ferro, J. M., and Santos, M. E. (1984). Associative visual agnosia: A case study, *Cortex, 20,* 121–134.

Finke, R. A. (1981). Interpretation of imagery-induced McCollough effects. *Perception and Psychophysics, 30,* 94–95.

Fisher, D. L., and Tan, K. C. (1989). Visual displays: the highlighting paradox. *Human Factors, 31,* 17–30.

Flanagan, P.; Cavanagh, P.; and Favreau, O. E. (1988). "Perceived colour shift in equiliminant chromatic gratings: adaptable colour-opponent channels." Paper given at the 11th European Conference on Visual Perception, Bristol, September.

Foard, C. F., and Kemler Nelson, D. G. (1984). Holistic and and analytic modes of processing: The multiple determinants of perceptual analysis. *Journal of Experimental Psychology: General, 113,* 94–111.

Fodor, J. A. (1983). *The Modularity of Mind.* Cambridge, Mass.: Bradford Books, MIT Press.

Fodor, J. A., and Pylyshyn, Z. (1981). How direct is visual perception? *Cognition, 9,* 139–196.

Foreit, K. G., and Ambler, B. A. (1978). Induction of the McCollough effect 1: Figural variables. *Perception and Psychophysics, 24,* 295–302.

Foster, D. H. (1990). *Vision and Visual Dysfunction.* Vol. 7, *Inherited and Acquired Colour Vision Deficiencies.* London: Macmillan.

Foster, J. J., and Bruce, M. (1982). Looking for entries in videotex tables: A comparison of four color formats. *Journal of Applied Psychology, 67,* 611–615.

Fraisse, P. (1969). Why is naming longer than reading? *Acta Psychologica, 30,* 96–103.

Freud, S. (1891/1935). *On Aphasia.* (Translated by E. Stengel.) London: Imago.

Freud, S. (1900/1938). The interpretation of dreams. In A. A. Brill (Ed.). *The Basic Writings of Sigmund Freud.* New York: Modern Library.

Freund, D. C. (1889). Ueber optische Aphasie und Seelenblindheit. *Archiv fuer Psychiatrie und Nervenkrankheiten, 20,* 276–297; 371–416.

Frisby, J. P., and Clatworthy, J. L. (1975). Illusory contours: Curious cases of simultaneous brightness contrast. *Perception, 4,* 349–357.

Fukuzawa, K.; Itoh, M.; Sasanuma, S.; Suzuki, T.; and Fukusako, Z. (1988). Internal representations and the conceptual operation of color in pure alexia with color naming defects. *Brain and Language, 34,* 98–126.

Fuld, K., Werner, J. S., and Wooten, B. R. (1983). The possible elemental nature of brown. *Vision Research, 23,* 631–637.

Funnell, E. (1987). Object concepts and object names: Some deductions from acquired disorders of word processing. In G. W. Humphreys and M. J. Riddoch (Eds.). *Visual Object Processing*. London: Lawrence Erlbaum Associates.

Fuster, J. M. (1988). Attentional modulation of inferotemporal neuron responses to visual features. *Society for Neuroscience Abstracts, 14*, 8.5, 18th Annual meeting, Toronto, November.

Galton, F. (1883). *Inquiries into the Human Faculty and its Development*. London: Macmillan.

Gardner, H. (1973). The contribution of operativity to naming capacity in aphasic patients. *Neuropsychologia, 11*, 213–220.

Garner, W. R. (1974). *The Processing of Information and Structure*. New York: Wiley.

Garner, W. R. (1983). Asymmetric interactions of stimulus dimensions in perceptual information processing. In T. J. Tighe and B. E. Shepp (Eds.). *Interactions: Perception, Cognition and Development: A Second Dartmouth Multi-Perspective Conference*. Hillsdale, N.J.: Erlbaum.

Garner, W. R. (1988). Facilitation and interference with a separable redundant dimension in stimulus comparison. *Perception and Psychophysics, 44*, 321–330.

Garner, W. R., and Felfoldy, G. L. (1970). Integrality of stimulus dimensions in various types of information processing. *Cognitive Psychology, 1*, 225–241.

Garro, L. C. (1986). Language, memory, and focality: A rexamination. *American Anthropologist, 88*, 128–136.

Gathercole, S. E., and Broadbent, D. E. (1984). Combining attributes in specified and categorized target search: Further evidence for strategic differences. *Memory and Cognition, 12*, 329–337.

Gathercole, S. E., and Broadbent, D. E. (1987). Spatial factors in visual attention: Some compensatory effects of location and time of arrival of nontargets. *Perception, 16*, 433–443.

Gelb, A. (1921). Ueber den Wegfall der Wahrnehmung von "Oberflaechenfarben." *Zeitschrift fuer Psychologie, 84*, 193–257.

Geller, E. S. (1977). Latencies to name one of three stimulus dimensions: A study of probability effects and dimension integrality. *Perception and Psychophysics, 22*, 70–76.

Geschwind, N., and Fusillo, M. (1966). Color-naming defects in association with alexia. *Archives of Neurology, 15*, 137–146.

Gibson, J. J. (1959). Perception as a function of stimulation. In: S. Koch (Ed.). *Psychology: A Study of a Science*. New York: McGraw-Hill.

Gibson, J. J. (1979). *The Ecological Approach to Visual Perception*. Boston: Houghton Mifflin.

Gibson, J. J., and Radner, M. (1937). Adaptation, after-effect, and contrast in the perception of tilted lines. 1. Quantitative studies. *Journal of Experimental Psychology, 20*, 453–467.

Gil, R., Pluchon, C., Toullat, G., Michenau, D., Rogez, R., and Levevre, J. P. (1985). Disconnexion visuo-verbale (aphasie optique) pour les objets, les images, les couleurs, et les visages avec alexie "abstractif." *Neuropsychologia, 23*, 333–349.

Gilbert, P. (1987). Westphal and Wittgenstein on White. *Mind, 96*, 399–403.

Gilchrist, A. L. (1979). The perception of surface blacks and whites. *Scientific American, 240*, March, 88–97.

Gilinsky, A. S. (1968). Orientation-specific effects of patterns of adapting light on visual acuity. *Journal of the Optical Society of America, 58*, 13–17.

Glaser, W. R., and Duengelhoff, F-J. (1984). The time course of picture-word interference. *Journal of Experimental Psychology: Human Perception and Performance, 10*, 640–654.

Gloning, I.; Gloning, K.; and Hoff, H. (1968). *Neuropsychological Symptoms and Syndromes in Lesions of the Occipital Lobe and Adjacent Areas*. Paris: Gauthiers-Vittars.

Goldenberg, G., and Artner, C. (1991). Visual imagery and knowledge about the visual appearance of objects in patients with posterior cerebral artery lesions. *Brain and Cognition* (in press).

Goldenberg, G., Podreka, I.; Steiner, M.; and Willmes, K. (1987). Patterns of regional cerebral blood flow related to memorising of high and low imagery words: An emission computer tomography study. *Neuropsychologia, 25,* 473–486.

Goldenberg, G.; Podreka, I.; Steiner, M.; and Willmes, K.; Suess, E., Deecke, L. (1989). Regional cerebral blood flow patterns in visual imagery. *Neuropsychologia, 27,* 641–664.

Goldman-Rakic, P. S. (1987). Circuitry of the primate prefontal cortex and the regulation of behavior by representational knowledge. Section I, V, 373–417. In E. Plum (Ed.). *Handbook of Physiology, the Nervous System, Higher Functions of the Brain.* Bethesda, Md.: American Physiological Society.

Goldstein, K. (1942). Some experimental observations concerning the influence of color on the function of the organism. *Occupational Therapy, 21,* 147–151.

Goldstein, K. (1948). *Language and Language Disturbances: Aphasic Symptom Complexes and Their Significance for Medicine and Theory of Language.* New York: Grune and Stratton.

Goldstein, L. H., and Oakley, D. A. (1986). Color versus orientation discrimination in severely brain-damaged and normal adults. *Cortex, 22,*261–266.

Goodfellow, R. A., and Smith, P. C. (1973). Effects of environmental color on two psychomotor tasks. *Perceptual and Motor Skills, 37,* 296–298.

Goodglass, H. (1980). Disorders of naming following brain injury. *American Scientist, 68,* 647–655.

Goodglass, H.; Barton, M. E.; and Kaplan, E. (1968). Sensory modality and object naming in aphasia. *Journal of Speech and Hearing Research, 11,* 488–496.

Goodglass, H.; Klein, B.; Carey, P.; and James, K. J. (1966). Specific semantic word categories in aphasia. *Cortex, 2,* 74–89.

Gorea, A., and Papathomas, T. V. (1989). Motion processing by chromatic and achromatic visual pathways. *Journal of the Optical Society of America, A., 6,* 590–602.

Gottwald, R. L., and Garner, W. R. (1972). Effects of focusing strategy on speeded classification with group, filtering, and condensation tasks. *Perception and Psychophysics, 11,* 179–182.

Gouras, P., and Kruger, J. (1979). Responses of cells in foveal visual cortex of the monkey to pure color contrast. *Journal of Neurophysiology, 42,* 850–860.

Graham, C. H., and Brown, J. L. (1965). Color contrast and color appearance: Brightness constancy and color constancy. In C. H. Graham (Ed.). *Vision and Visual Perception.* New York: Wiley.

Granger, E. M., and Heurtley, J. C. (1973). Visual chromaticity-modulation transfer function. *Journal of the Optical Society of America, 63,* 1173–1174.

Granger, G. W. (1955). The prediction of preference for colour combinations. *Journal of General Psychology, 52,* 213–222.

Green, B. F.; and Anderson, L. K. (1956). Color coding in a visual search task. *Journal of Experimental Psychology, 51,* 19–24.

Green, M. (1986). What determines correspondence strength in apparent motion? *Vision Research, 26,* 599–607.

Green, M., and Odom, J. V. (1986). Correspondence matching in apparent motion: Evidence for three-dimensional spatial representation. *Science, 233,* 1427–1429.

Greenblatt, S. H. (1973). Alexia without agraphia or hemianopsia. *Brain, 96,* 307–316.

Greene, T. C., and Bell, P. A. (1980). Additional considerations concerning the effects of "warm" and "cool" colors on energy conservation. *Ergonomics, 23,* 949–954.

Greene, T. C.; Bell, P. A.; and Boyer, W. N. (1983). Coloring the environment: Hue arousal and boredom. *Bulletin of the Psychonomic Society, 21,* 253–254.

186   References

Greenstein, J. J., and Fleming, R. A. (1984). The use of color in command control electronics status boards. In C. P. Gibson (Ed.). *Colour Coded vs Monochrome Electronic Displays. Proceedings of a NATO Workshop.* London: HMSO.

Gregory, R. L. (1970). *The Intelligent Eye.* London: Weidenfeld and Nicolson.

Gregory, R. L. (1977). Vision with equiluminant color contrast. 1. A projection technique and observations. *Perception, 6,* 113–119.

Gregory, R. L. (1980). Perception as hypotheses. *Philosophical Transactions of the Royal Society of London, B290,* 181–197.

Grewal, B. S.; Haward, L. R.; and Davies, I. R. (1987). The role of color discriminability in the Weigl test. *IRCS Medical Science: Psychology and Psychiatry, 14,* 693–694.

Grinberg, D. L., and Williams, D. R. (1985). Stereopsis with chromatic signals from the blue-sensitive mechanism. *Vision Research, 25,* 531–537.

Gross, C. G.; Desimone, R.; Albright, T. D.; and Schwartz, E. L. (1985). Inferior temporal cortex and pattern recognition, 179–199. In C. Chagas, R. Gatass, and C. Gross (Eds.). *Pattern Recognition Mechanisms.* Berlin: Springer.

Grossberg, S. (1987a). Cortical dynamics of three-dimensional form, color, and brightness perception: 1. Monocular theory. *Perception and Psychophysics, 41,* 87–116.

Grossberg, S. (1987b). Cortical dynamics of three-dimensional form, color, and brightness perception: 2. Binocular theory. *Perception and Psychophysics, 41,* 117–158.

Grossberg, S., and Mingolla, E. (1985). Neural dynamics of form perception: Boundary completion, illusory figures, and neon color spreading. *Psychological Review, 92,* 173–211.

Grunau, M. W. von (1975a). The "fluttering heart" and spatio-temporal characteristics of color processing. I. Reversibility and the influence of luminance. *Vision Research, 15,* 431–436.

Grunau, M. W. von (1975b). The "fluttering heart" and spatio-temporal characteristics of color processing. II. Lateral interactions across the chromatic border. *Vision Research, 15,* 437–440.

Guenther, R. K., and Klatzky, R. L. (1977). Semantic classification of pictures and words. *Journal of Experimental Psychology: Human Learning and Memory, 3,* 498–514.

Guenther, R. K.; Klatzky, R. L.; and Putnam, W. (1980). Commonalities and differences in semantic decisions about pictures and words. *Journal of Verbal Learning and Verbal Behavior, 19,* 54–74.

Gumenik, W. E., and Glass, R. (1970). Effects of reducing the readability of the words in the Stroop color-word test. *Psychonomic Science, 20,* 247–248.

Guth, S. K., and Eastman, A. A. (1970). Chromatic contrast. *American Journal of Optometry and Archives of American Academy of Optometry, 47,* 526–534.

Haber, R. N. (1983). The impending demise of the icon: A critique of the concept of iconic storage in word information processing. *Behavioral and Brain Sciences, 6,* 1–54.

Hallett, P.; Jepson, A.; and Gershon, G. (1988). Color constancy is at the level of the cones. *Investigative Ophthalmology and Visual Science (Supplement), 29,* 163.

Hamwi, V., and Landis, C. (1955). Memory for color. *Journal of Psychology, 39,* 183–194.

Handel, S., and Imai, S. (1972). The free classification of analyzable and unanalyzable stimuli. *Perception and Psychophysics, 12,* 108–116.

Harms, L., and Bundesen, C. (1983). Color segregation and selective attention in a non search task. *Perception and Psychophysics, 33,* 11–19.

Harrison, N., and Boese, E. (1976). The locus of semantic interference in the "Stroop" color-naming task. *Perception and Psychophysics, 20,* 408–412.

Hart, J., Berndt, R. S., and Caramazza, A. (1985). Category-specific naming deficit following cerebral infarction. *Nature, 316,* 439–440.

Hartley, E. R., and Adams, R. G. (1974). Effect of noise on the Stroop test. *Journal of Experimental Psychology, 102*, 62–66.

Hatfield, F. M.; Howard, D.; Barber, J.; Jones, C.; and Morton, J. (1977). The facilitation of picture naming in aphasia: The lack of effect of context or realism. *Neuropsychologia, 15*, 717–727.

Hatta, T. (1981). Differential processing of Kanji and Kana stimuli in Japanese people. Some implications from Stroop tests. *Neuropsychologia, 19*, 87–93.

Hecaen, H., and de Ajuriaguerra, J. (1956). Agnosie visuelle pour les objets inanimes par lésion unilaterale gauche. *Revue Neurologique, 94*, 222–233.

Hecaen, H.; de Ajuriaguerra, J.; Magis, C.; and Angelergues, R. (1952). Le problème de l'agnosie des physionomies. *encephale, 41*, 322–355.

Hecaen, H.; Goldblum, M. C.; Masure, M. C.; and Ramier, A. M. (1974). Une nouvelle observation d'agnosie d'objet. Deficit de l'association ou de la categorisation, specifique de la modalité visuelle. *Neuropsychologia, 12*, 447–464.

Heider, E. R. (1971). "Focal" color areas and the development of color names. *Developmental Psychology, 4*, 447–455.

Heider, E. R., and Olivier, D. (1972). The structure of the color space in naming and memory for two languages. *Congitive Psychology, 3*, 337–354.

Heilman, K. M.; Tucker, D. M.; and Valenstein, E. (1976). A case of mixed transcortical aphasia with intact naming. *Brain, 99*, 415–426.

Helmholtz, H. L. F. von (1909/1962). *Treatise on Physiological Optics* Trans. J. P. C. Southall. New York: Dover.

Hendrick, C.; Wallace, G.; and Tappenbeck, J. (1968). Effect of cognitive set on color perception. *Journal of Personality and Social Psychology, 10*, 487–494.

Hendricks, I. M.; Holliday, I. E.; and Ruddock, K. H. (1981). A new class of visual defect. Spreading inhibition elicited by chromatic light. *Brain, 104*, 813–840.

Hepler, N. (1968). Color: A motion-contingent aftereffect. *Science, 162*, 376–377.

Hering, E. (1878/1964). *Outlines of a Theory of the Light Sense.* Trans. L. M. Hurvich and D. Jameson. Cambridge: Harvard University Press.

Herring, B., and Bryden, M. (1970). Memory color effects as a function of viewing time. *Canadian Journal of Psychology, 24*, 127–131.

Heuer, F.; Fischman, D.; and Reisberg, D. (1986). Why does vivid imagery hurt color memory? *Canadian Journal of Psychology, 40*, 161–175.

Heywood, C. A., and Cowey, A. (1987). On the role of cortical area V4 in the discrimination of hue and pattern in macaque monkeys. *Journal of Neuroscience, 7*, 2601–2617.

Heywood, C. A.; Shields, C.; and Cowey, A. (1988). The involvement of the temporal lobes in color discrimination. *Experimental Brain Research, 71*, 437–441.

Heywood, C. A.; Wilson, B.; and Cowey, A. (1987). A case study of cortical color "blindness" with relatively intact achromatic discrimination. *Journal of Neurology, Neurosurgery and Psychiatry, 50*, 22–29.

Hilbert, D. R. (1987). *Color and Color Perception.* Stanford, Calif.: Center for the Study of Language and Information.

Hilz, R., and Cavonius, C. R. (1970). Wavelength discrimination measured with square-wave gratings. *Journal of the Optical Society of America, 60*, 273–277.

Hilz, R. L.; Huppman, G.; and Cavonius, C. R. (1974). Influence of luminance contrast on hue discrimination. *Journal of the Optical Society of America, 64*, 763–766.

Hochberg, J. E. (1978) *Perception.* Englewood Cliffs, N.J.: Prentice Hall.

Hock, H. S., and Egeth, H. E. (1970). Verbal interference with encoding in a perceptual classification task. *Journal of Experimental Psychology, 83*, 299–303.

Holender, D. (1986). Semantic activation without conscious identification in dichotic listening, parafoveal vision, and visual masking: A survey and appraisal. *The Behavioral and Brain Sciences, 9,* 1–66.

Hoeffding, H. (1891). *Outlines of Psychology.* London and New York: Macmillan.

Holmes, C. B.; Fouty, H. E.; and Wurtz, P. J. (1985). Choice of Luscher's color violet in a psychiatric sample. *Perceptual and Motor Skills, 60,* 402.

Holmes, C. B.; Fouty, H. E.; Wurtz, P. J.; and Burdick, B. M. (1985). The relationship between color preference and psychiatric disorders. *Journal of Clinical Psychology, 41,* 746–749.

Holmes, G. (1918). Disturbances of vision by cerebral lesions. *British Journal of Ophthalmology, 2,* 353–384.

Holmes, G. (1950). Pure word blindness. *Folia Psychiatrica, Neurologica et Neurochirurgica Neerlandica, 53,* 279–288.

Homa, D.; Haver, B.; and Schwartz, T. (1976). Perceptibility of schematic face stimuli: Evidence for a perceptual Gestalt. *Memory and Cognition, 4,* 176–185.

Hotopf, W. H. N. (1966). The size constancy theory of visual illusions. *British Journal of Psychology, 57,* 307–318.

Horton, J. C., and Hubel, D. H. (1981). A regular patchy distribution of cytochrome-oxidase staining in primary visual cortex of the macaque moneky, *Nature, 292,* 762–764.

Houck, M. R., and Hoffman, J. E. (1986). Conjunction of color and form without attention: Evidence from an orientation-contingent color aftereffect. *Journal of Experimental Psychology: Human Perception and Performance, 12,* 186–199.

Huang, I., and Borter, S. J. (1987). The color isolation effect in free recall by adults with Down's syndrome. *American Journal of Mental Deficiency, 92,* 115–118.

Hubel, D. H., and Livingstone, M. S. (1987). Segregation of form, color, and stereopsis in primate area 18. *Journal of Neuroscience, 7,* 3378–3415.

Hubel, D. H., and Wiesel, T. N. (1965). Receptive fields and functional architecture in two non-striate visual areas (18 and 19) of the cat. *Journal of Neurophysiology, 28,* 229–289.

Huff, F. J.; Corkin, S.; and Growdon, J. H. (1986). Semantic impairment and anomia in Alzheimer's disease. *Brain and Language, 28,* 235–249.

Humphrey, N. K. (1972). Interest and pleasure: Two determinants of a monkey's visual preferences. *Perception, 1,* 395–416.

Humphreys, G. W., and Bruce, V. (1989). *Visual Cognition.* Hove: Lawrence Erlbaum Associates.

Humphreys, G. W., and Riddoch, M. J. (1984). Routes to object constancy: Implications from neurological impairments of object constancy. *Quarterly Journal of Experimental Psychology, 36A,* 385–415.

Humphreys, G. W., and Riddoch, M. J. (1987). The fractionation of visual agnosia. In: G. W. Humphreys and M. J. Riddoch (Eds.). *Visual Object Processing: A Cognitive Neuropsychological Approach.* London: Lawrence Erlbaum Associates.

Humphreys, G. W.; Riddoch, M. J.; and Quinlan, P. T. (1988). Cascade processes in picture identification. *Congitive Neuropsychology, 5,* 67–103.

Humphreys, G. W.; Quinlan, P. T.; and Riddoch, M. J. (1989). Grouping processes in visual search: Effects with single- and combined-feature targets. *Journal of Experimental Psychology: General, 118,* 258–279.

Hurvich, L. M. (1981). *Color Vision.* Sunderland, Mass.: Sinauer.

Huttenlocher, J., and Kubicek, L. F. (1983). The source of relatedness effects on naming latency. *Journal of Experimental Psychology: Learning, Memory and Cognition, 9,* 486–496.

Indow, T. (1988). Multidimensional studies of Munsell Color Solid. *Psychological Review*, 95, 456–470.

Ingling, C. R., and Martinez, E. (1983). The spatiochromatic signal of the R-G channel. In J. D. Mollon and L. T. Sharpe (Eds.). *Vision: Physiology and Psychophysics*, 433–444. New York: Academic Press.

Ingram, F., and Lieberman, L. R. (1985). Effects of expectancy on the performance of hand grip after viewing selected hues. *Perceptual and Motor Skills*, 46, 187–190.

Intons-Peterson, M., and Roskos-Ewoldsen, B. B. (1989). Sensory-perceptual quality of images. *Journal of Experimental Psychology: Learning, Memory and Cognition*, 15, 188–199.

Intraub, H., and Nicklos, S. (1985). Levels of processing and picture memory: The physical superiority effect. *Journal of Experimental Psychology: Learning, Memory and Cognition*, 11, 284–298.

Itten, J. (1961). *The Art of Color*. New York: Van Nostrand.

Ives, H. E. (1923). A chart of the flicker photometer. *Journal of the Optical Society of America*, 7, 363–365.

Jackendoff, R. (1987). *Consciousness and the Computational Mind*. Cambridge, Mass.: Bradford/MIT Press.

Jackendoff, R. (1988). Conceptual semantics. In: U. Eco, M. Santambrogio, and P. Violi (Eds.). *Meaning and Mental Representations*. Bloomington: Indiana University Press.

James, W. (1890). *Principles of Psychology, vol. 1*. New York: Holt.

Jameson, D., and Hurvich, L. M. (1955). Some quantitative aspects of an opponent-colors theory. 1. Chromatic responses and spectral saturation. *Journal of the Optical Society of America*, 45, 546–552.

Jameson, D., and Hurvich, L. M. (1989). Essay concerning color constancy. *Annual Review of Psychology*, 40, 1–22.

Javadnia, A., and Ruddock, K. H. (1988). Simultaneous processing of spatial and chromatic components of patterned stimuli by the human visual system. *Spatial Vision*, 3, 115–127.

Jeffreys, D. A. (1971). Cortical source locations of pattern-related evoked potentials recorded from the human scalp. *Nature*, 229, 502–504.

Jenkins, B., and Ross, J. (1977). McCollough effect depends upon perceived organization. *Perception*, 6, 399–400.

Johnston, A., and Venables, P. H. (1982). Specificity of attention in the Stroop test: An EP study. *Biological Psychology*, 15, 75–83.

Jolicoeur, P.; Gluck, M. A.; and Kosslyn, S. M. (1984). Pictures and names: Making the connection. *Cognitive Psychology*, 16, 243–275.

Jones, P. D., and Holding, D. H. (1975). Extremely long term persistence of the McCollough effect. *Journal of Experimental Psychology: Human Perception and Performance*, 1, 323–327.

Jordan, T. C., and Rabbitt, P. M. A. (1977). Response times to stimuli of increasing complexity as a function of ageing. *British Journal of Psychology*, 68, 189–201.

Judd, D. B. (1960). Appraisal of Land's work on two-primary color projections. *Journal of the Optical Society of America*, 50, 254–268.

Julesz, B. (1965). Texture and visual perception. *Scientific American*, 212, (Feb.) 38–48.

Kahneman, D., and Chajczyk, D. (1983). Tests of the automaticity of reading: Dilution of Stroop effects by color-irrelevant stimuli. *Journal of Experimental Psychology: Human Perception and Performance*, 9, 497–509.

Kahneman, D., and Henik, A. (1981). Perceptual organization and attention. In: M. Kubovy and J. R. Pomerantz (Eds.). *Perceptual Organization*. Hillsdale, N.J.: Erlbaum.

Kahneman, D.; Treisman, A. M.; and Burkell, J. (1983). The cost of visual filtering. *Journal of Experimental Psychology: Human Perception and Performance, 9,* 510–522.

Kaiser, P. K. (1984). Physiological response to color: A critical review. *Color Research and Application, 9,* 29–36.

Kaiser, P. K.; Herzberg, P. A.; and Boynton, R. M. (1971). Chromatic border distinctness and its relation to saturation. *Vision Research, 11,* 953–968.

Kanisza, G. (1979). *Organization in Vision: Essays on Gestalt Perception.* New York: Praeger.

Kaplan, E., and Shapley, R. M. (1986). The primate retina contains two types of ganglion cells, with high and low contrast sensitivity. *Proceedings of the National Academy of Sciences USA, 83,* 2755–2757.

Kappauf, W. E., and Yeatman, F. R. (1970). Visual on-off latencies and handedness. *Perception and Psychophysics, 8,* 46–50.

Katz, D. (1935). *The World of Colour.* London: Kegan Paul, Trench, Trubner & Co.

Katz, R. B. (1986). Phonological deficiencies in children with reading disability: Evidence from an object naming test. *Cognition, 22,* 225–257.

Kay, J., and Ellis, A. W. (1987). A cognitive neuropsychological case study of anomia: Implications for psychological models of word retreival. *Brain, 110,* 613–629.

Kay, P., and Kempton, W. (1984). What is the Sapir-Whorf hypothesis? *American Anthropologist, 86,* 65–79.

Kay, P., and McDaniel, C. (1978). The linguistic significance of the meanings of basic color terms. *Language, 54,* 610–646.

Keele, S. W. (1972). Attention demands of memory retrieval. *Journal of Experimental Psychology, 93,* 245–248.

Keele, S. W.; Cohen, A.; Ivry, R.; Liotti, M. and Yee, P. (1988). Tests of a temporal theory of attentional binding. *Journal of Experimental Psychology: Human Perception and Performance, 14,* 444–452.

Kelley, D. (1986). *The Evidence of the Senses.* Baton Rouge: Louisiana State University Press.

Kellogg, R. S.; Kennedy, L. S.; and Woodruff, R. R. (1984). Comparison of color versus black-and-white visual displays as indicated by bombing and landing performance in the 2535 TA-4J flight simulator. *US Air Force Technical Report,* 84–22, July.

Kelly, D. H. (1983). Spatiotemporal variation of chromatic and achromatic contrast thresholds. *Journal of the Optical Society of America, 73,* 742–750.

Kelly, D. H., and Van Norren, D. (1977). Time-based model of heterochromatic flicker. *Journal of the Optical Society of America, 67,* 1081–1091.

Kelter, S.; Groetzbach, H.; Freiheit, R.; Hoehle, B.; Wutzig, G.; and Diesch, E. (1984). Object identification: The mental representation of physical and conceptual attributes. *Memory and Cognition, 12,* 123–133.

Kertesz, A. (1979). Visual agnosia: The dual deficit of perception and recognition. *Cortex, 15,* 403–419.

Kinsbourne, M., and Warrington, E. K. (1964). Observations on colour agnosia. *Journal of Neurology, Neurosurgery and Psychiatry, 27,* 296–299.

Kirshner, H. S.; Webb, W. G.; and Kelly, M. P. (1984). The naming disorder of dementia. *Neuropsychologia, 22,* 23–30.

Klein, G. S. (1964). Semantic power measured through the interference of words with color naming. *American Journal of Psychology, 77,* 576–578.

Koffka, K. (1935). *Principles of Gestalt Psychology.* New York: Harcourt Brace.

Koffka, K., and Harrower M. R. (1931). Colour and organization. *Psychologische Forschung, 15,* 145–191; 193–273.

Kolers, P. A., and Brison, S. J. (1984). On pictures, words, and their mental representation. *Journal of Verbal Learning and Verbal Behavior, 23,* 105–111.

Kolers, P. A., and Green, M. (1984). Color logic of apparent motion. *Perception, 13*, 249–254.

Kolers, P. A., and von Grunau, M. (1976). Shape and color in apparent motion. *Vision Research, 16*, 329–335.

Kolers, P. A., and Pomerantz, J. R. (1971). Figural change in apparent motion. *Journal of Experimental Psychology, 87*, 99–108.

Konorski, J. (1967). *Integrative Activity of the Brain: An Interdisciplinary Approach.* Chicago: University of Chicago Press.

Kosslyn, S. M. (1981). The medium and the message in mental imagery. *Psychological Review, 88*, 46–66.

Kosslyn, S. M. (1983). *Image and Mind.* Cambridge,: Harvard University Press.

Krauskopf, J. (1957). Effect of retinal image motion on contrast thresholds for maintained vision. *Journal of the Optical Society of America, 47*, 740–744.

Krebs, M. J., and Wolf, J. D. (1979). Design principles for the use of color in displays. *Proceedings of the Society for Information Displays, 20*, 10–15.

Kreindler, A., and Ionasescu, V. (1961). A case of "pure" word blindness. *Journal of Neurology, Neurosurgery and Psychiatry, 24*, 275–280.

Kremin, H. (1986). Spared naming without comprehension. *Journal of Neurolinguistics, 2*, 131–150.

Kroll, J. F., and Potter, M. C. (1984). Recognizing words, pictures, and concepts: A comparison of lexical, object, and reality decisions. *Journal of Verbal Learning and Verbal Behavior, 23*, 39–66.

Kroll, N. E.; Parks, T.; Parkinson, S. R.; Bieber, S. L.; and Johnson, A. L. (1970). Short-term memory while shadowing: Recall of visually and aurally presented letters. *Journal of Experimental Psychology, 85*, 220–224.

Kroll, N. E., and Ramskov, C. B. (1984). Visual memory as measured by classification and comparison tasks. *Journal of Experimental Psychology: Learning, Memory, and Cognition, 10*, 395–420.

Kruger, J., and Gouras, P. (1980). Spectral sensitivity of cells and its dependence on slit length in the monkey visual cortex. *Journal of Neurophysiology, 43*, 1055–1069.

Kuffler, S. (1953). Discharge patterns and functional organization of mammalian retina. *Journal of Neurophysiology, 16*, 37–68.

Kunishima, M., and Yanase, T. (1985). Visual effects of wall colors in living rooms. *Ergonomics, 28*, 869–882.

Kuschel, R., and Monberg, T. (1974. "We don't talk much about colour here": The semantics of color naming on Bellona Island, *Man, 9*, 213–242.

Lachman, R. (1973). Uncertainty effects on time to access the internal lexicon. *Journal of Experimental Psychology, 99*, 199–208.

Land, E. H. (1977). The retinex theory of color vision. *Scientific American, 237*, December, 108–128

Land, E. H.; Hubel, D. H.; Livingstone, M. S.; Perry, S. H.; and Burns, M. M. (1983). Color-generating interactions across the corpus callosum. *Nature, 303*, 616–618.

Landis, T.; Assal, G.; and Perret, E. (1979). Opposite cerebral hemispheric superiorities for visual associative processing of emotional facial expressions and objects. *Nature, 278*, 739–740.

Landis, T.; Cummings, J. L.; Christen, L.; Bogen, J. E.; and Imhof, H-G. (1986). Are unilateral right posterior cerebral lesions sufficient to cause prosopagnosia? Clinical and radiological findings in six additional findings. *Cortex, 22*, 243–252.

Lange, J. (1936, 1989). Agnosia and apraxia. In J. W. Brown (Ed.). *Agnosia and Apraxia: Selected Papers of Liepmann, Lange, and Poetzl.* New York: Institute for Research in Behavioral Neuroscience.

Lantz, D., and Stefflre, V. (1964). Language and cognition revisited. *Journal of Abnormal and Social Psychology, 69*, 472–481.

Larrabee, G. J.; Levin, H. S.; Huff, F. J.; Kay, M. C.; and Guinto, F. C. (1985). Visual agnosia contrasted with visual disconnection. *Neuropsychologia, 23*, 1–12.

Lehmann, A. (1904). Die irradiation als Ehrsache geometrische-optische. *Tauschungen Pfluegers Arch., 103*, 84–106.

Levine, D. N. (1978). Prosopagnosia and visual object agnosia: A behavioral study. *Brain and Language, 5*, 341–365.

Levine, D. N.; Warach, J.; and Farah M. (1985). Two visual systems in visual imagery. *Neurology, 35*, 1010–1018.

Levy, J., and Trevarthen, C. (1976). Metacontrol of hemispheric function in human split brain patients. *Journal of Experimental Psychology: Human Perception and Performance, 2*, 299–312.

Lewandowsky, M. (1908a). Abspaltung des Farbensinnes durch Herderkramgung des Gehirns, 402–407. In G. A. M. van Weyenburg (Ed.). *Compte Rendu des Travaux du 1er Congrès International de Psychiatrie, de Neurologie, de Psychologie et de l'Assistance des aliénés.* Amsterdam: J. H. de Bussy.

Lewandowsky, M. (1908b). Ueber Abspaltung des Farbensinnes. *Monatsschrift fuer Psychiatrie und Neurologie, 23*, 488–510.

Lewinski, R. J. (1938). An investigation of individual responses to chromatic illumination. *Journal of Psychology, 6*, 155–160.

Lhermitte, F., and Beauvois, M-F., (1973). A visual-speech disconnection syndrome: Report of a case with optic-aphasia, agnosic alexia, and color agnosia. *Brain, 96*, 695–714.

Lhermitte, F.; Chain, F.; Aron, D.; Leblanc. M.; and Souty, O. (1969). Troubles de la vision dans les lésions du cerveau. *Revue Neurologique, 121*, 1–29.

Lhermitte, F.; Chedru, F.; and Chain, T. (1973). À propos d'un cas d'agnosie visuelle. *Revue Neurologique, 128*, 301–322.

Lhermitte, F., and Pillon, B. (1975). La prosopagnosie. Rôle de l'hemisphere droit dans la perception visuelle. *Revue Neurologique, 131*, 791–812.

Lissauer, H. (1890). Ein Fall von Seelenblindheit nebst einem Beitrage zur Theorie derselben. *Archiv fuer Psychiatrie und Nervenkrankheiten, 21*, 222–270.

Livingstone, M. S. (1988). Art, illusion, and the visual space. *Scientific American*, January, 78–85.

Livingstone, M. S., and Hubel, D. H. (1984). Anatomy and physiology of a color system in the primate visual cortex. *Journal of Neuroscience, 4*, 2830–2835.

Livingstone, M. S., and Hubel, D. H. (1987a). Psychophysical evidence for separate channels for the perception of form, color, movement, and depth. *Journal of Neuroscience, 7*, 3416–3468.

Livingstone, M. S., and Hubel, D. H. (1987b). Connections between layer 4B of area 17 and the thick cytochrome oxide stripes of area 18 in the squirrel monkey. *Journal of Neuroscience, 7*, 3371–3377.

Lockhead, G. R. (1972). Processing dimensional stimuli: A note. *Psychological Review, 79*, 410–419.

Loftus, E. F. (1977). Shifting human color memory. *Memory and Cognition, 5*, 696–699.

Loftus, G. R., and Ginn, G. (1984). Perceptual and conceptual masking of pictures. *Journal of Experimental Psychology: Learning, Memory and Cognition, 10*, 435–441.

Loftus, G. R.; Hanna, A. M.; and Lester, L. (1988). Conceptual masking: How one picture captures attention from another picture. *Cognitive Psychology, 20*, 237–282.

Logan, G. D. (1980). Attention and automaticity in Stroop and priming tasks: Theory and data. *Cognitive Psychology, 12*, 523–553.

Logie, R. H. (1986). Visuo-spatial processing in working memory. *Quarterly Journal of Experimental Psychology, 38A,* 349–368.

Lu, C., and Fender, D. H. (1972). The interaction of color and luminance in stereoscopic vision. *Investigative Ophthalmology, 11,* 482–490.

Lueck, C. J.; Zeki, S.; Friston, K. J.; Deiber, M-P.; Cope, P.; Cunningham, V. J.; Lammertsma, A. A.; Kennard, C.; and Frackowiak, R. S. J. (1989). The color centre in the cerebral cortex of man. *Nature, 340,* 386–389.

Lucy, J. A., and Shweder, R. A. (1979). Whorf and his critics: Linguistic and nonlinguistic influences on color memory. *American Anthropologist, 81,* 581–615.

Lucy, J. A., and Shweder, R. A. (1988). The effect of incidental conversation on memory for focal colors. *American Anthropologist, 90,* 923–931.

Luder, C. B., and Barber, P. J. (1984). Redundant color coding on airborne CRT displays. *Human Factors, 26,* 19–32.

Lupker, S. J. (1988). Picture naming: An investigation of the nature of categorical priming. *Journal of Experimental Psychology: Learning, Memory and Cognition, 14,* 444–455.

Lupker, S. J., and Katz, A. N. (1981). Input, decision, and response factors in picture-word interference. *Journal of Experimental Psychology: Human Learning and Memory, 7,* 269–282.

Luria, A. R. (1976). *Cognitive Development: Its Cultural and Social Foundations.* Cambridge: Harvard University Press.

MacDonald, W. A., and Cole, B. L. (1988). Evaluating the role of color in a flight information cockpit display. *Ergonomics, 31,* 13–37.

Mack, J. L., and Boller, F. (1977). Associative visual agnosia and its related deficits: The role of the minor hemisphere in assigning meaning to visual perceptions. *Neuropsychologia, 15,* 345–351.

Mackay, D. M. (1957). Moving visual images produced by regular stationary patterns. *Nature, 180,* 849–850.

Mackay, G., and Dunlop, J. C. (1899). The cerebral lesions in a case of complete acquired color-blindness. *Scottish Medical Surgery Journal, 5,* 503–517.

MacKinnon, D. P.; Geiselman, E.; and Woodward, J. A. (1985). The effects of effort on Stroop interference. *Acta Psychologica, 58,* 225–235.

MacLaury, R. E. (1987). Color-category evolution and Shuswap yellow-with-green. *American Anthropologist, 89,* 107–124.

Macnamara, J. (1972). Cognitive basis of language learning in infants. *Psychological Review, 79,* 1–13.

MacRae, D., and Trolle, E. (1956). Defect of function in visual agnosia. *Brain, 79,* 94–110.

Malcolm, N. (1963). *Knowledge and Certainty.* Ithaca, N.Y.: Cornell University Press.

Maloney, L. (1986). Evaluation of linear models of surface spectral reflectance with small number of parameters. *Journal of the Optical Society of America, 3A,* 1673–1683.

Malpeli, J. G.; Schiller, P. H.; and Colby, C. L. (1981). Response properties of single cells in monkey striate cortex during reversible inactivation of individual lateral geniculate laminae. *Journal of Neurophysiology, 46,* 1102–1119.

Marc, R. E., and Sperling, H. G. (1977). Chromatic organization of primate cones. *Science, 196,* 454–456.

Marcel, A. J. (1983). Conscious and unconscious perception: An approach to the relation between phenomenal experience and perceptual process. *Cognitive Psychology, 15,* 197–237.

Mariani, A. P. (1984). Bipolar cells in monkey retina selective for the cones likely to be blue-sensitive. *Nature, 308,* 184–186.

Marin, O. S. M.; Glenn, C. G.; and Rafal, R. D. (1983). Visual problem solving in the absence of lexical semantics: Evidence from dementia. *Brain and Cognition, 2,* 285–311.

Marks, L. E. (1975). On colored-hearing synesthesia: Cross-model translations of sensory dimensions. *Psychological Bulletin, 82,* 303–331.

Marr, D. (1982). *Vision: A Computational Investigation into the Human Representation and Processing of Visual Information.* San Francisco: W. H. Freeman & Co.

Marshall, J. C., and Halligan, P. W. (1988). Blindsight and insight in visuo-spatial neglect. *Nature, 336,* 766–767.

Marshall, J. C., and Newcombe, F. (1973). Patterns of paralexia: A psycholinguistic approach. *Journal of Psycholinguistic Research, 2,* 175–199.

Martin, A. (1987). Representation of semantic and spatial knowledge in Alzheimer's patients: Implications for models of preserved learning in amnesia. *Journal of Clinical and Experimental Neuropsychology, 9,* 191–224.

Martin, K. A. C. (1988). The lateral geniculate strikes back. *Trends in the Neurosciences, 11,* 192–194.

Martin, M. (1978). Speech recoding in silent reading. *Memory and Cognition, 6,* 108–114.

Martindale, C., and Moore, K. (1988). Priming, prototypicality, and preference. *Journal of Experimental Psychology: Human Perception and Performance, 14,* 661–670.

Matthews, M. L. (1987). The influence of color on CRT reading performance and subjective comfort under operational conditions. *Applied Ergonomics, 18,* 323–328.

Maudarbocus, A. Y., and Ruddock, K. H. (1973). The influence of wavelength on visual adaptation to spatially periodic stimuli. *Vision Research, 13,* 993–998.

Maurer, D., and Adams, R. J. (1987). Emergence of the ability to discriminate a blue from a gray at one month of age. *Journal of Experimental Child Psychology, 44,* 147–156.

Mayhew, J. E. W., and Anstis, S. M. (1972). Movement aftereffects contingent on color, intensity, and pattern. *Perception and Psychophysics, 12,* 77–85.

McCann, J.; McKee, S., and Taylor, T. (1976). Quantitative studies in retinex theory. *Vision Research, 16,* 445–458.

McCarthy, R., and Warrington, E. K. (1986). Visual associative agnosia: A clinico-anatomical study of a single case. *Journal of Neurology, Neurosurgery and Psychiatry, 49,* 1233–1240.

McClelland, J. L. (1979). On the time relations of mental processes: An examination of systems of processes in cascade. *Psychological Review, 86,* 287–330.

McClelland, J. L., and Rumelhart, D. E. (1981). An interactive activation model of context effects in letter perception: Part 1. An account of basic findings. *Psychological Review, 88,* 375–407.

McClelland, J. L., and Rumelhart, D. E. (1985). Distributed memory and the representation of general and specific information. *Journal of Experimental Psychology: General, 114,* 159–188.

McCollough, C. (1965). Color adaptation of edge-detectors in the human visual system. *Science, 149,* 1115–1116.

McKenna, P., and Warrington, E. K. (1978). Category-specific naming preservation: A single case study. *Journal of Neurology, Neurosurgery and Psychiatry, 41,* 571–574.

McLean, J. P.; Broadbent, D. W.; and Broadbent, M. H. (1982). Combining attributes in rapid serial visual presentation tasks. *Quarterly Journal of Experimental Psychology, 35A,* 171–186.

McLean, M. V. (1965). Brightness contrast, color contrast, and legibility. *Human Factors, 7,* 521–526.

McLeod, P.; Driver, J.; and Crisp, J. (1988). Visual search for a conjunction of movement and form in parallel. *Nature, 332,* 154–155.

McManus, I. C.; Jones, A. L.; and Cottrell, J. (1981). The aesthetics of colour. *Perception*, 10, 651–666.

Meador, D.E. (1984). Effects of color on visual discrimination of geometric symbols by severely and profoundly mentally retarded individuals. *American Journal of Mental Deficiency*, 89, 275–286.

Meadows, J. C. (1974). Disturbed perception of colors associated with localized cerebral lesions. *Brain*, 97, 615–632.

Mehta, Z.; Newcombe, F.; and Ratcliff, G. (1988). Patterns of hemispheric asymmetry set against clinical evidence. In J. Crawford and D. Parker (Eds.). *Developments in Clinical and Experimental Neuropsychology*. New York: Plenum Press.

Melara, R. D. (1989). Dimensional interaction between color and pitch. *Journal of Experimental Psychology: Human Perception and Performance*, 15, 69–79

Menaud-Buteau, C., and Cavanagh P. (1984). Localisation de l'interference forme/couleur au niveau perceptual dans une tache de type Stroop avec des stimuli-dessins. *Canadian Journal of Psychology*, 38, 421–439.

Merrill, M. K., and Kewman, D. G. (1986). Training of colour and form identification in cortical blindness: A case study. *Archives of Physical Medicine and Rehabilitation*, 67, 479–483.

Mervis, C. B.; Catlin, J.; and Rosch, E. (1975). Development of the structure of color categories. *Developmental Psychology*, 11, 54–60.

Metelli, F. (1974). The perception of transparency. *Scientific American*, 230, April, 90–98.

Meyer, G. E., and Dougherty, T. (1987). Effects of flicker-induced depth on chromatic subjective contours. *Journal of Experimental Psychology: Human Perception and Performance*, 13, 353–360.

Meyer, G. E., and Phillips, D. (1980). Faces, vases, subjective contours, and the McCollough effect. *Perception*, 9, 603–606.

Mial, R. P.; Smith, P. C.; Doherty, M. E.; and Smith, D. W. (1974). The effect of memory color on form identification. *Perception and Psychophysics*, 16, 1–3.

Michael, C. R. (1988). Retinal afferent arborization patterns, dendritic field orientations, and the segregation of function in the lateral geniculate nucleus of the monkey. *Proceedings of the National Academy of Science, USA*, 85, 4914–4918.

Michel, F.; Schott, B.; Boucher, M.; and Kopp, N. (1979). Alexie sans agraphie chez un malade ayant un hemisphere déafferente. *Revue Neurologique*, 135, 347–364.

Milewski, A. E.; Iaccino, J.; and Smith, D. (1980). Checkerboard-specific color afterefects: A failure to find effects of perceptual organisation. *Perception and Psychophysics*, 28, 329–336.

Miller, G. A., and Johnson-Laird, P. N. (1976). *Language and Perception*. Cambridge: Harvard University Press.

Milner, A. D., and Heywood, C. A. (1989). A disorder of lightness discrimination in a case of visual form agnosia. *Cortex*, 25, 489–494.

Milner, B. (1958). Psychological defects produced by temporal lobe excisions. *Proceedings of Association for Research in Nervous and Mental Disease*, 36, 244–257.

Mishkin, M. (1978). Memory in monkeys severely impaired by combined but not by separate removal of the amygdala and hippocampus. *Nature*, 273, 297–298.

Mishkin, M.; Ungerleider, L. G.; and Macko, K. A. (1983). Object vision and spatial vision: Two cortical pathways. *Trends in the Neurosciences*, 6, 414–417.

Mitchell, D. B., and Brown, A. S. (1988). Persistent repetition priming in picture naming and its dissociation from recognition memory. *Journal of Experimental Psychology: Learning, Memory and Cognition*, 14, 213–222.

Modreski, R. A., and Goss, A. E. (1969). Young children's initial and changed names for form-color stimuli. *Journal of Experimental Child Psychology*, 8, 402–409.

Mohr, J. P.; Leicester, J.; Stoddard, L. T.; and Sidman, M. (1971). Right hemianopsia with memory and color deficits in circumscribed left posterior cerebral artery territory infarction. *Neurology, 21*, 1104–1113.

Mollon, J. D. (1982). Color vision. *Annual Review of Psychology, 33*, 41–85.

Mollon, J. D. (1986). Understanding colour vision. *Nature, 321*, 12–13.

Mollon, J. D. (1987). John Elliot, MD (1747–1787). *Nature, 329*, 19–20.

Mollon, J. D. (1988). Review of Goethe contra Newton: Polemics and the project for a new science by D. L. Sepper. *Nature, 336*, 433.

Mollon, J. D. (1990). The club-sandwich mystery. *Nature, 343*, 16–17.

Mollon, J. D., and Cavonius, C. R. (1986). The dicriminability of colors on C.R.T. displays. *Journal of the Institution of Electronic and Radio Engineers, 56*, 107–110.

Mollon, J. D.; Newcombe, F.; Polden, P. G.; and Ratcliff, G. (1980). On the presence of three cone mechanisms in a case of total achromatopsia, 130–135. In: G. Verriest, (Ed.). *Colour Vision Deficiencies.* Bristol: V. Hilger.

Moreland, J. D. (1980). Spectral sensitivity measured by motion photometry. 299–305. In: G. Verriest, (Ed.). *Colour Vision Deficiencies.* Bristol: V. Hilger.

Morgan, B. B., Jr., and Alluisi. E. A. (1967). Effects of discriminability and irrelevant information on absolute judgements. *Perception and Psychophysics, 2*, 54–58.

Morgan, M. J., and Aiba, T. S. (1985). Positional acuity with chromatic stimuli. *Vision Research, 25*, 689–695.

Morton, J. (1979). Word recognition. In J. Morton and J. C. Marshall (Eds.). *Psycholinguistics* (Series 2). London: Elek.

Morton, J. (1985). Naming. In S. Newman and R. Epstein (Eds.). *Current Perspectives in Dysphasia.* Edinburgh: Churchill Livingstone.

Morton, J., and Chambers, S. M. (1973). Selective attention to words and colors. *Quarterly Journal of Experimental Psychology, 25*, 387–397.

Mullen, K. T. (1985). The contrast sensitivity of human color vision to red-green and blue-yellow chromatic gratings. *Journal of Physiology, 359*, 381–400.

Mullen, K. T., and Baker, C. L. (1985). A motion aftereffect from an isoluminant stimulus. *Vision Research, 25*, 685–688.

Mullen, K. T., and Kulikowski, J. J. (1990). Wavelength discrimination at detection threshold. *Journal of the Optical Society of America, 7A*, 733–742.

Mullen, K. T., and Plant, G. T. (1986). Color and luminance vision in human optic neuritis. *Brain, 109*, 1–13.

Muller, H. J., and Findlay, J. M. (1987). Sensitivity and criterion effects in the spatial cuing of visual attention. *Perception and Psychophysics, 42*, 383–399.

Munsell, A. H. (1905). *A Color Notation.* Baltimore, Md.: Munsell Color Co.

Murch, G. M., and Hirsch, J. (1972). The McCollough effect created by complimentary afterimages. *American Journal of Psychology, 85*, 241–247.

Murphy, G. L., and Smith, E. E. (1982). Basic-level superiority in picture categorization. *Journal of Verbal Learning and Verbal Behavior, 21*, 1–20.

Murray, E. A., and Mishkin, M. (1985). Amygdalectomy impairs crossmodal association in monkeys. *Science, 228*, 604–606.

Nagel, W. A. (1906). Observations on the color-sense of a child. *Journal of Comparative Neurology and Psychology, 16*, 217–230.

Naish, P. L. N. (1985). The locus of the Stroop effect: One site masquerading as two? *British Journal of Experimental Psychology, 76*, 303–310.

Nakayama, K., and Silverman, G. H. (1986). Serial and parallel processing of visual feature conjunctions. *Nature, 320*, 264–265.

Narborough-Hall, C. S. (1985). Recommendations for applying color coding to air traffic control displays. *Displays: Technology and Application, 6*, 131–137.

Nathans, J.; Piantanida, T. P.; Eddy, R. L.; Shows, T. B.; and Hogness, D. S. (1986). Molecular genetics of inherited variation in human color vision. *Science, 232*, 203–210.

Nathans, J.; Thomas, D.; and Hogness, D. S. (1986). Molecular genetics of inherited variation in human color vision: Genes encoding blue, green, and red pigments. *Science, 232*, 193–202

Neisser, U. (1967). *Cognitive Psychology*. New York: Appleton Century Crofts.

Neisser, U. (1987). From direct perception to conceptual structures. In U. Neisser (Ed.) *Concepts and Conceptual Development*. Cambridge: Cambridge University Press.

Nelson, D. L.; Reed, V. S., and Walling, J. R. (1976). Pictorial superiority effect. *Journal of Experimental Psychology: Human Learning and Memory, 2*, 523–528.

Nelson, T. O.; Reed, V. S.; and McEvoy, C. L. (1977). Learning to order pictures and words: A model of sensory and semantic encoding. *Journal of Experimental Psychology: Human Learning and Memory, 3*, 485–497.

Neri, D. F.; Luria, S. M.; and Kobus, D. A. (1986). The detection of various color combinations under different chromatic ambient illuminations. *Aviation, Space and Environmental Medicine, 57*, 555–560.

Netley, C. (1974). Color aphasia: A case report. *Cortex, 10*, 388–394.

Neumann, K. M., and D'Agostino, P. R. (1981). Specificity of mental color codes. *American Journal of Psychology, 94*, 451–459.

Newcombe, F., and Marshall, J. C. (1980). Transcoding and lexical stabilization in deep dyslexia. In M. Coltheart, K. E. Patterson, and J. C. Marshall (Eds.). *Deep Dyslexia*. London: Routledge.

Newcombe, F., and Ratcliff, G. (1974). Agnosia: A disorder of object recognition. In: F. Michel and B. Schott (Eds.). *Les syndromes de disconnexion calleuse chez l'homme*. Lyon: Colloque International de Lyon.

Newcombe, F., and Russell, W. R. (1969). Dissociated visual perceptual and spatial deficits in focal lesions of the right hemisphere. *Journal of Neurology, Neurosurgery and Psychiatry, 32*, 73–81.

Newhall, S. M.; Burnham, R. W., and Clark, J. R. (1957). Comparison of successive with simultaneous color matching. *Journal of the Optical Society of America, 47*, 43–56.

Nielson, J. M. (1946). *Agnosia, Apraxia, Aphasia: Their Value in Cerebral Localization*. New York: Hoeber.

Nilsson, T. H., and Nelson, T. M. (1981). Delayed monochromatic hue matches indicate characteristics of visual memory. *Journal of Experimental Psychology: Human Perception and Performance, 7*, 151–156.

Noble, M., and Sanders A. F. (1980). Searching for traffic signals while engaged in compensatory tracking. *Human Factors, 22*, 89–102.

Norman, D. A. (1968). Toward a theory of memory and attention. *Psychological Review, 75*, 522–536.

O'Connell, B. J.; Harper, R. S.; and McAndrew, F. T. (1985). Grip strength as a function of exposure to red or green visual stimulation. Perceptual stimulation. *Perceptual and Motor Skills, 61*, 1157–1158.

Ogden, J. A. (1985). Autotopagnosia: Occurrence in a patient without nominal aphasia and with an intact ability to point to parts of animals and objects. *Brain, 108*, 1009–1022.

Oldfield, R. C., and Wingfield, A. (1965). Response latencies in naming objects. *Quarterly Journal of Experimental Psychology, 17*, 273–281.

Osgood, C. E. (1960). The cross-cultural generality of visual-verbal synaesthetic tendencies. *Behavioral Science, 5*, 146–169.

198   References

Ostergaard, A. L., and Davidoff, J. B. (1985). Some effects of color on naming and recognition of objects. *Journal of Experimental Psychology: Learning, Memory and Cognition, 11,* 579–587.

Overmyer, S. P., and Simon, J. R. (1985). The effect of irrelevant cues on "same-different" judgments in a sequential information processing task. *Acta Psychologica, 58,* 237–249.

Oxbury, J. M.; Oxbury, S. M.; and Humphrey, N. K. (1969). Varieties of color anomia. *Brain, 92,* 847–860.

Oyama, T. (1962). The effect of hue and brightness on the size-illusion of concentric circles. *American Journal of Psychology, 75,* 41–55.

Paivio, A. (1971). *Imagery and Verbal Processes.* London: Holt, Rinehart & Winston.

Paivio, A. (1975). Perceptual comparisons through the mind's eye. *Memory and Cognition, 3,* 635–647.

Pallis, C. A. (1955). Impaired identification of faces and places with agnosia for colors. *Journal of Neurology, Neurosurgery and Psychiatry, 18,* 212–224.

Palmer, G. (1777). *Theory of Light.* London: Leacroft.

Palmer, S. E., Rosch, E., and Chase, P. (1981). Canonical perspective and the perception of objects. In J. Long and A. D. Baddeley (Eds.). *Attention and Performance.* IX. Hillsdale, N.J.: Lawrence Erlbaum Associates.

Pantle, A., and Sekuler, R. W. (1968). Size detecting mechanisms in human vision. *Science, 162,* 1146–1148.

Park, D. C., and Mason, D. A. (1982). Is there evidence for automatic processing of spatial and color attributes present in pictures and words? *Memory and Cognition, 10,* 76–81.

Pashler, H. (1987). Detecting conjunctions of color and form: Re-assessing the serial search hypothesis. *Perception and Psychophysics, 41,* 191–201.

Pearlman, A. L.; Birch, J.; and Meadows, J. C. (1979). Cerebral color blindness: An acquired defect in hue discrimination. *Annals of Neurology, 5,* 253–261.

Pease, P. L. (1978). On color Mach bands. *Vision Research, 18,* 751–755.

Pellegrino, J. W.; Rosinski, R. R.; Chiesi, H. L.; and Siegel, A. (1977). Picture-word differences in decision latency: An analysis of single and dual memory models. *Memory and Cognition, 5,* 383–396.

Pena-Casanova, J.; Roig-Rovira, T.; Bermudez, A.; and Tolosa-Sarro, E. (1985). Optic aphasia, optic apraxia, and loss of dreaming. *Brain and Language, 26,* 63–71.

Pennal, B. E. (1977). Human cerebral asymmetry in color discrimination. *Neuropsychologia, 15,* 563–568.

Pentland, A. (1986). Perceptual organization and the representation of natural form. *Artificial Intelligence, 28,* 293–331.

Perenin, M. T.; Ruel, J.; and Hecaen. H. (1980). Residual visual capacities in a case of cortical blindness. *Cortex, 16,* 605–612.

Perlmutter, M. (1980) A developmental study of semantic elaboration and interpretation in recognition memory. *Journal of Experimental Child Psychology, 29,* 413–327.

Perry, V. H.; Oehler, R.; and Cowey, A. (1984). Retinal ganglion cells that project to the dorsal lateral geniculate nucleus in the macaque monkey. *Neuroscience, 12,* 1101–1123.

Peterhans, E., and Von der Heydt, R. (1989). Mechanisms of contour perception in monkey visual cortex. 11. Contours bridging gaps. *Journal of Neuroscience, 9,* 1749–1763.

Pfendler, C., and Widdel, H. (1986). Vigilance performance when using color on electronic displays. *Perceptual and Motor Skills, 63,* 939–944.

Pfister, M. (1951). *Colour Pyramid Test (Der Farbpyramiden-Test).* Bern: Verlag Hans Huber.

Philipsen, G. (1990). Half valid color highlighting and visual search in menu options. Paper presented at The Second International Conference on Visual Search, Durham, U.K., September.

Phillips, W. A. (1974). On the distinction between sensory storage and short term visual memory. *Perception and Psychophysics, 16,* 283–290.

Piaget, J. (1926). *The Language and Thought of the Child.* New York: Harcourt, Brace & World.

Pickford, R. W. (1972). *Psychology and Visual Aesthetics.* London: Hutchinson.

Pieron, H. (1931) La sensation chromatique. Données sur la latence propre et l'établissement des sensations de couleur. *Annee Psychologique, 32,* 1–29.

Piggins, D., and Nichols, R. D. (1982). The pink room effect: Tranquilization or methodological transgression. *Atti della Fondazione Giorgio Ronchi, 37,* 281–286.

Pillon, B.; Signoret, J. L.; and Lhermitte, F. (1981). Agnosie visuelle associative. Role de l'hemisphere gauche dans la perception visuelle. *Revue Neurologique, 137,* 831–842.

Pinker, S. (1985). Visual cognition: An introduction. In: S. Pinker (Ed.). *Visual Cognition.* Cambridge: MIT Press.

Poeck, K. (1984). Neuropsychological demonstration of splenial interhemispheric disconnection in a case of "optic anomia." *Neuropsychologia, 22,* 707–713.

Poetzl, O. (1928). *Die optisch-agnostischen Storungen.* Liepzig-Vienna: F. Deuticke.

Pohl, W. (1973). Dissociation of spatial discrimination deficits following frontal and parietal lesions in monkeys. *Journal of Comparative and Physiological Psychology, 82,* 227–239.

Pokorny, J., and Smith, V. C. (1986). Colorimetry and color discrimination. In K. R. Boff, L. Kaufman, and J. P. Thomas (Eds.) *Handbook of Perception and Human Performance.* New York: Wiley.

Pokorny, J.; Smith, V. C.; and Verriest, G. (1979). Congenital color defects. 183–241. In J. Pokorny, V. C. Smith, G. Verriest, and A. J. L. G. Pinckers (Eds.). *Congenital and Acquired Colour Vision Defects.* New York: Grune & Stratton.

Poppel, E. (1986). Long-range color generating interactions across the retina. *Nature, 320,* 523–525.

Poppel, E.; Held, R.; and Frost, D. (1973). Residual visual function after brain wounds involving the central visual pathways in man. *Nature, 243,* 295–296.

Poppelreuter, W. (1923). Zur Psychologie und Pathologie der optischen Wohr nehmung. *Zeitschrift ges. Neurol. Psychiat., 83,* 26–152.

Posner, M. I. (1980). Orienting of attention. *Quarterly Journal of Experimental Psychology, 32,* 3–25.

Posner, M. I., and Keele, S. W. (1967). Decay of visual information from a single letter. *Science, 158,* 137–139.

Posner, M. I., and Rothbart, M. K. (1989). *The evolution and development of the brain's attention system.* Paper presented at the Experimental Psychology Society, Cambridge, U.K. July.

Posner, M. I., and Snyder, C. R. R. (1975). Attention and cogniyive control. 55–58. In R. L. Solso (Ed.). *Information Processing and Cognition: The Loyola Symposium.* Hillsdale, N.J.: Lawrence Erlbaum Associates.

Posner, M. I.; Snyder, C. R. R.; and Davidson, B. J. (1980). Attention and the detection of signals. *Journal of Experimental Psychology: General, 109,* 160–174.

Posner, M. I.; Walker, J. A.; Friedrich, F. J.; and Rafal, R. D. (1984). Effects of parietal lobe injury on covert orienting of visual attention. *Journal of Neuroscience, 4,* 1863–1874.

Potter, M. C. (1976). Short-term conceptual memory for pictures. *Journal of Experimental Psychology: Human Learning and Memory, 2,* 109–122.

Potter, M. C., and Faulconer, B. A. (1975). Time to understand pictures and words. *Nature, 253,* 437–438.

Poulton, E. C., and Edwards, R. S. (1977). Perceptual load in searching for sloping colored lines camouflaged by colored backgrounds: A separate-groups investigation. *Journal of Experimental Psychology: Human Perception and Performance, 5,* 136–150.

Prazdny, K. (1985). On the nature of inducing forms generating perceptions of illusory contours. *Perception and Psychophysics, 37,* 237–242.

Previc, F. H., and Harter, M. F. (1982). Electrophysiological and behavioral indicants of selective attention to multifeature gratings. *Perception and Psychophysics, 32,* 465–472.

Price, C. J., and Humphreys, G. W. (1989). The effects of surface detail on object categorization and naming. *Quarterly Journal of Experimental Psychology, 41A,* 797–827.

Price, H. H. (1933). *Perception.* New York: McBride.

Prinzmetal, W., and Keysar, B. (1989). Functional theory of illusory conjunctions and neon colors. *Journal of Experimental Psychology: General, 118,* 165–190.

Prinzmetal, W., and Millis-Wright, M. (1984). Cognitive and linguistic factors affect visual feature integration. *Cognitive Psychology, 16,* 305–340.

Prinzmetal, W.; Presti, D. E.; and Posner, M. I. (1986). Does attention affect visual feature integration? *Cognitive Psychology, 16,* 305–340.

Pritchatt, D. (1968). An investigation into some of the underlying associative verbal processes of the Stroop colour effect. *Quarterly Journal of Experimental Psychology, 20,* 351–359.

Pylyshyn, Z. (1973). What the mind's eye tells the mind's brain: A critique of mental imagery. *Psychological Bulletin, 80,* 1–24.

Quinlan, P., and Humphreys, G. W. (1987). Visual search for targets defined by combinations of color, shape, and size: An examination of the task constraints on feature and conjunction searches. *Perception and Psychophysics, 41,* 55–72.

Quinn, P. C.; Rosano, J. L.; and Wooten, B. R. (1988). Evidence that brown is not an elemental color. *Perception and Psychophysics, 43,* 156–164.

Ramachandran, V. S. (1987). Interactions between color and motion in human vision, *Nature, 328,* 645–647.

Ramachandran, V. S., and Anstis, S. M. (1983) Perceptual organization in moving patterns. *Nature, 304,* 529–531.

Ramachandran, V. S., and Anstis, S. M. (1986). The perception of apparent motion. *Scientific American, 254,* June, 102–109.

Ramachandran, V. S., and Cavanagh, P. (1985). Subjective contours capture stereopsis. *Nature, 317,* 527–530.

Ramachandran, V. S., and Gregory, R. L. (1978) Does color provide an input to human motion perception? *Nature, 275,* 55–56.

Rapp, B. C., and Caramazza, A. (1989). General to specific access to word meaning: A claim reexamined. *Cognitive Neuropsychology, 6,* 251–272.

Ratliff, F. (1976). On the psychophysiological bases of universal color names. *Proceedings of the American Philosophical Society, 120,* 311–330.

Redies, C., and Spillman, L. (1981) The neon color effect in the Ehrenstein illusion. *Perception, 10,* 667–681.

Reeves, A., and Sperling, G. (1986). Attention gating in short-term visual memory. *Psychological Review, 93,* 180–206.

Reid, T. (1813/1970). *An Enquiry into the Human Mind.* Chicago: University of Chicago Press.

Reynolds, R. I. (1978). The microgenetic development of the Ponzo and Zollner illusions. *Perception and Psychophysics, 23,* 231–236.

Ribe, N. M. (1985). Goethe's critique of Newton: A reconsideration. *Studies in History and Philosophy of Science, 16,* 315–335.

Riddoch, G. (1917). Dissociation of visual perception due to occipital injuries, with especial reference to appreciation of movements. *Brain, 40,* 15–57.

Riddoch M.J., and Humphreys, G. W. (1987a). A case of integrative visual agnosia. *Brain, 110,* 1431–1462.

Riddoch, M. J, and Humphreys, G. W. (1987b). Picture Naming. In: G. W. Humphreys and M. J. Riddoch (Eds.) *Visual Object Processing: A Cognitive Neuropsychological Approach.* London: Lawrence Erlbaum Associates.

Riddoch, M. J., and Humphreys, G. W. (1987c). Visual object processing in optic aphasia: A case of semantic access agnosia. *Cognitive Neuropsychology, 4,* 131–185.

Riddoch, M. J.; Humphreys, G. W.; Coltheart, M.; and Funnell, E. (1988). Semantic systems or system? Neuropsychological evidence re-examined. *Cognitive Neuropsychology, 5,* 3–25.

Ridley, D. R. (1987). A neo-Whorfian revisitation of color memory. *Perceptual and Motor Skills, 64,* 103–110.

Riggs, L. A.; White, K. D., and Eimas, P. D. (1974). Establishment and decay of orientation-contingent after effects of color. *Perception and Psychophysics, 16,* 535–542.

Rivers, W. H. R. (1901). Primitive color vision. *Popular Science Monthly, 59,* 44–58.

Rizzo, M., and Damasio, H. (1985). Impairment of stereopsis with focal brain lesions. *Annals of Neurology, 18,* P112.

Rizzo, M., and Eslinger, P. J. (1989). Colored hearing synesthesia: An investigation of neural factors. *Neurology, 39,* 781–784.

Robinson, J. O. (1972). *The Psychology of Visual Illusion.* London: Hutchinson.

Rochford, G. (1971) A study of naming errors in dysphasic and in demented patients. *Neuropsychologia, 9,* 437–443.

Rock, I., and Gutman, D. (1981). Effects of inattention on form perception. *Journal of Experimental Psychology: Human Perception and Performance, 7,* 275–285.

Rollman, G. B., and Nachmias, J. (1972). Simultaneous detection and recognition of chromatic flashes. *Perception and Psychophysics, 12,* 308–314.

Rosch, E. (1975a). Cognitive representations of semantic categories. *Journal of Experimental Psychology: General, 104,* 192–233.

Rosch, E. (1975b). The nature of mental codes for color categories. *Journal of Experimental Psychology: Human Perception and Performance, 1,* 303–322.

Rosch, E.; Mervis, C. B.; Gray, W.; Johnson, D.; and Boyes-Braem, P. (1976) Basic objects in natural categories. *Cognitive Psychology, 8,* 382–439.

Roth, I., and Frisby, J. (1986). *Perception and Representation: A Cognitive Approach.* Milton Keynes: Open University Press.

Rovamo, J.; Hyvarinen, L.; and Hari, R. (1982) Human vision without luminance-contrast system: Selective recovery of the red-green color-contrast system from acquired blindness. In G. Verriest (Ed.). *Colour Vision Deficiencies VI,* The Hague: W. Junk.

Rubens, A., and Benson, D. (1971). Associative visual agnosia. *Archives of Neurology, 24,* 305–316.

Rubin, E. (1921). *Visuell wahrgenommene Figuren Gyldendalske.* Copenhagen: Boghandel.

Ruddock, K. H., and Waterfield, V. A. (1978). Selective loss of function associated with a central visual field defect. *Neuroscience Letters, 8,* 93–98.

Rumelhart, D. E., and McClelland, J. L. (1986). *Parallel Distributed Processing. Vol. 1, Foundations.* Cambridge: MIT Press.

Sacks, O.; Wasserman, R. L.; Zeki, S.; and Siegel, R. M. (1988). *Sudden color blindness of cerebral origin*. Presented at the Annual Meeting of the Society for Neurosciences, Toronto. Abstract 502.3.

Saito, T. (1983). Latent spaces of color preference with and without a context: Using the shape of an automobile as the context. *Color Research and Application, 8,* 101–113.

Samelsohn, J. (1881). Zur Frage des Farbensinnzentrums. *Centralblatt fuer die medicinischen Wissenschaften, 19,* 850–853.

Santucci, G.; Menu, J. P.; and Valot, C. (1982). Visual acuity in color contrast on cathode ray tubes: Role of luminance, hue, and saturation contrasts. *Aviation, Space and Environmental Medicine, 53,* 478–484.

Sapir, E. (1921). *Language,* New York: Harcourt, Brace.

Sartori, G., and Job, R. (1988). The oyster with four legs: A neuropsychological study on the interaction of visual and semantic information. *Cognitive Neuropsychology, 5,* 105–132.

Sasanuma, S. (1974). Kanji versus Kana processing in alexia with transient agraphia: A case report. *Cortex, 10,* 89–97.

Saunders, B. A. C., and Van Brakel, J. (1988). Against basic color terms. *Collegium Antropologicum, 12,* 295–296.

Savoy, R. L. (1987). Contingent after effects and isoluminance: Psychophysical evidence for separation of color, orientation, and motion. *Computer Vision, Graphics, and Image Processing, 37,* 3–19.

Scanlon, B. A. (1985). Race differences in selection of cheese color. *Perceptual and Motor Skills, 61,* 314.

Schank, R. C., and Abelson, R. (1977). *Scripts, Plans, Goals, and Understanding.* Hillsdale, N.J.: Erlbaum.

Schauss, A. G. (1985). The physiological effect of color on the suppression of human aggression: Research on Baker-Miller pink. *International Journal of Biosocial Research, 7,* 55–64.

Schein, S. J.; Marrocco, R. T.; and DeMonasterio, F. M. (1982). Is there a high concentration of color-selective cells in area V4 of monkey visual cortex? *Journal of Neurophysiology, 47,* 193–213.

Schiller, P. H., and Colby, C. L. (1983). The responses of single cells in the lateral geniculate nucleus of the rhesus monkey to color and luminance contrast. *Vision Research, 23,* 1631–1641.

Schiller, P. H., Logothetis, N. K., and Charles, E. R. (1990). Functions of the colour-opponent and broad-band channels of the visual system. *Nature, 343,* 68–70.

Schneider, G. E. (1969). Two visual systems: Brain mechanisms for localization and discrimination are dissociated by tectal and cortical lesions. *Science, 163,* 895–902.

Schneider, W., and Shiffrin, R. M. (1977). Controlled and automatic human information processing: 1. Detection, search, and attention. *Psychological Review, 84,* 1–66.

Schwartz, M. F.; Marin, O. S. M.; and Saffran, E. M. (1979) Dissociations of language in dementia: A case study. *Brain and Language, 7,* 277–306.

Scott, I. (1970) *The Luscher Test.* London: Cape.

Scotti, G., and Spinnler, H. (1970). Color imperception in unilateral hemisphere-damaged patients. *Journal of Neurology, Neurosurgery and Psychiatry, 33,* 22–28.

Scoville, W. B., and Milner, B. (1957). Loss of recent memory after bilateral hippocampal lesions. *Journal of Neurology, Neurosurgery and Psychiatry, 20,* 11–22.

Selfridge, O. G. (1959). Pandemonium: A paradigm for learning. In: *The Mechanization of Thought Processes.* London: HMSO

Serjent, J., and Lorber, E. (1983) Perceptual categorization in the cerebral hemispheres. *Brain and Cognition, 2,* 39–54.

Seymour, P. H. K. (1977). Conceptual encoding and the locus of the Stroop effect. *Quarterly Journal of Experimental Psychology, 29*, 245–265.

Seymour, P. H. K. (1979). *Human Visual Cognition.* London: Collier Macmillan.

Seymour, P. H. K. (1980) Semantic and structural coding of the months. *British Journal of Psychology, 71*, 379–393.

Shallice, T. (1988a) *From Neuropsychology to Mental Structure.* Cambridge: Cambridge University Press.

Shallice, T. (1988b) Specialization within the semantic system. *Cognitive Neuropsychology, 5*, 133–142.

Shallice, T., and Jackson, M. (1988). Lissauer on agnosia. *Cognitive Neuropsychology, 5*, 153–192.

Shallice, T.; McLeod, P.; and Lewis, K. (1985) Isolating cognitive modules with the dual-task paradigm: Are speech perception and production separate processes? *Quarterly Journal of Experimental Psychology, 37A*, 507–532.

Shanon, B. (1982) Color associates to semantic linear orders. *Psychological Research, 44*, 75–83.

Siple, P., and Springer, R. M. (1983) Memory and preference for the colors of objects. *Perception and Psychophysics, 34*, 363–370.

Sittig, O. (1921) Stoerungen im Verhalten gegenueber Farben bei Aphasischen. *Monatsschrift fuer Psychiatrie und Neurologie, 49*, 63–68; 169–187.

Slaughter, M. M., and Miller, R. F. (1983). An excitatory amino acid antagonist blocks cone input to the sign-conserving second-order retinal neurons. *Science, 219*, 1230–1232.

Smets, G. (1969). Time expression of red and blue. *Perceptual and Motor Skills, 29*, 511–514.

Smith, E. E.; Balzano, G. J.; and Walker, J. (1977). Nominal, perceptual, and semantic codes in picture categorization. In J. Cotton and R. L. Klatzky (Eds.) *Semantic Factors in Cognition.* Hillsdale, N.J.: Lawrence Erlbaum Associates.

Smith, E. L.; Levi, D. M.; Harwerth, R. S.; and White, J. M. (1982). Color vision is altered during the suppression phase of binocular rivalry. *Science, 218*, 802–804.

Smith, M. C., and Magee, L. E. (1980). Tracing the time course of picture-word processing. *Journal of Experimental Psychology: General, 109*, 373–392.

Smith, S. L. (1962). Color coding and visual search. *Journal of Experimental Psychology, 64*, 434–440.

Smith, S. L., and Thomas, D. W. (1964). Color versus shape coding in information displays. *Journal of Applied Psychology, 48*, 137–146.

Snodgrass, J. G. (1984). Concepts and their surface representations. *Journal of Verbal Learning and Verbal Behavior, 23*, 3–22.

Snodgrass, J. G., and McCullough, B. (1986). The role of visual similarity in picture categorization. *Journal of Experimental Psychology: Learning, Memory and Cognition, 12*, 147–154.

Snowling, M., van Wagtendonk, B., and Stafford, C. (1988). Object-naming deficits in developmental dyslexia. *Journal of Research in Reading, 11*, 67–85.

Snyder, C. R. R. (1972). Selection, inspection, and naming in visual search. *Journal of Experimental Psychology, 92*, 428–431.

Sperber, R. D.; McCauley, C.; Ragain, R.; and Weil, C. (1979). Semantic priming effects on picture and word processing. *Memory and Cognition, 7*, 339–345.

Sperling, G. (1960). The information available in brief visual presentations. *Psychological Monographs, 74, (11, Whole no. 498).*

Spitzer, H.; Desimone, R.; and Moran, I. (1988). Both behavioral and neuronal performance are improved by increased attention. *Society for Neuroscience, Abstracts, 14*, 8.5. 18th Annual Meeting, Toronto, November.

Spreen, O.; Benton, A. L.; and Van Allen, M. W. (1966). Dissociation of visual and tactile naming in amnesic aphasia, *Neurology, 16*, 807–814.

Stabell, B., and Stabell, U. (1981). Absolute spectral sensitivity at different eccentricities. *Journal of the Optical Society of America, 71*, 836–840.

Stachowiak, F.-J., and Poeck, K. (1976). Functional disconnection in pure alexia and color naming deficit demonstrated by facilitation methods. *Brain and Language, 3*, 135–143.

Stalmeier, P. F. M., and DeWeert, C. M. M. (1988). Large color differences measured by spontaneous Gestalt formation. *Color Research and Application, 13*, 209–218.

Steffan, P. H. (1881). Beitrag zur Pathologie des Farbsinnes. *Archiv fuer Ophthalmologie, 27*, 1–24.

Stefurak, D. L., and Boynton, R. M. (1986). Independence of memory for categorically different colors and shapes. *Perception and Psychophysics, 39*, 164–174.

Stemberger, J. P. (1984). Structural errors in normal and agrammatic speech. *Cognitive Neuropsychology, 1*, 281–313.

Stengel, E. (1948). The syndrome of visual alexia with color anomia. *Journal of Mental Sciences, 94*, 46–58.

Sternberg, S., and Knoll, R. L. (1973). The perception of temporal order: Fundamental issues and a general model. In S. Kornblum (Ed.). *Attention and Performance IV*. New York: Academic Press

Stiles, W. S., and Crawford, B. H. (1933). The liminal brightness increment as a function of wavelength for different conditions of the foveal and parafoveal retina. *Proceedings of the Royal Society of London, Series B, 117*, 496–530.

Stoerig, P. (1987). Chromaticity and achromaticity. Evidence for a functional differentiation in visual field defects. *Brain, 110*, 869–886.

Strawson, P. F. (1979). Perception and its objects. In G. McDonald (Ed.). *Perception and Identity: Essays Presented to A. J. Ayer*. London: Macmillan.

Stromeyer, C. F., and Dawson, B. M. (1978). Form-color aftereffects: Selectivity to local luminance contrast. *Perception, 7*, 407–418.

Stromeyer, C. F., and Mansfield, R. J. W. (1970). Colored aftereffects produced with moving edges. *Perception and Psychophysics, 7*, 108–114.

Stroop, J. R. (1935). Studies of interference in serial verbal reactions. *Journal of Experimental Psychology, 18*, 643–662.

Styles, E. A., and Allport, D. A. (1986). Perceptual integration of identity, location, and color. *Psychological Research, 48*, 189–200.

Suchman, R. G., and Trabasso, T. (1966) Color and form preference in young children. *Journal of Experimental Child Psychology, 3*, 177–187.

Sun, R. K. (1983). Perceptual distances and the basic color term encoding sequence. *American Anthropologist, 85*, 387–391.

Svinicki, J.; Meier, S.; and Svinicki, M. D. (1976). Stimulus label and generalization in children as a function of age. *Journal of Experimental Child Psychology, 21*, 282–288.

Symonds, C., and Mackenzie, I. (1957). Bilateral loss of vision from cerebral infarction. *Brain, 80*, 415–456.

Tansley, B. W., and Boynton, R. M. (1978). Chromatic border perception: The role of red-and-green-sensitive cones. *Vision Research, 18*, 683–697.

Tansley, B. W.; Robertson, H. W.; and Maughan, K. E. (1983). Chromatic and achromatic border perception: A two-cone model accounts for suprathreshold border distinctness judgments and cortical pattern-evoked response amplitudes to the same stimuli. In J. D. Mollon and R. T. Sharpe (Eds.). *Colour Vision: Physiology and Psychophysics, 445–454. New York: Academic Press*.

Taylor, A. M., and Warrington, E. K. (1971). Visual agnosia: A single case report, *Cortex, 7*, 152–161.

Teller, D. Y., and Bornstein, M. H. (1985). Color vision and color perception in infancy. In L. B. Cohen and P. Salapatek (Eds.). *Handbook of Infant Perception*. New York: Academic Press.

Te Linde, J. (1982). Picture-word differences in decision latencies: A test of common coding assumptions. *Journal of Experimental Psychology: Learning, Memory and Cognition. 8*, 584–598.

Te Linde, J., and Paivio, A. (1979). Symbolic comparison of color similarity. *Memory and Cognition, 7*, 141–148.

Teuber, H.-L.; Battersby, W. S.; and Bender, M. B. (1960). *Visual Field Defects after Penetrating Missile Wounds of the Brain*. Cambridge: Harvard University Press.

Thompson, P., and Latchford, G. (1986) Color-contingent aftereffects are really wavelength contingent. *Nature, 320*, 525–526.

Thorell, L. G., DeValois, R. L., and Albrecht, D. G. (1984). Spatial mapping of monkey V1 cells with pure color and luminance stimuli. *Vision Research, 24*, 751–769.

Tinbergen, N. (1951). *The Study of Instinct*. Oxford: Clarendon Press.

Titchener, E. B. (1908). *Lectures on the Elementary Psychology of Feeling and Attention*. New York: Macmillan.

Todd, J. T. (1985). Perception of structure from motion: Is projective correspondence of moving elements a necessary condition? *Journal of Experimental Psychology: Human Perception and Performance, 11*, 689–710.

Todd, J. T., and Mingolla, E. (1983). Perception of surface curvature and direction of illumination from patterns of shading. *Journal of Experimental Psychology: Human Perception and Performance, 9*, 583–595.

Tomikawa, S. A., and Dodd, D. H. (1980). Early word meanings: Perceptually or functionally based? *Child Development, 51*, 1103–1109.

Tootell, R. B.; Hamilton, S. L.; and Silverman, M. S. (1985). Topography of cytochrome oxidase activity in owl monkey cortex. *Journal of Neuroscience, 5*, 2786–2800.

Tootell, R. B.; Silverman, M. S.; DeValois, R. L.; and Jacobs, G. H. (1983). Functional organization of the second cortical visual area in primates. *Science, 220*, 737–739.

Towne, R. L., and Banick, P. L. (1989). The effect of stimulus color on naming performance of aphasic adults. *Journal of Communication Disorders, 22*, 397–405.

Treisman, A. M. (1982). Perceptual grouping and attention in visual search for features and objects. *Journal of Experimental Psychology: Human Perception and Performance, 8*, 194–214.

Treisman, A. M. (1986). Properties, parts, and objects. In K. R. Boff, L. Kaufman, and J. P. Thomas (Eds.). *Handbook of Perception and Human Performance*. New York: Wiley.

Treisman, A. M. (1988). Features and Objects. *Quarterly Journal of Experimental Psychology, 40A*, 201–237.

Treisman, A. M., and Fearnley, S. (1969). The Stroop test: Selective attention to colors and words. *Nature, 222*, 437–439.

Treisman, A. M., and Gelade G. (1980). A feature integration theory of attention. *Cognitive Psychology, 12*, 97–136.

Treisman, A. M.; Kahneman, D.; and Burkell, J. (1983). Perceptual objects and the cost of filtering. *Perception and Psychophysics, 33*, 527–532.

Treisman, A. M., and Schmidt, H. (1982). Illusory conjunctions in the perception of objects. *Cognitive Psychology, 14*, 104–141.

Treisman, A., and Souther, J. (1985). Search asymmetry: A diagnostic for preattentive processing of separable features. *Journal of Experimental Psychology: General, 114*, 285–310.

Treitel, T. (1879). Ueber den Werth der Gesichtsfeldmessung mit Pigmenten fuer die Auffassung der Krankheiten des nervoesen Sehaparates. *Albrecht von Graefes Archiv fuer Ophthalmologie, 25*, Abteilung 11, 29–51; Abteilung 111, 47–110.

Troscianko, T. (1987). Perception of random-dot symmetry and apparent movement at and near isoluminance. *Vision Research, 27*, 547–554.

Troscianko, T., and Fahle, M. (1988). Why do isoluminant stimuli appear slower? *Journal of the Optical Society of America (A), 5*, 871–880.

Troscianko, T., and Harris, J. P. (1988). Phase discrimination in compount chromatic gratings. *Vision Research, 28*, 1041–1049.

Tsal, Y. (1983). On interpreting the effects of location preknowledge: A critique of Duncan. *Perception and Psychophysics, 34*, 297–298.

Tsao, Y.; Wu, M.; and Feustel, T. (1981) Stroop interference: Hemispheric differences in Chinese speakers. *Brain and Language, 13*, 372–378.

Tullis, T.S. (1981). An evaluation of alphanumeric, graphic, and color information displays. *Human Factors, 23*, 541–550.

Turvey, M. T. (1973). On peripheral and central processes in vision: Inferences from an information-processing analysis of masking with patterned stimuli. *Psychological Review, 80*, 1–52.

Uchikawa, K., and Ikeda, M. (1981). Temporal deterioration of wavelength discrimination with successive comparison method. *Vision Research, 21*, 591–595.

Uchikawa, K.; Uchikawa, H.; and Boynton, R. M. (1989). Partial color constancy of isolated surface colors examined by a color-naming method. *Perception, 18*, 83–91.

Uhlarik, J.; Pringle, R.; and Brigell, M. (1977). Color aftereffects contingent on perceptual organization. *Perception and Psychophysics, 22*, 506–510.

Ullman, S. (1984). Visual routines. *Cognition, 18*, 97–159.

Ullman, S. (1989). Aligning pictorial descriptions: An approach to object recognition. *Cognition, 32*, 193–254.

Van der Horst, G. J. C. (1969). Chromatic flicker. *Journal of the Optical Society of America, 59*, 1213–1217.

Van Tuijl, H. F. J. M. (1975). A new visual illusion: Neonlike color spreading and complimentary color induction between subjective contours. *Acta Psychologica, 39*, 441–445.

Van Tuijl, H. F. J. M., and De Weert, C. M. M. (1979). Sensory contours for the occurrence of the neon spreading illusion. *Perception, 8*, 211–215.

Varley, H. (1980). *Colour*. London: Marshall Editions.

Varney, N. R. (1982). Color association and "colour amnesia" in aphasia. *Journal of Neurology, Neurosurgery and Psychiatry, 45*, 248–252.

Varney, N. R., and Digre, K. (1983). Color amnesia without aphasia. *Cortex, 19*, 551–555.

Verrey, D. (1888). Hemiachromatopsie droite absolue. *Archives d'Ophthalmologie* (Paris), *8*, 289–300.

Von der Heydt, R.; Peterhans, E.; and Baumgartner, G. (1984). Illusory contours and cortical neuron responses. *Science, 224*, 1260–1262.

Von Kries, J. (1905). Die Gesichtsempfindungen. In W. Nagel (Ed.). *Handbuch der Physiologie der Menschen*. Brunswick: Wieweg.

Von Restorff, H. (1933). Ueber die Wirkung von Bereichsbildungen im Spurenfeld. *Psychol. Forsch. 18*, 299–342.

Von Seggern, H. (1881). Achromatopsie bei homonymer Hemianopsie mit voller Seherschaerfe. *Klinischer Monatsblaetter fuer Augenheilkunde, 71*, 101–104.

Von Wright, J. M. (1970). On selection in visual immediate memory. *Acta Psychologica, 33*, 280–292.

Walls, G. L. (1954). The filling-in process. *American Journal of Optometry, 31*, 329–341.

Walls, G. L. (1956). The G. Palmer Story. *Journal of the History of Medicine, 11*, 66–96.

Walters, J. W., and Harwerth, R. S. (1978). The mechanisms of brightness enhancement. *Vision Research, 18*, 777–779.

Wapner, W.; Judd, T.; and Gardner, H. (1978). Visual agnosia in an artist. *Cortex, 14,* 343–364.

Ward, T. B.; Foley, C. M.; and Cole, J. (1986). Classifying multidimensional stimuli: Stimulus, task, and observer factors. *Journal of Experimental Psychology: Human Perception and Performance, 12,* 211–225.

Ward, T. B., and Vela, E. (1986). Classifying color materials: Children are less holistic than adults. *Journal of Experimental Child Psychology, 42,* 273–302.

Ware, C., and Beaty J. C. (1988). Using color dimensions to display data dimensions. *Human Factors, 30,* 127–142.

Ware, C., and Cowan, W. B. (1987). Chromatic Mach bands: Behavioral evidence for lateral inhibition in human color vision. *Perception and Psychophysics, 41,* 173–178.

Warren, C. E. J., and Morton, J. (1982). The effects of priming on picture recognition. *British Journal of Psychology, 73,* 117–130.

Warrington, E. K. (1975). The selective impairment of semantic memory. *Quarterly Journal of Experimental Psychology, 27,* 635–657.

Warrington, E. K. (1985). Visual deficits associated with occipital lobe lesions in man. In *Pattern Recognition Mechanisms,* 247–261. C. Chagas, R. Gatass, and C. Gross (Eds.). Berlin: Springer.

Warrington, E. K., and James, M. (1967). Disorders of visual perception in patients with localised cerebral lesions. *Neuropsychologia, 5,* 253–266.

Warrington, E. K., and James, M. (1986). Visual object recognition in patients with right hemisphere lesions: Axes or features. *Perception, 15,* 355–366.

Warrington, E. K., and James, M. (1988). Visual apperceptive agnosia: A clinico-anatomical study of three cases. *Cortex, 24,* 13–32.

Warrington, E. K., and McCarthy, R. (1983). Category specific access dysphasia. *Brain, 106,* 859–878.

Warrington, E. K., and McCarthy, R. (1987). Categories of knowledge: Further fractionation and an attempted integration. *Brain, 110,* 1273–1296.

Warrington, E. K., and Shallice, T. (1984). Category specific semantic impairments. *Brain, 107,* 829–853.

Warrington, E. K., and Taylor, A. M. (1973). The contribution of the right parietal lobe to object recognition. *Cortex, 9,* 152–164.

Warrington, E. K., and Taylor, A. M. (1978). Two categorical stages of object recognition. *Perception, 7,* 695–705.

Watanabe, T., and Sato, T. (1989). Effects of luminance contrast on color spreading and illusory contour in the neon spreading effect. *Perception and Psychophysics, 45,* 427–430.

Watts, F. N.; McKenna, F. P.; Sharrock R.; and Tresize, L. (1986). Color naming of phobia related words. *British Journal of Psychology, 77,* 97–108.

Webster, W. R., Day, R. H.; and Willenberg, K. (1988). Orientation-contingent color aftereffects are determined by real color, not induced color. *Perception and Psychophysics, 44,* 43–49.

Wedell, J., and Alden, D. G. (1973). Color versus numeric coding in a keep-track task: Performance under varying load conditions. *Journal of Applied Psychology, 57,* 154–159.

Weiskrantz, L. (1986). *Blindsight.* Oxford: Clarendon Press.

Weiskrantz, L. (1987). Residual vision in a scotoma: A follow-up study of "form" discrimination. *Brain, 110,* 77–92.

Werner, H. (1940). *The Comparative Psychology of Mental Development.* New York: Harper.

Westphal, J. (1987). *Colour: Some Philosophical Problems for Wittgenstein.* Oxford: Blackwell.

White, C. W., and Montgomery, D. A. (1976). Memory colors in afterimages: A bicentennial demonstration. *Perception and Psychophysics, 19,* 371–374.

Whitehouse, P.; Caramazza, A.; and Zurif, E. (1978). Naming in aphasia: Interacting effects of form and function. *Brain and Language, 6,* 63–74.

Whorf, B. L. (1956). *Language, Thought and Reality.* Ed. J. B. Carroll. Cambridge: MIT Press.

Wickens, C. D., and Andre, A. D. (1990). Proximity, compatability and information display: Effects of color, space, and objectness on information integration. *Human Factors, 32,* 61–71.

Wiesel, T. N., and Hubel, D. H. (1966). Spatial and chromatic interactions in the lateral geniculate body of the rhesus monkey. *Journal of Neurophysiology, 29,* 1115–1156.

Wild, H. M.; Butler, S. R.; Carden, D.; and Kulikowski, J. J. (1985). Primate cortical area V4 important for colour constancy but not wavelength discrimination. *Nature, 313,* 133–135.

Williams, C. (1974). The effect of an irrelevant dimension on "same-different" judgements of multi-dimensional stimuli. *Quarterly Journal of Experimental Psychology, 26,* 26–31.

Williams, E. (1977). The effects of amount of information in the Stroop color word test. *Perception and Psychophysics, 22,* 463–470.

Williams, L. G. (1966). The effect of target specification on objects fixated during visual search. *Perception & Psychophysics, 1,* 315–318.

Willows, D. M., and McKinnon, G. E. (1973). Selective reading: Attention to the "unattended" lines. *Canadian Journal of Psychology, 27,* 292–304.

Wilson, G. D. (1966). Arousal properties of red versus green. *Perceptual and Motor Skills, 23,* 947–949.

Wilson, M.; Kaufman, H. M.; Zieler, R. E.; and Lieb, J. P. (1972). Visual identification and memory on monkeys with circumscribed inferotemporal lesions. *Journal of Comparative, Physiological and Comparative Psychology, 78,* 173–183.

Wingfield, A. (1968). Effects of frequency on identification and naming of objects. *American Journal of Psychology, 81,* 226–234.

Wiseman, S., and Neisser, U. (1974). Perceptual organization as a determinant of visual recognition memory. *American Journal of Psychology, 87,* 675–681.

Wittgenstein, L. (1978). *Remarks on Colour.* Ed. G. E. M. Anscombe. Trans. L. McAlister and M. Schaettle. Oxford: Blackwell.

Wolfe, J. M.; Cave, K. R.; and Franzel, S. L. (1989). Guided search: An alternative to the feature integration model for visual search. *Journal of Experimental Psychology: Human Perception and Performance, 15,* 419–433.

Wolford, G. (1975). Perturbation model for letter identification. *Psychological Review, 82,* 184–199.

Wolin, L. R.; Massopust, L. C.; and Meder, J. (1966). Differential color responses from the superior colliculus of squirrel monkeys. *Vision Research, 6,* 637–644.

Wong-Riley, M. T. T. (1978). Reciprocal connections between striate and prestriate cortex in squirrel monkey as demonstrated by combined peroxidase histochemistry and autoradiography. *Brain Research, 147,* 159–164.

Worthey, J. (1985). Limitations of color constancy. *Journal of the Optical Society of America, 2A,* 1708–1712.

Wright, B., and Rainwater, L. (1962). The meaning of color. *Journal of General Psychology, 67,* 89–99.

Wright, P., and Fox, K. (1970). Presenting information in tables. *Applied Ergonomics, 1,* 234–242.

Wyke, M., and Holgate, D. (1973). Color-naming defects in dysphasic patients. A qualitative analysis. *Neuropsychologia, 11,* 451–461.

References   209

Wyszecki, G. (1986). Color appearance. In K. R. Boff, L. Kaufman, and J. P. Thomas (Eds.). *Handbook of Perception and Human Performance*. New York: Wiley.

Yamadori, A., and Albert, M. L. (1983). Word category aphasia. *Cortex, 9,* 112–125.

Yarbus, A. L. (1967). *Eye Movements and Vision*. New York: Plenum Press.

Young, A. W.; Hay, D. C.; and Ellis, A. W. (1986). Getting semantic information from familiar faces. In H. D. Ellis, M. A. Jeeves, F. Newcombe, and A. W. Young (Eds.). *Aspects of Face Processing*. Dordrecht: Martinus Nijhoff.

Young, R. S. L.; Fishman, G. A.; and Chen, F. (1980). Traumatically acquired color vision defect. *Investigative Ophthalmology and Visual Science, 19,* 545–549.

Young, T. (1802). On the Theory of Light and Colours. *Philosophical Transactions of the Royal Society of London, 92,* 12–48.

Young, T. (1814). Review of *Zur Farbenlehre*, by Johann Wolfgang von Goethe. *Quarterly Review (Edinburgh), 10,* no 20., Jan., 427.

Yukie, M., and Iwai, E. (1981). Direct projection from the dorsal lateral geniculate nucleus to the prestriate cortex in macaque monkey. *Journal of Comparative Neurology, 201,* 81–97.

Zeki, S. M. (1974). Functional organization of a visual area in the posterior bank of the superior temporal sulcus of the rhesus monkey. *Journal of Physiology, 236,* 549–573.

Zeki, S. M. (1978). Functional specialisation of the visual cortex of the rhesus monkey. *Nature, 274,* 423–428.

Zeki, S. M. (1980). The representations of colors in the cerebral cortex. *Nature, 412–418.*

Zeki, S. M. (1983). Colour coding in the cerebral cortex: The reaction of cells in monkey visual cortex to wavelengths and colours. *Neuroscience, 9,* 741–765.

Zeki, S. M. (1989). Functional specialisation and multi-stage integration in the visual cortex. Paper presented at the Fifth International Symposium of the Northern Eye Institute. Bristol, U.K. July.

Zihl, J.; Roth, W.; Kerkhoff, G.; and Heywood, C. A. (1988). The influence of homonymous visual field disorders on color sorting performance in the FM 100-hue test. *Neuropsychologia, 26,* 869–876.

Zihl, J., and von Cramon, D. (1986). *Zerebrale Sehstoerung*. Stuttgart: Kohlhammer.

Zihl, J.; von Cramon, D.; and Mai, N. (1983). Selective disturbance of movement vision after bilateral brain damage. *Brain, 106,* 313–340.

Zohary, E., and Hochstein, S. (1989). How serial is serial processing in vision? *Perception, 18,* 191–200.

Zollinger, H. (1988). Biological aspects of color naming. In I. Rentschler, B. Herzberger, D. Epstein (Eds.) *Beauty and the Brain*. Basel: Birkhaeuser Verlag.

Zurif, E. B.; Caramazza, A.; Myerson, R.; and Galvin, J. (1974). Semantic feature representations for normal and aphasic language. *Brain and Language, 1,* 167–187.

Zwaga, H. J. G., and Duijnhouwer, F. (1984). The influence of a fixed background in a VDU display on the efficiency of color and shape coding. In C. P. Gibson (Ed.). *Colour Coded vs Monochrome Electronic Displays*. London: HMSO.

Index

Achromatopsia, 7, 31–40, 137, 169
Acuity, 32, 35–40, 42–45, 82
Adams, R. J., 148–149
Adler, A., 93, 124, 133, 156
Aesthetics of color, 115–118
Aftereffects
  contingent, 58, 126
  McCollough effect, 58–59, 61, 72, 125–126
  motion, 46–47, 58, 62, 66
  tilt, 66
Afterimages, 3, 16, 58, 78
Agnosia, 82, 92–94, 100–101, 109–110, 156–157
Agraphia, 157
Albers, J., 78
Albert, M. L., 92, 95, 101
Alexia, 36, 93, 157
Allport, D. A., 85, 96, 101, 146
Anomia, 143, 159–162. See also Optic aphasia, Color anomia
Anstis, S. M., 47, 58, 62, 65, 80
Aphasia, 36, 92, 129, 131–132, 142–146, 148, 157
Apperception, 39–40, 52–53, 81–83, 92–93, 124
Apraxia, 35
Arguin, M., 59–61, 65–67
Assimilation, 43, 72–73, 78, 126
Attention, 3, 5, 7, 41, 53–60, 63, 82, 84–85, 97, 104, 126, 150, 164–166
  attentional spotlight, 54–57, 84
  feature integration, 58–60
  pop-out, 53–54, 66–67, 69
  prior entry, 56–58

Baker-Miller pink, 113–114
Barbur, J. L., 25, 62
Barlow, H. B., 6, 13–14

Barrow, H. G., 66, 70
Bartram, D. J., 52, 139
Basso, A., 131, 134, 138, 159–160
Baylis, G. C., 13, 85
Beauvois, M-F., 73, 110, 131–134, 136, 138, 143–144, 148, 160–162
Beck, J., 3, 64
Bender, M. B., 25, 33
Benham top, 81
Benson, D. F., 39, 82, 92, 133, 162
Benton, A. L., 144–145
Berlin, B., 150–153, 155
Berndt, R. S., 95, 145
Bertulis, A., 70–71, 84
Biederman, I., 88, 97, 121–123, 167
Binocular vision, 1, 4, 13, 19, 23–25, 28, 40–41, 48, 59, 61–62, 66, 71–72, 75, 82, 87. See also Depth perception
Birch, J., 32, 160
Bisiach, E., 138, 145, 146
Blakemore, C., 48, 66
Blindness, 37, 53, 91, 148
Blindsight, 12, 25–26, 62
Blob cells, 19–23, 25–26, 43, 72, 75, 77, 79, 170
Boller, F., 133, 162
Bornstein, M. H., 106, 109, 149, 150, 159
Boucher, M., 135, 157, 161
Boundary-contours, 2, 24, 62–65, 70–73, 75, 78–79, 83–84, 93, 96–97, 121, 123, 125. See also Domains
Boynton, R. M., 65, 75–76, 109, 153
Broadbent, D. E., 7, 53, 57–58, 85
Brown, R. W., 108, 154–155
Bruce, M., 45, 64
Bruce, V., 89, 99, 141
Bruner, J. S., 127, 129
Bryden, M., 129, 167
Bundesen, C., 57, 64

Callaghan, T. C., 64, 70–71
Campbell, F. W., 45, 66
Campion, J., 82, 94
Capitani, E., 39, 131
Caramazza, A., 94–95, 99, 145
Carr, T. H., 91, 141
Cascade model. *See* Object knowledge
Case studies
  AB, 94
  MP, 110, 134, 136, 160, 161, 162
  RV, 73, 110, 131–133, 136, 160
  VER, 95
  YOT, 95
Category-specific impairments. *See* Disorders of object knowledge
Cavanagh, P., 7, 47, 59–67, 75, 122, 127, 150, 165
Cavonius, C. R., 44, 65, 79
Charnallet, A., 38, 82
Christ, R. E., 64, 123
Cohen, R., 131–132
Color agnosia (disorders of the internal color space), 109–111
Color anomia, 156–159
Color and depth, 81
Color and form, 42–45, 47, 69, 72, 125–126. *See also* Color contrast
Color and luminance, 25, 28, 79–80
  Abney effect, 79
  Bezold-Brucke effect, 79
  Helmholtz-Kohlrausch effect, 80
  Retinex model, 77, 80
Color and motion, 80–81
Color and object recognition, 121–124
Color blindness, 31–32, 65, 110. *See also* Achromatopsia
Color center, 1, 27, 37, 137
Color constancy, 24, 27, 38, 75–77, 80, 149
Color contrast, 77–78
Color naming, 147–167
  cross-cultural aspects, 150–156
  development, 9, 109, 140, 148–150, 159, 172
  disorders (color anomia), 109–110, 133–135, 156–159
Color-opponent cells, 15–16, 19–21, 26, 148–149
Coltheart, M., 51, 144
Complex cells, 19, 22, 24, 27–28, 72

Concrete representations. *See* Object knowledge
Cones, 14–17, 21, 25, 28, 31, 32, 45, 48, 76–81, 89
Conjunctions. *See* Feature conjunctions
Connectionism, 5–6, 89
Consciousness, 5, 12, 25, 53, 55, 73, 75, 107, 124, 155, 171
Contours. *See* Boundary-contours
Coslett, H. B., 134, 160
Cowey, A., 1, 13, 15, 22, 23, 26, 27, 35, 40
Cramon, D. von, 32–33, 35, 40
Critchley, M., 35, 52
Cross-cultural differences for colors, 115, 118–119, 151, 153, 170, 171
  Bellona Islanders, 155–156
  Dani, 106
  Japanese, 111, 115, 153, 163, 167
  Murray Islanders, 154
  Shuswap, 152
  Tarahumara, 154–155
  Uzbek, 152
  Zuni, 108, 154
Cross-modal associations. *See* Synaesthesia

D'Agostino, P. R., 107–109, 116
Damasio, A. R., 32–33, 35–38, 40, 114, 134, 145–146, 157, 159–162
Dannemiller, J. L., 77, 149
Davidoff, J. B., 39, 57, 89–90, 93, 98, 104, 108–109, 122, 124, 130, 136, 140, 150, 156, 159, 161
Dean, P., 27, 40
Denckla, M. B., 148, 159
Depth perception, 3–4, 35, 42, 48, 75, 81, 121. *See also* Binocular vision
DeRenzi, E., 38–39, 110, 131–132, 137–138, 156, 159–160
Derrington, A. M., 16, 23, 47
Desimone, R., 13, 27, 56, 72
DeValois, K. K., 44, 49, 66
DeValois, R. L., 23, 25, 28, 72
Development. *See* Color naming, Object knowledge
DeVreese, L. P., 136, 148, 159, 163
DeWeert, C. M. M., 48, 65, 78, 104
DeYoe, E. A., 7, 13, 26–28
Disconnection accounts, 138, 156, 157, 159

Disorders of boundary perception. *See* Apperception

Disorders of color vision. *See* Achromatopsia

Disorders of face perception. *See* Prosopagnosia

Disorders of form perception. *See* Apperception

Disorders of imagery, 35–36, 132–138, 159–162. *See also* Imagery

Disorders of naming. *See also* Anomia, Disconnection accounts

Disorders of object knowledge. *See also* Agnosia
  associative visual disorders, 82, 92–94, 98–101, 124
  category-specific impairments, 94–96
  loss of abstract attitude, 110, 131–132

Disorders of object recognition (associative visual disorders). *See* Agnosia, Apperception

Dissociations, 25, 39–40, 52, 81, 110, 114, 129, 160–162. *See also* Double dissociations

Dixon, N. F., 73, 107, 113

Domains, 7, 50, 60–67, 69, 72, 75, 169. *See also* Boundary-contours

Double dissociations, 9, 40, 138

Double-opponent cells, 20, 21, 23, 24, 26, 72, 77

Drawing ability, 82–83, 123, 130, 135, 145

Dreaming in color, 36

Driver, J., 59, 85

Duncan, J., 69, 70, 84

Dyer, F. N., 164–166

Dyschromatopsia. *See* Achromatopsia

Dyslexia, 145, 148

Edge-based representations. *See* Object knowledge

Edges. *See* Boundary-contours

Egeth, H. E., 103, 164

Ekehammar, B., 118–119

Elliot, J., 2, 14

Ellis, A. W., 82, 90, 93, 141–142

Ellis, H. D., 123

Emotional reaction to colors, 113–115, 171

Endstopped cells, 19, 22, 24, 72

Entry level. *See* Object knowledge

Equiluminance, 41–49, 61–62, 65–66, 72, 75, 84

Eriksen, C. W., 55, 64

Ettlinger, G., 133, 160, 162

Face perception, 8, 35, 89, 93, 123, 126, 141. *See also* Prosopagnosia

Faglioni, P., 110, 131, 159

Farah, M. J., 29, 128, 135–138, 160–162

Favreau, O. E., 47, 58, 66

Feature conjunctions, 55–60

Feature-contours, 70–73, 78–79, 96, 121. *See also* Boundary-contours

Feature integration, 2, 52–60, 84, 169

Features of objects, 1, 3, 7, 53–61, 64–67, 83, 85, 93, 95, 101, 126

Fechner, G., 115, 117

Felsten, G., 15, 26

Ferro, J. M., 115, 131, 133, 160, 162

Focal colors, 106–107, 109, 125, 127, 147, 151–153, 170. *See also* Internal color space

Fodor, J. A., 1, 6, 29, 90

Form perception, 13, 19, 25, 27–28, 47, 49, 52, 58–67, 69, 72, 103, 105–107, 144, 169–170. *See also* Apperception

Foster, J. J., 45, 64

Frequency. *See* Spatial frequency, Word frequency

Freud, S., 82, 128

Freund, D. C., 143, 157

Frisby, J. P., 75, 88, 90

Fukuzawa, K., 110–111, 133, 135, 157, 160, 162

Functional modularity. *See* Internal color space, Modularity

Funnell, E., 140, 144

Fuster, J. M., 56, 126

Ganglion cells, 14–15, 26

Gardner, H., 146, 160

Garner, W. R., 71, 103–104

Garro, L. C., 109, 114

Gelb, A., 52, 110

Geschwind, N., 135, 157, 160–162

Gesturing, 144

Gibson, J. J., 5, 66, 144

Gil, R., 134, 157, 160, 162

Goethe, 2–3, 114

Goldenberg, G., 135–138

Goldstein, K., 94, 110, 113, 131

Goodglass, H., 95, 142, 156
Gorea, A., 47, 49, 65
Gouras, P., 16, 27–28
Gregory, R. L., 44, 46–48, 62, 75, 90, 126
Gross, C. G., 13, 29, 56, 79
Grossberg, S., 70–73, 78–79, 82–83, 93, 97, 121
Grunau, M. W. von, 61, 65, 80–81
Guenther, R. K., 91, 99, 161

Harms, L., 57, 64
Hart, J., 95, 100
Hecaen, H., 25, 92, 94, 143, 160
Heider, E. R. (Rosch), 106, 149
Helmholtz, H. L. F. von, 16, 55, 72, 75
Hering, E., 3, 16, 126, 149
Heywood, C. A., 27, 35, 37, 39–40, 160
Hilz, R., 44, 79
Holmes, G., 33, 35, 135, 162
Holmgren wool test, 110–111
Homa, D., 89, 98, 122
Hubel, D. H., 7, 13, 15–17, 19–29, 41–49, 52, 61, 66–67, 72–73, 79–80
Humphrey, N. K., 118, 159
Humphreys, G. W., 54, 59, 69–70, 82–83, 89–90, 92, 94, 99–101, 122, 124, 134-135, 137–139, 143–144, 160, 162
Hurvich, L. M., 16, 75, 77
Hypercomplex cells. See Endstopped cells

Illusions, 43–44, 45–46, 48, 51. See also Aftereffects, Assimilation, Motion
Illusory conjunctions, 55, 57, 60, 125–126
Illusory contours, 72–73, 75
Imagery, 107, 147, 126–128, 157, 170. See also Disorders of imagery
Integral dimensions, 104
Integration. See Feature integration
Interblobs, 22, 24, 28, 42–43
Internal color space, 8–9, 105–111, 113–118, 125, 138, 140, 147, 149–156, 170-171
    development of, 104–106, 112, 170
Ishihara test, 62, 65, 110
Isoluminance. See Equiluminance

Jackendoff, R., 6, 140
James, M., 82, 83, 93, 138
Jameson, D., 75, 77
Johnson-Laird, P. N., 141, 149–150
Judd, D. B., 80, 160

Kahneman, D., 55, 60, 164
Kaiser, P. K., 75, 113–114
Kaplan, E., 15, 26
Katz, D., 3, 52
Kay, P., 150–155
Keele, S. W., 52, 55, 164
Kelley, D., 3, 5–6
Kelly, D. H., 44–45
Kelter, S., 52, 131–132, 141
Kennard, C., 25, 37
Kertesz, A., 93, 110, 133
Kinsbourne, M., 110, 132, 134, 159–163
Klatzky, R. L., 91, 161
Koffka, K., 42, 59, 126
Kolers, P. A., 80–81, 90
Kosslyn, S. M., 88, 128
Krauskopf, J., 16, 42, 44, 73
Kroll, J. F., 90–91, 98
Kruger, J., 27–28
Kulikowski, J. J., 27, 109, 151
Kunishima, M., 114–115

Landis, T., 38, 96, 108
Landmark colors. See Focal colors
Lange, J., 82, 87, 132, 161
Larrabee, G. J., 131, 133, 134, 160, 162
Lateral geniculate nucleus, 12–13, 15–22, 25–26, 77, 107
Lehmann, A., 42–43
Lenneberg, E. H., 108, 154, 155
Lennie, P., 16, 77
Levine, D. N., 29, 82, 92, 94, 110, 124, 132–133, 135, 156
Lewandowsky, M., 129–132, 135, 138, 150, 156, 161–162
Lhermitte, F., 131, 133, 134, 143, 144, 160, 162, 163
Lightness, 35, 39, 103–104, 107, 115, 130, 132. See also Luminance
Lissauer, H., 39, 81–82, 92, 94, 129
Livingstone, M. S., 7, 13, 15, 17, 19, 20–29, 41–49, 52, 61, 66–67, 72–73, 79–80
Livingstone and Hubel streams, 7, 13-14, 19–20, 22, 24–29, 40–49, 52, 57, 61, 65–67, 151, 169
Locke, 2, 7
Loftus, E. F., 97, 99, 109
Lueck, C. E., 37, 137
Luminance, 16–17, 42, 44–49, 51, 60–63, 65–66, 70, 73, 75, 77, 79–80, 83–84, 123, 151. See also Lightness

Luscher test, 118–119
Luzzatti, C., 131, 138

McCarthy, R., 92, 95, 101, 133, 141, 162
McClelland, J. L., 6, 89, 94, 99–100, 117, 139
McCollough effect. *See* Aftereffects
Mach, 4, 44, 149
McKee, J., 35, 114
McKenna, P., 95, 164
McLeod, P., 47, 59, 139
Magnocellular pathway, 15–19, 22, 25, 40–42, 45, 79
Malcolm, N., 6, 67
Marin, O. S. M., 39, 93
Marr, D., 60, 70, 82, 88, 121
Marshall, J. C., 25, 94, 145
Martindale, C., 116–118
Meadows, J. C., 35, 37–38, 160
Memory. *See also* Object recognition
  for colors, 105, 108–109, 114, 127, 129, 131–132, 155
  for object colors, 110, 127, 129, 133–135
Menaud-Bateau, C., 127, 150, 165
Mervis, C. B., 88, 106, 149
Michel, F., 157, 161
Miller, G. A., 141, 149–150
Milner, B., 112, 138
Mime, 144
Mind-blindness. *See* Agnosia, Apperception
Mingolla, E., 70–72, 78–79, 83, 93, 97, 121
Mishkin, M., 13, 29, 112
Modularity
  compared to nonmodular approaches, 69–85, 169
  functional, 103–111, 114–115, 117, 137–138, 156, 170–171 (*see also* Internal color space)
  neurophysiology of, 11–29
  neuropsychology of, 31–40
  studied by equiluminance, 41–50
  and temporary representations, 51–67
Mohr, J. P., 108, 135, 157, 159, 162
Mollon, J. D., 2–3, 14, 27, 31–32, 44, 62, 65, 160
Moran, J., 27, 56
Morton, J., 91, 98, 139, 141–142, 164, 165
Motion
  aftereffects, 46–47, 58, 62, 66
  apparent, 45–48, 61, 65, 80, 132

and color (*see* Color and motion)
flicker and, 18, 31, 45, 80–81
and luminance, 46
module, 40, 45–49, 53
neurophysiology of, 20, 24, 27–28
Mullen, K. T., 33, 44, 47, 109, 151
Munsell colors, 79, 104, 116, 152, 155
Music, 111–112

Nachmias, J., 66, 73
Names, 8–9, 88, 91, 139–146. *See also* Color naming
Neisser, U., 51, 53, 56, 87–88, 90
Netley, C., 135, 159–161
Newcombe, F., 25, 29, 31, 92, 94, 138, 145
Newton, 2–3, 14

Object colors, 121–138
Object knowledge. *See also* Form perception
  Allport's model, 96, 101
  associative knowledge, 92, 141, 171
  cascade model, 100–101, 139
  concrete representations, 94, 128, 145, 167
  development, 87, 129
  disorders (*see* Disorders of object knowledge)
  edge-based representations, 121–122, 128, 140, 171
  entry level representations, 8, 87–91, 93–95, 97–101, 106–107, 121–125, 128–129, 137, 139–146, 147, 171
  function (*see* Object knowledge, isa)
  hasa, 8–9, 97–102, 106, 108, 114–115, 122–124, 127–129, 132, 136–138, 140–148, 150, 156, 159–163, 166, 171
  isa, 8, 9, 91–92, 97–102, 124, 140, 141–146, 171
  kinesthetic associations, 96, 146, 157
  sensory (*see* Object knowledge, hasa)
  top-down effects of, 70, 124–127
  typicality, 98–100, 107, 116–117
  verbal vs. visual code, 91, 94, 98, 124, 148
Object recognition, 27, 62, 70, 81–85, 87–90, 98
Object recognition and color, 121–124
Opponent processes, 15–16, 20–21, 23, 26–27, 32, 44, 46–47, 66, 75, 77–78, 107, 109, 149, 151, 170

Optic aphasia, 143–145, 160, 171
Orientation, 14, 19, 21–25, 27, 35, 49, 53, 58, 62, 66, 105, 170
Ostergaard, A. L., 108–109, 122, 124, 136, 140, 150, 159, 161
Oxbury, J. M., 133–134, 159–162

Paivio, A., 91, 94, 124, 148
Palmer, G., 14
Parvocellular pathways, 15–19, 25–26, 42–43, 79
Pena-Casanova, J., 134, 162
Perry, V. H., 15, 24, 26
Phrenology, 1
Pictorial register, 8–9, 51–52, 60, 67, 69–70, 73, 81, 83–85, 87–90, 96–99, 103–104, 107–111, 121, 124–129, 159–160, 164, 167, 171–172
Piecemeal perception, 89, 124
Pillon, B., 133, 160, 162
Podreka, I., 135, 137
Poeck, K., 134, 143, 162
Poetzl, O., 53, 82, 161
Pokorny, J., 6, 31–32, 79
Poppel, E., 24, 25
Poppelreuter, W., 13, 82, 84
Positional uncertainty hypothesis. See Spatial uncertainty hypothesis
Posner, M. I., 52, 55–56, 59, 85, 166
Postman, L., 127, 129
Potter, M. C., 90–91, 96–98, 141, 163
Poulton, E. C., 64
Priming, 90–91, 98, 107, 117, 125, 127, 139, 141, 145, 147
Prinzmetal, W., 55–56, 125–126
Prosopagnosia, 35, 36, 38, 132, 133
Pylyshyn, Z., 6, 91

Quinlan, P., 54, 59, 99

Ramachandran, V. S., 46–47, 62, 65, 75, 80
Rapp, B. C., 94, 99
Ratcliff, G., 31, 92, 138
Reading (preserved), 92, 101
Reed, V. S., 91, 139
Representationalism, 5–8
Retinex theory, 77, 80
Ribe, W. B., 2–3
Riddoch, G., 40, 53

Riddoch, M. J., 59, 82–83, 90, 92, 94, 99–101, 134–135, 137–138, 143–144, 160, 162
Ridley, D. R., 109, 114, 129
Rizzo, M., 40, 112
Rock, I., 84–85
Rods, 14, 25, 32, 79, 81
Rosch, E., 84, 88, 98–99, 106–107, 116–117, 141, 147, 151–152
Roth, I., 39, 88, 90
Rubens, A., 92, 133, 162
Ruddock, K. H., 25, 52, 62, 66
Rumelhart, D. E., 6, 89, 94, 99, 117

Saffran, E. M., 93, 134, 160
Saillant, B., 73, 110, 131–134, 136, 138, 143, 148, 160–162
Samelsohn, J., 32–33
Sapir, E., 153–154
Sasanuma, S., 110, 159
Saturation, 75, 78–79, 103–105, 107, 115, 131–132
Savoy, R. L., 49, 61
Schiller, P. H., 15, 19, 27
Schneider, G. E., 11–13
Schott, B., 157, 161
Schwartz, M. F., 13, 89, 93
Scotti, G., 39, 110, 131
Segmentation. See Boundary-contours
Semantics. See Object knowledge
Separable dimensions, 103
Seymour, P. H. K., 91, 99, 115, 127, 129, 165–166
Shallice, T., 39–40, 81, 90, 92, 94–95, 99, 101, 129, 139, 144, 159
Shape perception. See Form perception
Silverman, M. S., 23, 27
Simple cells, 19, 22, 27, 72
Siple, P., 108, 129
Sittig, O., 109–110
Smith, E. E., 99, 141
Smith, M. C., 91, 97, 165
Smith, P. C., 114, 122
Smith, S. L., 64, 119
Smith, V. C., 6, 31, 79
Snyder, C. R. R., 55–56
Spatial frequency, 15, 27, 44–47, 49, 59, 78–79
Spatial uncertainty hypothesis, 44–47
Sperber, R. D., 91, 141
Sperling, G., 45, 51, 57

Spinnler, H., 38, 39, 110, 131, 138, 156, 159–160
Spitzer, H., 56, 126
Split-brain patients, 96
Stabilized retinal images, 42, 73, 80
Stachowiak, F. J., 134, 162
Stalmeier, P. F. M., 65, 104
Steffan, P. H., 32–33, 35
Steiner, M., 135, 137
Stengel, E., 110, 135, 137, 160, 161
Stereopsis. See Binocular vision
Stiles, W. S., 44, 81
Stoerig, P., 25–26
Streams. See Livingstone and Hubel streams
Stromeyer, C. F., 59, 61
Stroop effect, 127, 163–167
Sun, R. K., 151–152
Surface colors, 2–5, 7–8, 52–53, 60, 69–84, 99, 103–105, 108–109, 121–128, 137, 140, 151, 162–163, 170–172. See also Feature-contours
Switkes, E., 44, 49, 61
Synaesthesia, 111–113

Tansley, B. W., 63, 65, 75
Taylor, A. M., 70, 82, 83, 96, 133, 138, 142, 160
Te Linde, J., 91, 148
Temporary representation. See Pictorial register
Texture, 28, 61, 63, 65–66, 108, 121, 123, 170
Thorell, L. G., 28, 72
Tilt aftereffect. See Aftereffects
Todd, J. T., 67, 70
Transparent surfaces, 3–5
Treisman, A. M., 1, 7, 53–56, 58–60, 64–67, 85, 125, 164
Tritanopia, 78
Troscianko, T., 43–44, 46
Typicality. See Object knowledge

Uchikawa, K., 76, 108
Ungerleider, L. G., 13, 27

Van Essen, D. C., 7, 13, 26–28
Van Tuijl, H. F. J. M., 78, 126
Varney, N. K., 131, 135, 160–161
Verrey, D., 32–33, 37

Von Bezold spreading effect. See Assimilation
Von Kries, J., 76–77
Von Seggern, H., 32–33

Walls, G. L., 14, 78
Wapner, W., 133, 160
Ware, C., 44, 65
Warren, C. E. J., 91, 98
Warrington, E. K., 7, 39, 70, 82–83, 92–96, 101, 110, 132–134, 138, 141–142, 159–163
Waterfield, V. A., 25, 62
Weiskrantz, L., 12, 25
Werner, H., 150–151
Whorf-Sapir hypothesis, 153–155
Wickens, C. D., 64, 84
Wiesel, T. N., 13, 16, 19, 25
Williams, L. G., 56, 85
Willmes, K., 135, 137
Wilson, B., 35, 93
Wingfield, A., 84, 98, 107, 139
Wittgenstein, L., 4–5
Word frequency, 98, 100, 107, 139, 151, 153
Wyke, M., 91, 112, 133, 146, 148, 160, 162
Wyszecki, G., 6, 80

Young, T., 3, 14, 16
Young, A. W., 25, 82, 90, 93, 141

Zeki, S. M., 1, 7, 13, 24, 27, 37, 38
Zihl, J., 32–33, 35, 39, 40
Zollinger, H., 106, 127, 151, 153